Advanced C Programming by Example

John W. Perry
De Anza College

I(T)P An International Thomson Publishing Company

Boston • Albany • Bonn • Cincinnati • London
Melbourne • Mexico City • New York • Paris
San Francisco • Singapore • Tokyo • Toronto • Washington

PWS Publishing Company
20 Park Plaza, Boston, MA 02116–4324

I(T)P
an International Thomson Publishing company
The trademark ITP is used under license.

Sponsoring Editor: *David Dietz*
Production Editor: *Andrea Goldman*
Manufacturing Buyer: *Andrew Christensen*
Marketing Manager: *Nathan Wilbur*
Copyeditor: *Connie Day*
Composition: *Argosy*
Cover Design: *Jeff Cosloy*
Interior Design: *Octal Publishing*
Text Printer and Binder: *Quebecor/Fairfield*
Cover Printer: *Phoenix Color Corp.*

This book is printed on recycled, acid-free paper.

Printed in the United States of America.
98 99 00 01 — 10 9 8 7 6 5 4 3 2 1

Library of Congress Cataloging-in-Publication-Data

Perry, John W.
Advanced C programming by example / John W. Perry
Includes index.
ISBN 0–534–95140–6
1. C (Computer program language) I. Title.
QA76.73.C15P462 1998
005.13'3–dc21 97-31818
CIP

For more information, contact:
PWS Publishing Company
20 Park Plaza
Boston, MA 02116

International Thomson Publishing Europe
Berkshire House
168-173 High Holborn
London WC1V 7AA
England

Thomas Nelson Australia
102 Dodds Street
South Melbourne, 3205
Victoria, Australia

Nelson Canada
1120 Birchmont Road
Scarborough, Ontario
Canada M1K 5G4

International Thomson Editores
Campos Eliseos 385, Piso 7
Col. Polanco
11560 Mexico D.F., Mexico

International Thomson Publishing GmbH
Königswinterer Strasse 418
53227 Bonn, Germany

International Thomson Publishing Asia
221 Henderson Road
#05-10 Henderson Building
Singapore 0315

International Thomson Publishing Japan
Hirakawacho Kyowa Building, 31
2-2-1 Hirakawacho
Chiyoda-ku, Tokyo 102
Japan

Contents

Chapter 3

Chapter 4

Chapter 5

Chapter 6

Chapter 7

Appendix

Preface

This book attempts to fill a gaping void in the C textbook literature. At De Anza College (my current employer) we have often felt it was ironic that our Advanced C Programming course, a core course in our curriculum, had no textbook despite the ready availability of numerous C language texts. A cursory look at the available books reveals that the vast majority of them are either beginner books or reference manuals. Other candidate texts are really data structures books rather than true Advanced C texts.

This book does *not* shun discussion of data structures (such as lists, trees, arrays of lists, and so on), but when it ventures into this area, it does so with an ever-watchful eye on the bottom-up mechanics of implementing these structures in C.

The "purists" in programming would have it that the language of algorithm implementation is secondary to the thinking behind the algorithm itself. This flies in the face of human experience. Everyone has heard that Eskimos have dozens of words for snow, but in programming, we have failed to appreciate the fact that language shapes perception just as much as perception shapes language. Thus our experience with human languages should call for a balanced approach somewhere between the extremes of pure algorithmic thinking and the hacking of a "syntax junkie."

An anecdote will highlight the need for balance between a "top-down" and "bottom-up" approach. A graduate student was giving a testimonial about the virtues of the purely algorithmic approach of her department at a symposium on educational computing. The fact that her department's approach to teaching language syntax was not to teach it at all but rather to throw a reference manual at students was seen as enlightened. During a break, a private conversation with this student revealed the truth—she was having trouble at a job she currently held. Why? She did not know C well enough. All that algorithmic knowledge in her brain could not be expressed! This book will try to strike a balance between theory and syntax, between "top-down" and "bottom-up," between abstraction and implementation.

In keeping with this "blue-collar" realism, *Advanced C Programming by Example* focuses on areas of greatest practical application. Above all, a good C programmer must not fear pointers; this construct is the heart and soul of C and also the source of its great expressiveness and blazing speed of execution. Thus, after discussing style issues in Chapter 1, we proceed immediately to a thorough review of basic pointer arithmetic in Chapter 2. All that follows is contingent on mastery of the material in this chapter—it is a pivot around which the rest of the book turns.

Before we discuss the book's contents after Chapter 2, a word about prerequisite knowledge is in order. After all, the book is an *advanced* C text, so knowledge about C is presumed. However, because no two schools will agree on what knowledge an intermediate-level C programmer should have, what this book presumes is outlined below.

- C looping and conditional statements—that is, `if`, `switch`, `while`, `do...while`, and `for`.
- Assignment operations: =, +=, *=, and so on.
- ANSI-style functions: prototyping, function calling, and parameter passing.
- The `static`, `automatic`, and `extern` storage classes.
- The `break`, `goto`, and `continue` branching statements.
- Prefix and postfix ++ and `--`. Basic arithmetic operations and operator precedence.
- Relational operators and Boolean conditions.
- The text-oriented `stdio.h` functions `scanf()`, `fscanf()`, `sscanf()`, `printf()`, `fprintf()`, `sprintf()`, `gets()`, `fgets()`, `puts()`, `fputs()`, `getchar()`, `fgetc()`, `putchar()`, `fputc()`, and `fopen()`.
- The fundamental scalar data types, one-dimensional arrays, structures, and unions.
- The use of pointers to traverse simple arrays and to pass parameters to functions.
- The `ctype.h` library, such as `isupper`, `tolower`, `isalpha`, `isdigit`, and so on.
- The elementary `string.h` functions `strcmp`, `strcpy`, and `strcat`.
- The `#define` and `#include` preprocessor statements.

Of course, some people will have a little less knowledge than this and some a little more. Rest assured that any of these items that is missing from the reader's personal knowledge list will be used and explained in plenty of examples!

Now a little explanation of the book's contents and ordering of material. After users have dusted the cobwebs off their pointer knowledge, we will put it to use immediately in Chapter 3 in a discussion of the linear dynamic data structures and memory management. After discussing stacks, queues, and lists, we will show readers how to control the destiny of memory usage in their programs rather than leaving it up to the designer of the `malloc()` and `free()` functions. The chapter ends with a discussion of lists of lists and arrays of lists and their use in memory hashing.

Chapter 4 is truly an Advanced C chapter that you won't find in any algorithm or data structures book—it addresses advanced string handling. Students will learn how to (1) parse user input with `strtok()` and/or `strpbrk()`, (2) convert text strings to numbers with error checking via `strtol()`, `strtoul()`, and `strtod()`, (3) search strings with `strchr()`, `strrchr()`, and `strstr()`, (4) use pointer *expressions* and not just pointer *variables* as arguments to `string.h` functions, (5) create, initialize, and traverse arrays of strings, and (6) grow and shrink arrays of strings via `realloc()`.

Chapter 5 is all about advanced file input/output. Here we teach about binary files, random access files, disk hashing and indexing, advanced `printf()` formatting, and the proper way to read from terminals.

Chapter 6 examines bit manipulation. Bit manipulation is used in such diverse applications as cryptography, industrial automation, and graphics. The reader will discover how to turn bits and bit sequences on and off, overlay bit patterns on memory, test bits, rotate bits, and "toggle" bits.

Chapter 7 deals with recursion—the idea that a function can call itself. It also deals with the data structure most often manipulated via recursion: binary trees. Most important, students will learn how expensive recursion is, how to avoid it, and when to avoid it. Code examples show how to convert recursive code to iterative code. We also show when recursion is worth the cost. A discussion of input randomization is included so that the reader can construct trees that have good worst-case performance while sidestepping the complexities and inefficiencies created by tree-balancing algorithms.

Chapter 8 is all about arrays of dimension two or higher: creating them, moving around them, initializing them, and assigning them. Students are introduced to C's memory model for multidimensional arrays and techniques to minimize the inherent costs of array indexing. Included in the discussion of multidimensional arrays is a discussion of "ragged" arrays (rows of unequal length) usually represented as arrays of pointers to non-`char` data types. Much complexity lurks in this apparently simple topic—a fact that this chapter clearly reveals.

Chapters 9 and 10 are entitled "Potpourri: Part One" and "Potpourri: Part Two." These chapters deal with topics that are important but not extensive enough to warrant their own separate chapters. Chapter 9 discusses the functions from the `time.h` library, pointers to functions, functions with variable-length argument lists, and the reading and writing of difficult C declarations.

Among the C library functions, the `time.h` functions are used, arguably, in the most varied settings. Databases, operating systems, business reports, and quality assurance (especially benchmarking) all require keeping time and/or the timestamping of events. Pointers to functions are a neglected area in C, even though operating system libraries on any platform often require them as function arguments.

Variable-length argument lists for functions enable users to discover how functions like `printf()` work. Functions with variable-length argument lists also allow for the possibility that these functions may have different data types from one call to the next. This makes possible a degree of flexibility similar to the template concept of C++. All functions that deal with unnamed arguments are in the `stdarg.h` library and are discussed in full.

The final section of Chapter 9, on reading and writing difficult C declarations, illustrates the right-left rule for evaluating and writing complex declarations like arrays of function pointers, functions that return a function pointer, and pointers to nonscalar entities such as `int(*p)[5]`, which will jump by five `int`s when you say `p++`.

Chapter 10, the second "Potpourri" chapter, covers the `qsort()` and `bsearch()` functions, signal and exception handling, and file-related functions that can rename files, remove files, create temporary files, and so on.

`Qsort()` and `bsearch()` are like cousins because they are often used together in the same application. `Qsort()` uses the "quicksort" algorithm to sort arrays. `Bsearch()` does a binary search of a sorted array. As usual, a realistic example supplements the discussion.

The sections on signal handling and file-related functions are included for completeness. However, these are the most problematic functions in the ANSI C library. That's because each operating system has its own platform-dependent file systems and its own idea of what event constitutes an interrupt. Nonetheless, many of the operations described in these sections of Chapter 10 may be performed portably and without risk. The reader is duly warned when something may not be portable or safe.

How to Read This Book

Above all, this is a *code-centered* book. This means that it relies heavily on offering lots of code examples and narratives discussing them. *Advanced C Programming by Example* is a reaction against large books full of verbose theory. For better or worse, most programmers and students of programming learn by example, and this book acknowledges and takes full advantage of that fact. I have tried to keep the narrative part of the text short and to the point so that people will actually read it!

The narratives that follow code examples dissect and explain the syntax of these examples and how they express what we wanted algorithmically. If code contains obscure or difficult syntax, diagrams are included to show how this code affects data structures or program output. Within text appearing outside of code examples, all variable names, function names, C reserved words, names of `.h` header files, and expressions used in code examples are set in a different typeface. Function names referred to in the narrative are always accompanied by parentheses—for instance, `printf()`.

In order to make it easy to distinguish between code examples and regular text, all code examples are introduced by a heading that describes their content and are followed by a solid line. Furthermore, code examples are given in a typeface different from that used in the narrative. Within code examples, output from the code is included where appropriate. A comment line (e.g., `/***** Output Below *****/`) separates the end of the code from the beginning of output. C comments on output lines are *not* part of the output but serve merely to help the reader link that output line with particular line(s) in the code above.

Each chapter of the book (except Chapters 1, 6, and 9) ends with "Facts About Functions" and "Exercises." "Facts About Functions" lists important facts about C library functions discussed in the current chapter. The functions are grouped under the `.h` file where they can be found. The facts listed include obvious material such as return values and argument lists, but unlike reference manuals, these sections also devote special attention to areas of applicability, pitfalls, and traps to be avoided when using a particular library function.

Exercises that are answered in the back of the book (the Appendix) are marked with a solid square (■). Rather than overwhelming the reader with 40 or 50 exercises, this text contains an average of about 12 carefully selected problems in each chapter. Some problems test the reader's understanding of C syntax and notation, some ask the reader to write a function using concepts from the current chapter, and some entail the writing of sizable programs where knowledge acquired from the current chapter and from preceding chapters must be used in one program.

The Current State of C Programming

Finally, like many authors of technology books, I am compelled to weigh in on The Great Language Debate and the past and future of computing. Computing *appears* to change rapidly, yet this impression is deceptive. Consider, for example, that Internet electronic mail and file transfer, though they have been in the public eye for only about the last five years, have existed since the early 1970s!

My intent here is to alleviate the natural tendency to become anxious and bewildered when confronted with proliferation of new languages and tools. Do I have to learn every hip, new language that comes down the pike? What's transient and what's here to stay? How long must I run at full speed just to stay in the same spot on the treadmill?

An impressive number of "experts" tell us that many new languages, especially those in the so-called object-oriented (OO) sector, are huge advancements over older, procedural languages. But their contentions, like those of the "pure algorithmic" camp mentioned earlier, fly in the face of common sense and human experience. Let us see why.

First, these languages are huge. They represent a doubling (or more) in the total number of syntactic elements (reserved words and operators). They have a litany of "must-be-memorized" side effects like the implicit invocation of copy constructors. They also introduce new variable scopes such as the "class scope" of C++ and Java, and C++'s idea of classes with shared `static` variables.

Class scope, alone, leads to program-reading difficulties similar to those seen in poorly written C programs that use global variables in functions. When you see a variable name in a "method" (function), its declaration may not be found in the function header or local declaration section because of class scope. You may have to look in the class definition or even further if the program uses inheritance.

In the author's opinion, supporters of many "new age/new paradigm" languages have failed to consider the obvious correlation between the size of a language and the difficulty of learning and using it. Some even maintain that these tools are *easier* to use than their ancestors. If we carry that argument into the domain of natural human languages, we can see how tenuous these claims are. Would anybody suggest that a student who is earning a D grade in Beginning French should jump to Advanced French immediately because of its larger vocabulary, syntax, and conceptual variety? Yet this is the kind of propaganda we are asked to swallow, whole and unsubstantiated.

Indeed, many Java books try to portray Java as a kind of "manageable" C++, clearly implying that C++ is unmanageable. The price you pay for this "leaner and meaner" C++ is that the OO paradigm is unavoidable—no function can exist outside of an object! This means that stand-alone utility functions cannot be written legally in Java. Is OO so demonstrably better than the procedural paradigm that this force-feeding is justified?

There is an impressive lack of experimental evidence that OO languages give us anything at all. Steve McConnell, in *Rapid Development* (Microsoft Press, Redmond, Washington), cites evidence that early OO projects succeeded only because they were staffed with "stars"—people who could program brilliantly in any language. When staffed with average industrial programmers, OO projects yielded only what could be expected with older tools, or worse.

Those interested in the "or worse" can read the January 1994 issue of *Software Technology Practitioner*, which includes an article by Robert L. Glass entitled "Object-Orientation Is Least Successful Technology." Richard Gabriel, in his book *Patterns of Software* (Oxford University Press, New York), analyzes the "habitability" of OO languages—a term he uses to describe a programmer's ability to move around comfortably in all parts of a language. He concludes that the "great object-oriented experiment" will not succeed.

Even in the area of code reusability, an area of renewed emphasis in the OO sector, no one has yet presented a cogent refutation of the idea of a simple function as a reusable entity. The simple ANSI C function library remains the greatest reusability success story to date.

C is a remarkably expressive and yet small language. By itself, it led to the rapid expansion in available software in the 1980s and 1990s, especially for personal computers. Since its nearly universal adoption in the mid-1980s, we have gone from a situation where the members of the entire universe of software products numbered a few dozen to a "code glut" of tens of thousands of products.

Are we good enough at using it yet? Clearly we are not. Is C a kind of Rosetta Stone of programming languages? No. It, too, has some imperfections and fuzzy edges. Have its competitors proved their right to "seize the throne"? My answer to that is given above, and I might add one more query: Why are the compilers of these "pretenders to the throne" written in C instead of using their own tongue as even the earliest C compilers did?

C is neither the end of the history of programming languages nor an ultimate solution to the challenges our discipline poses. It is merely better than its predecessors or its current would-be successors. It is my hope that through this book, the reader will discover the elegance and power in its sparseness, while enhancing his or her own mastery of its more advanced features. In the meantime, while the bewildered programmer is waiting for a worthy successor to emerge, he or she can rest assured that the foreseeable future of C is as bright as its past.

Acknowledgments

Special thanks go the staff at PWS Publishing Company, particularly Andrea Goldman and Connie Day.

I would also like to thank the following reviewers for their comments and suggestions:

- Cliff Green, *University of Washington*
- Clare Hamlet, *Pima College*
- Mike Holland, *Northern Virginia Community College*
- Bruce Mycroft, *Flathead Valley Community College*
- Rahul Roy-Chowdhury, *Columbia University*

Thanks also go to Behrouz Forouzan of De Anza College for the "right-left" rule for analyzing difficult C declarations.

John Perry
Palo Alto, California

Chapter 1

Optimal C Coding Style

1.1 Commenting, Whitespacing, and Other Style Issues

The issue of programming style has generated the sort of heated arguments usually reserved for debates on religion or politics. This is unfortunate because the extremity of opinions has discouraged many of the "silent majority" who simply want to get the job done without too much pain. It is also unfortunate because there is a genuine crisis of quality in the software industry.

This crisis was made unmistakably clear in "Software's Chronic Crisis" (W. Wayne Gibbs) in the September 1994 issue of *Scientific American*. This article reports that a study by the Software Engineering Institute revealed that, according to the self-assessment of 261 companies, only *two* had nearly perfect program development and evaluation methods, and 75 percent were functioning at the "chaos" level!

Because commercial programs are updated constantly, it is vital that the code be readable. Given the constant editing and upgrading of commercial products, an exquisitely readable program with a few functional flaws is preferable to a perfectly functional program that is incoherent. Every decision made in designing and coding a program is important. These decisions include answering the following questions:

- How should I phrase the language in comments?
- How much whitespace should I use and where should I use it?
- Is code indented consistently?

- Are functions too long (i.e., longer than a page)? Do some do too much?
- How can I make it easy to see where comments and code start and stop?
- How can I make subtasks within a function separate from other subtasks in an easy-to-visualize manner?

Comments should be written in clear English and not high-tech jargon. They should state what a function or code fragment does. They should be easily separable, at a glance, from surrounding code. Whitespace should be used liberally between functions and subtasks within functions. Whenever possible, functions should be *short;* ideally, they should take less than a page and should *not* straddle two pages on the printout.

It is the author's opinion that commenting styles leading to more comment than code, such as pseudocode, actually *detract* from program readability. When comment volume starts to dwarf code volume, it is time to create a separate document so that the code reader can see where the code is without straining. Judicious and plentiful use of whitespace is probably the greatest enhancement to program readability available to the programmer.

Here's an example that illustrates most of these suggestions.

Example 1.1 Demonstration of Block-Commenting Style and Whitespacing

```
/*****************************************************/
/*                                                   */
/*   This program does the following:                */
/*                                                   */
/*       1) Swaps two integers.                      */
/*       2) Prints the values of the newly swapped   */
/*          integers.                                */
/*       3) Adds the two integers.                   */
/*       4) Prints the result of the addition.       */
/*****************************************************/

#include <stdio.h>
main(void)
{
    int i = 5, j = 10;
    void swap(int *pi, int *pj);
    int add(int i, int j);

    swap(&i, &j);
    printf("i = %d     j = %d\n", i, j);
    printf("The sum of i and j is: %d\n", add(i,j));
}

/**********************************************/
/*                                            */
```

```
/*  The function below swaps the values of the     */
/*  two integer parameters.                        */
/**************************************************/
void swap(int *pi, int *pj)
{
    int temp;


    temp = *pi;
    *pi  = *pj;
    *pj  = temp;
}
/**************************************************/
/*                                                */
/*   The function below returns the sum of the */
/*   two integer parameters.                      */
/**************************************************/
int add(int i, int j)
{
    return (i + j);
}
```

Note the following aspects of the foregoing code:

- The clear visibility of comments.
- The common-sense descriptions, in clear English, of what the code does.
- The use of whitespace to separate all functions from one another.
- The faithful use of ANSI function prototypes (all functions should be prototyped in any function where they are called).
- By way of review, the fact that the format list of a `printf` can contain any legal expression as long as it matches the format descriptor (`%d` in this case).

This example is not intended to intimidate the reader into one style of commenting and code writing. It is merely my first opportunity to reinforce an idea that I will repeat like a mantra: *Every decision in a program counts!*

If your functions are jammed together with no whitespace between them, if your curly braces do not line up, if you indent two spaces in some code blocks and seven in others, or if the leftmost characters of all statements in a code block don't line up, your code will look terrible. This will hinder anyone's ability to maintain it or add functionality to it. Note that even the (seemingly) insignificant detail of lining up the assignment operators in the swap function makes it easier on the eye than if this was not done. Nothing is trivial enough to neglect in your work of programming art!

1.2 The Use of Short-Cut Notation: Good or Bad?

One area of controversy in C programming is the use of terse notation versus verbose notation. Here are a few examples using functions that should be familiar to you.

Example 1.2 Demonstration of Short-Cut Boolean Expressions in Loop Headers

```
while (fgets(line, MAXCHARS, filepointer))
{
    /*****  Block of code here.  *****/
}
```

versus,

```
while (fgets(line, MAXCHARS, filepointer) != NULL)
{
    /*****  Block of code here.  *****/
}
```

Which is better? Certainly the longer expression contains no ambiguity whatever and simply cannot be considered incorrect. But is the use of the shorter expression a programming "sin"? Given that we expect at least a modest level of language competence from future readers (who might be ourselves!), it is probably not too much to ask that the would-be reader know that only a zero expression value (same as the value of the built-in constant `NULL`) makes a loop conditional false. Thus, if this is a "sin," it is a very minor one indeed.

In fact, as we shall see, some programmers never use terse C expression forms, even when they sacrifice no readability at all. This is often due to a background in languages like Pascal and Fortran, wherein many expressions (such as Pascal procedure calls) can't return a value. Witness the following situation:

Example 1.3 The Use of the Ternary `?` Operator in a `Return`

```
if (a > b)
{
    return a;
}
else
{
    return b;
```

```
}
```

versus,

```
return a > b ? a : b;
```

The ternary operator ? is merely like a sideways `if` statement with the *true* expression to the left of the : and the *false* to the right of the :. It's certainly terse, but again, for whom are we writing our code? Other C programmers! In this case, I greatly favor the use of ? because it avoids the need to write two separate `return` statements. Like any other syntactic construct in C, however, ? can be abused or used in tricky ways that might compromise readability. Read on.

Example 1.4 Prevention of Code Redundancy Using the Ternary Operator

```
if (a > b)
{
    printf("%d\n", a);
}
else
{
    printf("%d\n", b);
}
```

versus,

```
printf("%d\n", a > b ? a : b);
```

and

```
if (palindrome(string))
{
    printf("%s is a palindrome!\n", string);
}
else
{
    printf("%s is not a palindrome!\n", string);
}
```

versus,

```
printf("%s is%s a palindrome!\n", string,
        palindrome(string) ? "" : " not");
```

The use of ? in the last code fragment prevents the duplication of two `printf`s that differ only in that one contains the word `"not"` in its output whereas the other doesn't. However, we are on much shakier ground here than in Example 1.3, where ? had no liabilities. Here the ternary expression is embedded in a `printf`, which renders it much less visible than it was in the `return` statement of Example 1.3. We can probably stop short of an outright condemnation of this trick, but its use is extremely questionable. Critical code must be visible!

Before we leave Example 1.4, note that the second code fragment in the example says

```
if (palindrome(string))
```

and not

```
if (palindrome(string) != 0)
```

The first form of the `if` looks more English-like ("If string is a palindrome, then do something...") and is more concise—a double advantage! If a function returns a value to be interpreted in a Boolean true/false fashion, there is no need for the relational operation !=, and it actually makes code *less* readable. Similarly, if you want to do some action if `string` is *not* a palindrome, it is actually more English-like to say

```
if (! palindrome(string))      /*** If not a palindrome, do
                                  something!  ***/
```

instead of

```
if (palindrome(string) == 0)
```

Another way in which novice C programmers fail to use Boolean expressions properly is demonstrated in the following example.

Example 1.5 Proper Use of a Relational Expression in a `Return` Statement

```
if (a > b)
{
    return 1;
}
else
{
    return 0;
}
```

versus,

```
return a > b;
```

Because any C programmer knows that all relational expressions (i.e., those using = or != or > or >= or < or <=) produce a value of one if true and zero if false, there is no good reason to use the coding style in the first code fragment of Example 1.5. It is verbose, does not use C's expressive power, and is no more readable than `return a > b`.

Let's summarize what is clear and what is open to debate in this section. What is clear is that Boolean return values from functions and Boolean expressions are often misused, as shown in Examples 1.4 and 1.5. The ternary operator ? is underused, but as is clear in the last code fragment of Example 1.4, it is easily abused.

Is there any other operator in C that is not properly appreciated? Yes—the comma operator! Look at the following examples.

Example 1.6 The Use of the Comma Operator in a Loop Conditional

```
getint(&i);
while (i != 0)
{
    /*  lots of code here */
    getint(&i);
}

void getint(int *pi)
{
    char line[80];

    printf("Enter an integer: ");
    gets(line);
    sscanf(line, "%d", pi);
}
```

versus,

```
while (getint(&i), i != 0)
{
    /* lots of code here */
}
/*****  Function getint shown above would go here.  *****/
```

The comma operator is shown in the final `while` loop conditional in Example 1.6. The value of a series of expressions separated by comma operators is the value of the rightmost expression. Thus, in the second `while` in Example 1.6, `i != 0` controls whether the `while` loop continues and *not* `getint(&i)`.

So why bother using the comma operator? If you inspect the code in Example 1.6, you will note that one reason for using the comma operator here is that `getint(&i)` is not repeated as it is in the first `while` loop of Example 1.6. However, programming is not a contest to see whose program can be typed in the fewest characters. Therefore, we expect another benefit. That benefit is readability. Loop headers, if well written, give the reader vital information about the flow of control in a program. Here, putting `getint(&i)` in the loop header really reveals what controls the loop (i.e., whether an integer just obtained from the user is zero or not).

However, you must remember that the comma operator is a highly abusable operator! It is rather tragicomic to see a `while` loop that has seven expressions comma-separated in its loop conditional with only one or two statements in the loop body itself. Restrict comma-delimited expressions in a loop header so that only those expressions involved in loop control are in the header. If the number of expressions exceeds two or three, avoid using the comma operator. Just remember the old adage: "Now that you have been given a hammer, remember that not everything is a nail!"

1.3 Flow of Control: How to Write "Flat" Rather Than "Deep" Programs

Every beginning programming student is instructed to *think* about programs long before writing the first line of code. Very few actually follow this advice. The result is that the code tends to be "dense" with doubly and trebly nested loops, deeply nested `if`s, and so on. Needless to say, nesting of loops and `if`s should be avoided whenever possible. If nesting is necessary, there is usually a right and a wrong way to do it. Look at the following code.

Example 1.7 An Incorrect Multi-way `If` Statement

```
if (score >= 60)
{
    if (score >= 70)
    {
        if (score >= 80)
        {
            if (score >= 90 )
            {
                printf("Excellent job!\n");
                grade = 'A';
            }
            else
            {
                printf("Good job!\n");
                grade = 'B';
```

```
            }
        }
        else
        {
            printf("Average job!\n");
            grade = 'C';
        }
    }
    else
    {
        printf("Poor job!\n");
        grade = 'D';
    }
}
else
{
    printf("Failing job!\n");
    grade = 'F';
}
```

Many readers may be rolling on the floor with laughter at this point, but I have seen such shoddy code countless times! Let's examine this code and pinpoint what is wrong with it. First, nesting forces you to "remember your past." That is, when you are inside the fourth nested `if`, you must remember the three prior conditions that had to be "true" to get you to this deeply nested level.

Second, this method of nesting does not put the *false* actions (those associated with the `else` clauses) immediately after the *true* actions (those associated with the `if` clauses). As a result, by the time you read the `else` clause, you may have forgotten what the `if` condition was because it occurred too far back in the program.

Contrast this disaster with the correct code shown in Example 1.8.

Example 1.8 A Correct Multi-way `If` Statement

```
if (score >= 90)
{
    printf("Excellent job!\n");
    grade = 'A';
}
else if (score >= 80)
{
    printf("Good job!\n");
    grade = 'B';
}
else if (score >= 70)
```

```
{
    printf("Average job!\n");
    grade = 'C';
}
else if (score >= 60)
{
    printf("Poor job!\n");
    grade = 'D';
}
else  /* Score is below 60! */
{
    printf("Failing job!\n");
    grade = 'F';
}
```

Note the following about the code in Example 1.8: (1) There is no nesting, so the `printf`s and assignments are all at the same level of indentation and thus are easy to read. (2) It is much easier to see what condition leads to the execution of the `printf`s and assignments, because they follow the condition *immediately*. (3) Because there is no nesting, readers do not have to remember a multitude of Boolean conditions that got them to the code they are currently reading—readers do not have to "remember their past."

Unnecessary `if` nesting also results when programmers simply forget that `if`s can have multiple Boolean conditions. Look at Example 1.9.

Example 1.9 Use of `&&` to Prevent `If` Nesting

```
if (a == b)
    if (b == c)
        if (c == d)
        {
            /* Do something in here. */
        }
```

versus,

```
if (a == b && b == c && c == d)
{
    /* Do something in here. */
}
```

Obviously the single `if` is better than the trebly nested `if`. Why "obviously"? For two reasons: The notion that the block of code is executed only if all three conditions are true is more obvious because of the commonsense meaning of *and*, and people read better from left to right than downward at an angle. The *and* is explicit in the single `if` because it is represented by the `&&` symbol, whereas it is merely implicit in the nested `if`. Explicit is usually better.

Loops (`while`s, `do...while`s, and `for`s) also are often unnecessarily nested, leading to poor program readability. Let's say you are supposed to output the contents of a file to the screen such that (1) each line is numbered, (2) each letter is encrypted by adding 2 to its ASCII value, and (3) each nonletter is simply sent unchanged to the screen. Assume that all lines of the file are newline (`'\n'`) terminated.

Many people would engage in the following plausible line of thinking: "I must deal with a file and with lines within a file, so I'll use a doubly nested `while` loop where the outer `while` deals with end-of-file and the inner `while` deals with end-of-line." Unfortunately, this thinking might result in code such as that shown in Example 1.10.

Example 1.10 A Literal, but Suboptimal, Conversion of a Problem Statement to Bad C Syntax

```
linenum = 1;
c = 'X';
while (c != EOF)
{
    printf("\n%-5d", linenum);
    linenum++;
    while ((c = fgetc(filepointer)) != '\n' && c != EOF)
    {
        if (isalpha(c)) c += 2;   /*** Encrypts "c"  ***/
        putchar(c);
    }
    if (c != EOF)
    {
        putchar(c);   /* Output the newline! */
    }
}
```

This code has an artificial, contrived look about it, and analysis bears this impression out. Note the strange initialization of `c`, the repeated `EOF` tests (one of which is necessary to keep the inner `while` from becoming an infinite loop when `EOF` occurs), and the general feel of near chaos created by this code.

It is simply amazing that such apparently logical thought could lead to such convoluted code. Nonetheless, it is bad code indeed. By contrast, the code in Example 1.11 uses no loop nesting, no repeated `EOF` test, and no repeat of the `putchar(c)` statement, and there is no need for a contrived initialization of `c`. It is clearly superior to the code in Example 1.10, and yet it does not just "drop out" of the language of the problem statement.

This is a kind of "proof-by-example" that knowing the syntax and idioms of a language may result in better code, with clearer structures and minimal nesting, if only we shape our thinking about the algorithm *in terms of the language's resources.* Yes, "bottom-up" syntactic considerations should have some influence on even the earliest phases of "top-down" design—a controversial assertion that the following code clearly affirms.

Example 1.11 A Translation of the Encryption Problem to Better C Syntax

```
linenum = 1;
printf("1    ");
while ((c = getchar()) != EOF)
{
    if (isalpha(c)) c += 2;
    putchar(c);
    if (c == '\n')
    {
        linenum++;
        printf("%-5d", linenum);
    }
}
```

The code in Example 1.11 can be designed easily if we remember at the outset that in C, unlike Pascal, newlines are just characters and not Boolean conditions (end-of-line is a Boolean function in Pascal that returns `"true"` or `"false"`). "Bottom-up" counts from beginning to end, and here it results in the waste-free code of Example 1.11 instead of the hodpepodge that is Example 1.10. Some algorithmic purists will object to this assertion, but nothing dispels such controversy better than an example that applies this philosophy.

1.4 Dogma Versus Reality on `Goto`, `Break`, and `Continue`

Ever since the structured programming movement condemned branching statements, avoiding `goto`, `break`, and `continue` has been fashionable. However, like much mindlessly followed dogma, it is almost correct but not completely correct. As usual, to produce optimal code you must analyze for yourself (1) why branching is generally bad, and (2) the exceptions to this principle and when those exceptions apply.

`Goto` and `break` in loops are almost always bad, because the loop conditional should tell the reader what terminates the loop. When `goto` or `break` is improperly used, it is generally because the programmer did not devote enough thought to loop design. The following code is a typical result.

Example 1.12 A Horrible Use of the `Break` Statement

```
while(1)
{
    /* Some code is here. */
    if (condition) break;
    /* Some code is here, too. */
}
```

When programmers read code, they usually look first at generalities, not specifics, to get the "big picture" of what the code does. Unless you understand the basic functioning of a program, the specifics are often meaningless. Yet code like that in Example 1.12 forces the reader to wade into the small details immediately, because loop control information is embedded deeply within the loop and surrounded by lots of code the reader would rather not think about at the outset.

However, the `continue` statement is another matter. Because it forces control to return to the loop condition, it actually forces the programmer to create proper loop control conditionals. `Continue` can also enhance readability if it enables us to dispense with odd conditions at the top of the loop body before we engage in processing "normal" situations. The following "pseudo-C" code illustrates a good use of `continue`.

Example 1.13 Pseudocode of an Acceptable Use of the `Continue` Statement

```
while(strcmp(user_input, "quit") != 0)
{
    if (user_input is all whitespace or just a newline)
    {
        continue;
    }
    if (user_input has non-letter characters)
    {
        printf("Invalid characters!\n");
        continue;
    }
    /* See if user-supplied word is in some table here. */
}
```

Computer programming is much like chess in that there are general principles that are *usually* true. However, we get into difficulties if we fail to be mindful of the exceptions. I have seen many chess games lost because a person unthinkingly played a move that conformed to general principles but was invalid in the circumstances at that time. Programming, like chess, requires vigilance at every step. That is why it is such a challenging, frustrating, and yet peculiarly rewarding activity.

Chapter 2

Review of Standard Pointer and Array Operations

2.1 One-Dimensional Array Manipulation, Pointer Arithmetic, and Indexing

As we noted in the Preface, it is no exaggeration to say that pointers are the heart and soul of the C programming language. No one can master the language without a thorough mastery of pointers. Thus it is essential that you feel completely comfortable with the material in this chapter before moving on to the rest of the book. Even if you feel comfortable with basic pointer manipulation, there may be gaps in your knowledge, so don't leave this chapter without satisfying yourself that you understand it fully.

A good place to begin is with the well-known `strlen()` function. It shows how to use a pointer to traverse a character array—one of the most common uses for a pointer.

Example 2.1 The Insides of the ANSI C `Strlen` Function

```
int strlen(char *string)
{
    char *ptr = string;

    while (*ptr != '\0') ptr++;
```

```
    return ptr - string;
}
```

Why does this work? Characters are guaranteed to occupy one byte of memory in the ANSI C standard. Therefore, the address held in `ptr` will be `strlen(string)` higher than the address held in `string` after the `while` loop terminates. Note that the `while` conditional could have been written as

```
while (*ptr)
```

Though terse, this is certainly readable to a seasoned programmer, because the value of the `'\0'` character is zero—the value that stops any loop! You may choose the less terse condition used in Example 2.1, but do not forget that you will *read* far more code than you *write* in your career as a programmer. Let's look at another well-known `string.h` library function, `strcmp()`.

Example 2.2 The Insides of the ANSI C `Strcmp` Function

```
int strcmp (char *s1, char *s2)
{
    while (*s1 == *s2)
    {
        if (*s1 == '\0') return 0;
        s1++;
        s2++;
    }
    return *s1 - *s2;
}
```

Remember the rule for how `strcmp()` works? It returns a positive number if the first string argument is greater than the second string argument, a zero if the two strings are the same, and a negative number if the first string argument is less than the second string argument.

The sense of *greater than* and *less than* can be understood only with reference to the ASCII character set. In this character set, all the digit characters precede all the uppercase letters, which precede all the lowercase letters. This means that a lowercase letter is "greater than" that an uppercase letter and that an uppercase letter is "greater than" a digit character.

This algorithm says, then, in English, "Keep looping while the characters being pointed at by `s1` and `s2` are the same." The `if` takes care of the case where both `*s1` and `*s2` are both `'\0'` and, therefore, we've reached the end of both identical strings. All other cases are taken care of by the `while` header. At this point, the ASCII value of `*s2` is subtracted from the ASCII value of `*s1`. Obviously, this number must be positive or negative. (Remember that the zero return is taken care of by the `if` inside the loop!)

Thus if s1 points at "Smith" and s2 points at "Smyth", then strcmp() will return a negative number because 'i' - 'y' (the point at which *s1 is not the same as *s2) is a negative number. What if s1 points at "Smith" and s2 points at "Smithers"? The tie between the values of *s1 and *s2 will be broken when s1 points at the '\0' character and s2 points at the 'e' in "Smithers". Obviously, '\0' - 'e' is a negative number because the ASCII value of '\0' is zero.

Are there any values for s1 in strlen() and strcmp(), or for s2 in strcmp(), that would cause these functions to blow up? Yes, if either of these pointers is NULL, it would cause these functions to dereference address zero—a fatal runtime error. However, all string.h functions expect you to be smart enough not to make this mistake.

It is crucial that you understand the difference between a pointer that is NULL and a pointer that points at an empty string (i.e., one that contains only the '\0' character). That '\0' character in an empty string definitely has an address in memory, and that address is never going to be zero. A NULL pointer has the address value zero stored in it, and you're always going to get in trouble if you try to dereference this address.

Another small but vital detail you must understand is the difference between a NULL pointer and an unassigned pointer. A NULL pointer has a value—zero. An unassigned pointer has no value at all. As we will see later, the stdlib.h function free() can be applied successfully (i.e., without a runtime failure) to a NULL pointer, but not to an unassigned pointer. Forgetting this apparently insignificant detail can mean the difference between a program that runs correctly and one that runs incorrectly or not at all.

Let us move now to a function that takes a pointer to an array of int. This function will assume that its purpose is to sum the elements of the int array so long as the element being pointed at does not have a zero value.

Example 2.3 Typical Traversal of a Non-Char Array with a Pointer

```
int sumints (int *pi)
{
    int sum = 0;

    while (*pi != 0)
    {
        sum += *pi++;
    }
    return sum;
}
```

This little piece of code illustrates a lot. Let's pick it apart. First, note that we initialized our accumulator variable sum to zero in the declaration—a common practice and a good one. Note the use of += instead of =. This can actually make the code run faster on some platforms. Note that after the value of `*pi` (i.e., the value in the address pointed at by `pi`) is added to `sum`, `pi`'s value is incremented.

It is critical that you understand this meaning of `*pi++` because the operation of lending a value to an expression and then incrementing the pointer is universal in C programs. It is `pi` that is incremented, not `*pi`. We must type `(*pi)++` to increment the value pointed to by `pi`. That's because the * has a lower precedence than the ++ and therefore does not bind to `pi` as closely as ++.

Now for the confusing part. Everyone knows that ++ in C means "increment by one." But hold on! If our program is running on a machine with four-byte integers, then how can I claim that the ++ in the code above moves to the next integer; that is, it is adding *four* to `pi`, not *one*? Here is where the intelligent design of the C language saves us. When you use ++ to increment a *pointer*, doing so actually increments its value *by the size of the thing being pointed at.* In this case, we are pointing at an `int`, which will be two, four, or eight bytes, depending on the host computer's hardware. It is no exaggeration to say that C would be a useless language if it did not have this feature.

Many students who are fearful of pointers are afraid to write code like that in Example 2.3. They would write it something like this:

Example 2.4 Traversing an Array by Indexing (Not Recommended!)

```
int sumints (int i[])
{
    int sum = 0, j = 0;

    while (i[j] != 0)
    {
        sum += i[j++];
    }
    return sum;
}
```

Although this code works, it is far inferior to Example 2.3. Why? To answer this, we must discuss assembly language for a moment. All assemblers have an "increment by one" instruction just as C does. When we use pointer arithmetic in Example 2.3, the ++ operator is all we use to move the pointer. However, in Example 2.4 we use indexing, and the C compiler turns `i[j++]` into `*(i + j)` followed by `j++`. We add `j` to `i`—an additional operation not done in Example 2.3 and, worse yet, one that takes at least three statements in assembly language. And we must still increment `j`!

Thus, in this small code space, we have introduced a variable, `j`, that is not needed and that greatly reduces the efficiency of the function. "But such a small function!" you may object. Yes, but remember that such small inefficiencies, if created routinely in a 10,000-line program, add up to a great deal of inefficiency.

Here is a good rule of thumb to remember: *When traversing an array, always use a pointer.* Of course, exceptions to this rule exist. For example, if you are not traversing an array linearly (i.e., if you are jumping back and forth), you may need an index variable to keep track of where you are in the array.

Let us return to the idea that `i[j]` is turned into `*(i + j)` by the compiler. Remember that an array name is the name of a *pointer constant.* Thus `*(i + j)` means "Add `j` to the address stored in `i` and then fetch the data stored in this computed address." Upon learning that `*(i + j)` is just an address arithmetic version of `i[j]`, some programmers fall into the trap known as "a little knowledge is dangerous" and create a function that combines the worst features of Examples 2.3 and 2.4. Look at the horrible code in Example 2.5.

Example 2.5 A Horrible Mixture of Pointer Arithmetic and Array Indexing

```
int sumints(int i[])
{
    int sum = 0, j = 0;

    while (*(i + j) != 0)
    {
        sum += *(i + j);
        j++;
    }
    return sum;
}
```

This disastrous code contains all the inefficiency of Example 2.4 (you're still doing that addition of `j` to `i`) and none of the readability of Example 2.3. In fact, I often jokingly refer to `*(i + j)` as "cheater indexing."

Why "cheater indexing"? Because you're still using an index variable, `j`, but are fooling yourself into thinking that you understand pointer arithmetic just because you wrote an expression, `*(i + j)`, that doesn't use index brackets (`[]`). Example 2.3 is the only code you should even consider as a correct way of solving the array element summing problem.

Remember that the code in Example 2.3 uses zero as a sentinel value (a value that warns us to stop processing data). When you traverse arrays, you must know when to stop. Otherwise, you will get a fatal runtime memory error (whether you use indexing or pointer arithmetic). Often, the sentinel method is no good, because in some applications, all array element values (including zero!) are valid data.

To write `sumints()` in the most general fashion possible, we would probably pass a second parameter telling us how many array elements to process. The optimal result is shown in Example 2.6.

Example 2.6 A Generalized Array Sum Function with Pointer Arithmetic

```
int sumints (int *pi, int num_elements)
{
    int sum = 0;

    while (num_elements-- > 0)
    {
        sum += *pi++;
    }
    return sum;
}
```

Finally, why not use the `sizeof()` function to compute the number of bytes in the array? Because an array, when passed to a function, *is always treated as a pointer regardless of the notation in the function header.* Therefore, when used in a function, `sizeof(pi)` will return the size of an `int` pointer, not the size of an `int` array.

2.2 Using Pointers as Function Parameters

As you know from beginning C, the parameter-passing mechanism in C is referred to as *call-by-value.* This means that the value of a parameter comes back to the calling environment unchanged unless you pass a pointer to it. Thus the function in Example 2.7 will not swap the values of the integers `i` and `j`.

Example 2.7 A Swap Function That Fails Because of Call-by-Value

```
void swap (int i, int j)
{
    int temp;

    temp = i;
    i = j;
    j = temp;
}
```

We know that the code in Example 2.7 does not work, because call-by-value means that copies of `i` and `j` are sent to the `swap()` function. These copies do not live in the same address in memory as the original `i` and `j` from the calling environment. Therefore, no matter what we do in the function, the values of the parameters of `swap()` will not change when we return to the calling environment.

The correct code for `swap()` is shown in Example 2.8.

Example 2.8 A Correct Swapping Function Using Pointers

```
void swap (int *pi, int *pj)
{
    int temp;

    temp = *pi;
    *pi = *pj;
    *pj = temp;
}
```

Let's assume that we are swapping the values of variables `i` and `j` in the calling environment. From beginning C, we know that the proper call of swap looks like this:

```
swap(&i, &j);
```

Now we are directly manipulating what's in the addresses in memory where `i` and `j` live!

What will the call to the `sumints()` function (Examples 2.3 through 2.5) look like? Well, let's assume that we have an array `a` whose elements we wish to sum. Let's further assume that we wish to assign the `int` return value to a variable `i`. The call would look like this:

```
i = sumints(a);
```

This same call works no matter which of the three single-parameter versions of `sumints()` we use. Why? Because the name of a one-dimensional array is a pointer (address) to its first element. We are sending the address of the first element, so we are manipulating what is in that address directly (whether with pointer arithmetic or with indexing), not a copy that exists in another address.

Many beginning and intermediate-level C programmers forget this fact and pass `&a` to the function. This is a serious mistake for three reasons:

1. We don't want to change the address held in `a`. We still want it to hold the address of the first `int` in the array.
2. Because `a` is already a pointer, `&a` is a pointer to a pointer. Thus we would have a type mismatch between the actual and formal parameters.
3. Because `a` is a pointer constant, we risk the function trying to change `a`'s value—an illegal operation on any type of constant.

Surprisingly, I have seen compilers that would let such a type mismatch pass at compile time and runtime. Of course, making such a mistake invites bizarre runtime behavior. Later in this chapter, we will see a situation where we *want* to change a pointer's value in a function and must therefore pass a pointer to the pointer. But that's not what we want to do in `sumints()`.

By now you should have a handle on using pointers and arrays inside functions and from their calling environments. However, so far we have been dealing with simple, one-dimensional arrays of `int`s and `char`s. What about `struct`s and arrays of `struct`s?

First, it should be understood that you can send `struct`s to functions as parameters. Second, you should understand that the same *call-by-value rule* holds. In other words, the following code would not swap the two structure parameters back in the calling environment.

Example 2.9 Dysfunctional Attempt to Swap `Struct`s in a Function

```
void swapstruct (struct foo sf1, struct foo sf2)
{
    struct foo temp;

    temp  = sf1;  /* Yes, you can assign structs directly!*/
    sf1   = sf2;
    sf2   = temp;
}
```

In the calling environment, the two `struct` parameters would still have their original contents after the return from `swapstruct()`. The correct code to swap two structures is shown in Example 2.10.

Example 2.10 Correct Way to Swap Two `Struct`s in a Function

```
void swapstruct (struct foo *psf1, struct foo *psf2)
{
    struct foo temp;

    temp  = *psf1;
    *psf1 = *psf2;
    *psf2 = temp;
}
```

Note that the correct swapping code does not look any different from the code that swapped `int`s. That's because `struct`s can be assigned to other `struct`s just like `int`s. As we have already seen, arrays *cannot* be directly assigned. We will talk about array copying in Section 2.3.

Obviously, we cannot write a function similar to `sumints()` for an array of `struct`s, because an element of an array of `int` is simply one `int`, whereas an element of an array of `struct`s is a `struct`. As you already know, one `struct` can contain an unlimited amount of data—arrays, scalars, other `structs`, or any combination of these.

When dealing with arrays of `structs`, we may be interested in performing an operation on one component of each `struct` in the array. This component is often referred to as the *key* of the structure. Let us assume that we wish to sum the `int` component `i` of each structure in an array of `struct foos`. We will, as we did in our optimal `sumints()` code in Example 2.6, pass two parameters to our function—the address of the first array element and the number of elements.

Example 2.11 Summing Key Values of `Structs` Using Pointer Arithmetic

```
void sumstructs (struct foo *sfp, int num_elements)
{
    int sum = 0;

    while (num_elements-- > 0)
    {
        sum += sfp->i;
        sfp++;
    }
    return sum;
}
```

There are several important items to note in Example 2.11. When we say `sfp++`, the pointer `sfp` is moved to the next array element. Here we see a clear application of a principle stated earlier: When you increment a pointer via ++, the pointer is actually incremented by the number of bytes in the item being pointing at. In this case, `sfp` is incremented by the number of bytes in a `struct foo`. Also, you see a notation that you may not have seen before, `sfp->i`. What does it mean?

Suppose I have a set of declarations like these:

```
struct foo
{
    int  i;
    char  string[10];
};

struct foo  sfoo, *fooptr;
```

Recall, from beginning C, that I can access the component `i` of `sfoo` with the notation

```
sfoo.i
```

I can copy "hello" into sfoo's string component via

```
strcpy(sfoo.string, "hello");
```

What about fooptr? The first thing we have to worry about is that fooptr has not been allocated any space to point at something. Here's how we would take care of this task:

```
fooptr = (struct foo *) malloc(sizeof(struct foo));
```

Now the fooptr is pointing at a newly allocated struct foo that has not yet been filled up. Malloc(), a function we will use throughout this book, returns a void *. It turns out that void pointers are compatible with any pointer type. You should still cast malloc's return value so the reader knows what type of pointer fooptr is. Later, we will see what to do if malloc() cannot deliver memory to us successfully.

How can we assign 5 to the i component of the struct pointed at by fooptr? There are two ways:

```
(*fooptr).i  =  5;
fooptr->i  = 5;
```

The parentheses are necessary because . has higher precedence than *. Without the parentheses, C will look for a component i in a struct called fooptr and then dereference that. This is doubly wrong; fooptr is not a struct and i is not a pointer! However, because (*fooptr) is a clumsy notation, the -> operator was added to C. It's nice because it looks like it says "points at." In fact, fooptr->i means "the component i in the struct pointed at by fooptr."

Finally, how can we assign the string "hello" to our struct pointed at by fooptr?

```
strcpy(fooptr->string, "hello");
```

2.3 Assigning and Initializing One-Dimensional Arrays

As we have seen, arrays are the most troublesome data type in ANSI C in at least one respect. They cannot be assigned to one another as the scalar data types and structs can be. Why not? Well, suppose we have a program with the following declarations:

```
char s1[80] = "Hello", s2[80];
```

The following statement is not allowed:

```
s2 = s1;
```

Because s2 is declared as a true array, it is a pointer constant, not a pointer variable. Constants cannot be on the left side of an = operator. Suppose we try to get around this problem by declaring s2 as a pointer variable and assigning it some space to point at with the malloc() (memory allocation) function from the stdlib.h library via

```
char *s2 = (char *) malloc(80);    /* Malloc argument = bytes
                                       to allocate. */
```

And now suppose we say

```
s2 = s1;
```

Does this copy the string pointed at by s1 to s2? No! It merely puts the address of the "H" in "Hello" in s2. Here s1 and s2 are pointing at the same string in the same place in memory. As we all know, strcpy makes a true copy, so

```
strcpy(s2, s1);
```

is what we really want. Now s1 and s2 are pointing at their own copy of "Hello", each of which resides in a different place in memory. However, we have a dilemma if we try to copy arrays of types other than char. What do we do? We use the string.h library function memcpy(). Memcpy's syntax is

```
memcpy(destination_address, origin_address,
        num_bytes_to_copy);
```

Suppose we have two int arrays declared as follows:

```
int a1[10] = {1, 3, 5, 7, 9, 11},  a2[10];
```

We could copy the whole of a1 to a2 via

```
memcpy(a2, a1, 10 * sizeof(int));
```

Note that memcpy's syntax is identical to strcpy's except for the extra (third) parameter. In the official definition of C, you would find that the data type of the first two parameters of memcpy() is void *. Fortunately, a void * is compatible with any C pointer type. Thus, in English, this call to memcpy() says, "Copy 10 ints starting at the address in a1 to the addresses starting at a2."

Of course, it is crucial that a2 contain an address value. If a2 is declared as a true array, the storage for its elements are allocated at compile time. If a2 is a pointer, it must be allocated space via malloc() or calloc() (you can look at calloc on your own; we won't use it).

Finally, note that we have initialized a1 with only six values even though it holds ten. We will repeat the following many times: *If an array initialization contains fewer values than the number of elements in the array, the remaining (uninitialized) values are zero.* Thus a[6] through a[9] will all be zero.

Suppose that a2 is a true array declared via

```
int a2[10];
```

Doesn't this memcpy() violate the rule that you can't assign to an array because it is a pointer constant? No! When you try to assign an array via a2 = a1, you are trying to put a different address in a2—something you can't do to a pointer constant. However, if a2 is declared as a true array or as a pointer that is malloc'ed space, then memcpy() does not change the value of a2; it merely changes the values in the array pointed at by a2. Pointers hold address values, and the memcpy() isn't going to change that value.

Memcpy() is also very flexible. Suppose you want the first five ints of the a2 array to be equal to the last five ints of the a1 array, and you want the last five ints of the a2 array to be equal to the first five ints of the a1 array. Here's how to do it:

```
memcpy(a2, &a1[5], 5 * sizeof(int));
memcpy(&a2[5], a1, 5 * sizeof(int));
```

You may have guessed by now that giving a2 as an argument is identical to saying &a2[0]. However, the &a2[0] form is unnecessary, because the name of a one-dimensional array is always the address of the first element—i.e., the one with an index of zero.

Returning to array initialization again for a moment, here's a nifty and useful trick that many forget.

```
int a[100] = {0};   /** Yes, all 100 elements are zero!! **/
```

You don't need to use for loops for all array initializations! How about initializing an array of structs? Here's an example:

Example 2.12 Initializing an Array of Structs at Declaration Time

```
struct person
{
    int age;
    char name[40];
    float salary;
};
int main()
{
    struct person people[3] = { {45, "John Doe", 40123.34},
                             {39, "Jack Benny", 109987.88},
                           {100, "George Burns",  1000000.00}};
         /*** Remainder of main's code goes here.  ***/
```

Note that the order of declaration of the components of a struct person (age, then name, then salary) must be followed in the initialization. Just as with an array of any other type, if there are fewer initializers than array elements, then the remaining uninitialized structs are completely zeroed out. Thus, if we left out George Burns's entry above, people[2].age would be zero, people[2].name would be a string of '\0' characters, and people[2].salary would be 0.0.

Copying arrays of structs is no different from copying arrays of any other type. For example, if we wanted to copy the people array in Example 2.12 to the second, third, and fourth elements of a struct person array called folks (let's assume folks is pointing at some space allocated at declaration time or via malloc()), we would do this:

```
memcpy(&folks[1], people, 3 * sizeof(struct person));
```

We know that memcpy() works a lot like strcpy(), but it works for any array data type. Is there a mem analog to the strcmp() function? Yes, the memcmp() function. It too is in string.h. Here's its syntax:

```
memcmp(pointer1, pointer2, byte_length_of_comparison);
```

Memcmp() works just like strcmp() except that it compares bytes from any two array types. Thus two int arrays can be compared, or (ridiculous as it may sound) one int array and one char array. The array types of the first two arguments do not have to be the same. Generally, though, it would be an odd application if they were not. Here's an example of the use of memcmp():

```
int a[5] = {1, 3, 5, 7, 9}, b[5] = {1, 3, 5, 8, 9};
printf("Result of comparison is %d\n", memcmp(a, b, 5 *
        sizeof(int)));
```

What will the printf() print? Remember that it works just like strcmp() in that it returns a negative value if the first array is less than the second, a zero if the first array is the same as the second, and a positive number if the first array is greater than the second.

However, with non-char arrays, *greater than, less than,* and *equal* refer to the integer value of bytes rather than to the ASCII value of characters. Clearly, the printf() should print a negative value, because after the first three values are equal (1, 3, and 5), the fourth value of b is greater than the fourth value of a (8 versus 7). Note that the two arrays may be partially or wholly compared, because the third argument of memcmp() enables us to specify the byte length of the comparison.

This leads us to the introduction of the "n" versions of the string.h functions—the ones named strncmp(), strncpy(), and strncat(). These, like memcmp() and memcpy(), take a third parameter that enables us to compare, copy, and concatenate only the first "n" characters, where "n" is some int you give as the third argument. Let's demonstrate strncmp().

```
char s1[] = "Hello", s2[] = "Helicopter";
printf("%d\n", strncmp(s1, s2, 3));
```

What should the printf() print? It should print 0 (zero) because the first three characters of the two strings are identical.

2.4 An Example of Pointer Manipulation with Strings

A good exercise for practicing pointer manipulation with strings is to write a program that

1. Receives newline-terminated strings from a user until the user enters `"quit"`.
2. "Formats" the string by getting rid of whitespace and converting uppercase letters to lowercase.
3. Reverses the string (e.g., `"foobar"` becomes `"raboof"`) and outputs it to the screen.

Have you thought about the problem? Are you confused about where to start? Let's examine the problem algorithmically first. First, how many functions should there be besides `main()`? Your answer should be "at least two"—one to format the string and one to turn the string backwards. Here, in English, is the algorithm to format the string:

1. Initialize two pointers, `fast` and `slow`, so that they start out by pointing to the beginning of the string.
2. Let the `fast` pointer run ahead until it finds a non-whitespace character.
3. When `*fast` is a non-whitespace character, copy it to `*slow`.
4. Continue looping until `*fast` is the `'\0'` character.
5. After loop termination, copy the `'\0'` character to `*slow`.

An inexperienced C programmer would be tempted to use two `char` arrays to accomplish this—the entered string that is scanned by one pointer, and another string to receive a copy of the non-whitespace characters only. But you should use only one.

Now that you have a "formatted" string, how do you reverse the string? You can certainly guess that, once again, you use two pointers but only one string—the original "formatted" string. Here, in English, is the algorithm for reversing the string:

1. Initialize two pointers, `start` and `end`, so that they point at the first and last characters of the string (e.g., the `"f"` in `"foobar"` and the `"r"` in `"foobar"`).
2. Swap the values of `*start` and `*end`.
3. Move the `start` and `end` pointers toward one another by one character.
4. Continue steps 1 through 3 until the two pointers are equal or cross over.

Here's my solution to this exercise:

Example 2.13 Reversing a String in Place with Two Pointers and One String

```
#include <stdio.h>
#include <string.h>
#include <ctype.h>

/**************************************************/
/*                                                */
/*  Get strings from user, clean out whitespace   */
/*  and convert letters to lowercase, reverse string */
/*  and then output to screen.                    */
/**************************************************/

main()
{
    char word[512];
    void getword(char *), format(char *), reverse(char *);

    while (getword(word), format(word), strcmp(word,
            "quit"))
    {
        if (*word == '\0') continue;
        reverse(word);
        printf("Your original word reversed is \"%s\"\n\n",
                word);
    }
    return 0;
}


/********  Get user-entered string from terminal. ********/
void getword(char *string)
{
    printf("Please enter a string:  ");
    gets(string);
}


/**************************************************/
/*                                                */
/*   Remove whitespace from string.  Convert uppercase */
/*   letters to lowercase.                        */
/**************************************************/

void format(char *string)
{
    char *fast = string, *slow = string;
```

```
    while ( *fast )
    {
        if (!isspace(*fast)) *slow++ = tolower(*fast);
        fast++;
    }
    *slow = '\0';
}


/*****************************************************************/
/*                                                               */
/*      Reverse order of characters in string.                   */
/*****************************************************************/

void reverse(char *string)
{
    char *end, *start = string, tempchar;

    if (*string == '\0') return;
    end = string + strlen(string) - 1;
    while ( end > start)
    {
        tempchar = *end;
        *end = *start;
        *start = tempchar;
        start++; end--;
    }
}  /**** End of reverse. ****/

/************** Sample Program Session Below **************/

$ asg1e.exe

Enter a word or quit ->      /**** Immediate return here ****/
Enter a word or quit ->      /**** Mix of space/tab here ****/
Enter a word or quit -> f  oo bar
Your original word reversed is "raboof"

Enter a word or quit -> f7yABC   D
Your original word reversed is "dcbay7f"

Enter a word or quit -> l  e ve l
Your original word reversed is "level"

Enter a word or quit -> q  u  i  t
$
```

Let's analyze the code of `format()` and `reverse()`. `Format()` can be explained simply. The `fast` pointer simply runs ahead of the `slow` pointer until it finds a non-whitespace character (not a space, tab, or newline). Then the lowercase of `*fast` is copied into `*slow`. It continues doing this until `*fast` is the `'\0'` character. At that point, the loop conditional, `*fast`, becomes zero (the ASCII value of the `'\0'` character), and the loop terminates. Then the `'\0'` character is copied to `*slow`.

We will illustrate how `reverse()` works with a series of graphs showing the pointers and string values after each loop iteration. We will assume that the formatted string is `"hello"`.

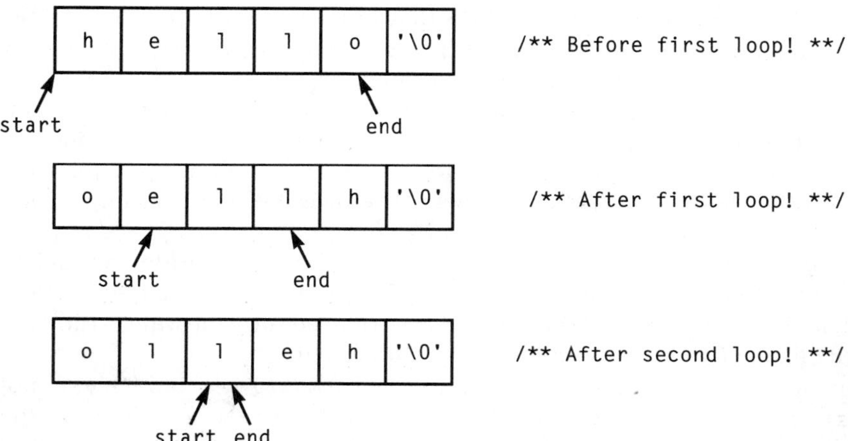

At this point, the `while` conditional `(end > start)` fails because the two pointers are now equal. If you don't understand `format()`, try drawing graphs like these for every loop iteration. When it comes to understanding pointers, a picture really is worth a thousand words.

Let's look at some of the details of the code in this program. Note the trick in `reverse()` that got the `end` pointer to the end of `"hello"`. That trick was

```
end = start + strlen(start) - 1;
```

Many people would use a loop such as

```
for (end = start; *end != '\0'; end++) ;
end--;    /*** We want to point at the "o" in "hello", not
              the '\0'.  ***/
```

You may have overheard programmers using the expression "reinventing the wheel" when describing a programmer who writes unnecessary code instead of using the power already in the language. Not to use `strlen()` to get the `end` pointer to its starting location is indeed reinventing the wheel in this situation.

Note that `gets()` was used to capture the user's input string. Here is another situation where a beginner reinvents the wheel or makes a serious mistake. Some would use this to capture the input string:

```
scanf("%s", word);
```

WRONG! This programmer has forgotten that `scanf()` will stop reading into `word` as soon as it encounters whitespace. Others would use `getchar()` in a loop to capture characters, one at a time, and stuff them into `word` until `'\n'` is encountered.

The beauty of `gets()` is that it captures *all characters up to, and including, the newline.* After it finds the newline, it overwrites it with `'\0'` in the captured string. The only danger with `gets()` is that your line may have more characters than allocated for `word`. That's why it's a good idea to give `word` a hefty allocation such as the 512 characters allocated for it in Example 2.13.

`Format()` removes whitespace and converts uppercase characters to lowercase as the algorithm states. Note that the `tolower()` function is called to convert the non-whitespace character to lowercase even if it is not uppercase. The ANSI C definition says that `tolower()` returns the character unchanged if it is not uppercase.

Also note that the `fast` pointer is *not* incremented inside the call to `tolower()`. This is because the function call parentheses have a higher priority than ++, and, in fact, this author has experienced difficulty when using the postfix form of ++ inside a function call. Don't do it!

Finally, note that the `while` condition in `format()` says only `*fast`, not `*fast != '\0'`. Why? Because if `*fast` is `'\0'` then its value is zero—the value that terminates a `while` loop. However, this is a gray area. If you find the wordier `while` condition more readable, use it. It is not worth quibbling over. However, you may have to read code written by others who use the terse form. Therefore, it is good to be conversant with both forms.

It is worth taking a moment to look at the testing session that accompanies the code in Example 2.13. You should always test all possible permutations of input, especially extreme input such as an empty string or one that contains whitespace only. Note that these conditions and all relevant "normal" input are, indeed, tested in the sample program session shown in Example 2.13.

While we are on the subject of testing and functionality, do `format()` and `reverse()` behave properly in the extreme cases of empty strings and strings that are all whitespace? They do. However, some of you may think that

```
end = start + strlen(start) - 1;
```

causes trouble on an empty string, because `end` will point one character to the left of `start`—a location clearly outside the string's boundaries. Remember this rule: *A pointer with an out-of-bounds address causes a problem only when it is dereferenced.* Because the `end > start` test will fail immediately, the function will never refer to `*end` when the string is empty.

2.5 Index and Pointer Trickery in C

Some of what I am about to show you is *awful.* I will show you tricks involving array indexing and pointer arithmetic that no sane person would use in their code. Why am I doing this? Two reasons. First, regrettably, you are likely to read much, much more code in your life than you will write. This means that you must be able to read all coding styles—the good, the bad, and the ugly! Second, this "awful" code is actually instructive in that it reveals more interesting truths about indexing and pointer arithmetic. Some of these truths will be quite surprising.

Let's say we have a program with the following declarations and initializations:

```
int a[] = {1, 3, 5, 7, 9, 11}, *b = &a[3];
```

Thus array `b` is an `int` pointer that points at the `int` in `a[3]`—that is, the 7. What is the value of `b[-1]`? First, is it legal to give `b` a negative index? You bet it is! Let's "pointerize" the expression as we did earlier in this chapter. The pointer version of `b[-1]` is `*(b - 1)`. The expression `*(b - 1)` says, "Subtract one `int` unit from the address in `b` and then fetch me the `int` in that address." Therefore, the expression `b - 1` gives us the address of the 5. The dereference operator (*) then fetches that 5. Let's look at a graph that summarizes all of this.

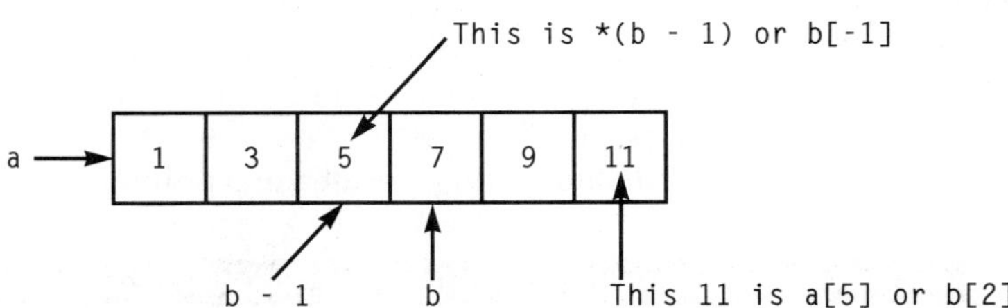

Now let me ask you another question. What is the value of `b - a`? If your answer is "It depends on the size of an `int`," then you are forgetting how address arithmetic works in C. Remember that when we add an `int` to, or subtract it from, a pointer, it adds or subtracts that `int` *times the size of the thing pointed to by the pointer.* Thus, in the previous paragraph, the value of `b - 1` is really `b - (1 * sizeof(int))` because `b` is an `int` pointer. Therefore, `b - a` is really `b - (a * sizeof(int))`. But there's an easier way to do this subtraction: Ask yourself how many `int`s separate `b` and `a`. The answer: 3.

A final trick I want to demonstrate is the use of the `sizeof()` function with arrays and pointers. If a variable is declared as a true array (e.g., `int a[5]`), then `sizeof()` will return the size of each element times the number of elements. Thus, if your computer had four-byte `int`s, then `sizeof(a)` would return `20` (5 * 4). However, if a variable is declared as a pointer, then `sizeof()` will return your machine's byte size for a pointer—generally 4.

It does not matter how much memory is `malloc`'ed to a true pointer; the `sizeof()` it will be just the pointer size for that machine. Finally, if you give `sizeof()` an element of an array as a parameter (e.g., `sizeof(a[5])`), it will simply return the size of `a[5]`'s data type—in this case, `sizeof(int)`.

Later in the book, when we look at multidimensional arrays, you will see how this knowledge can help you to understand tricks involving multiple indices and/or multiple levels of indirection. First, however, you must take the biggest leap of your programming career: understanding pointers to pointers.

2.6 Pointers to Pointers in Function Parameter Lists

Most people have little trouble understanding the use of pointers in functions because of call-by-value. For some reason, however, most students have great difficulty with the concept of a pointer to a pointer. My theory is that this problem arises because the concept is actually easy while it is expected to be difficult!

Remember that when you are passing a parameter to a function and you want this parameter to come back to the calling environment with a changed value, you must pass a pointer to it. What if the value being passed to the function is a pointer and you wish it to come back with a changed value? You guessed it—you have to give the address of the pointer, which is just another way of saying a pointer to the pointer.

Here's a simple piece of code illustrating the idea of a pointer to a pointer.

Example 2.14 A First Exposure to Code Using Pointers to Pointers

```
#include <stdio.h>
#include <stdlib.h>
int main()
{
    char *s1, *s2;

    if ((s1 = (char *) malloc(80)) == NULL ||
        (s2 = (char *) malloc(80)) == NULL)
    {
        printf("Fatal memory error!\n");
        exit(1);
    }
    strcpy(s1, "Hello");  strcpy(s2, "Goodbye");
    strswap(&s1, &s2);
```

```
    printf("s1 is now %s.  s2 is now %s.\n",  s1, s2);
    return 0;
}


void strswap (char **s1, char **s2)
{
    char *temp;

    temp = *s1;
    *s1  = *s2;
    *s2  = temp;
}
```

Study this code carefully. It contains many important chunks of basic knowledge. What does it do? As the function name would suggest, it swaps two strings. It does so *without copying a single character.* How it does so will be explained after we've cleared up a few points.

First, why are `s1` and `s2` declared as character pointers and not as character arrays? Remember that true arrays are pointer constants. However, in order to swap these two strings, we do so by changing the address contained in `s1` so that it contains the address of the `"G"` in `"Goodbye"` and by changing the address contained in `s2` so that it contains the address of the `"H"` in `"Hello"`. Because we are going to change the contents of `s1` and `s2`, they must be pointer variables, not pointer constants.

Next, after we've properly declared `s1` and `s2` as pointer variables, we must allocate some space for them via `malloc()`. `Malloc()` can fail at runtime if the computer is out of available memory. When `malloc()` fails, it returns `NULL` (zero) as the return value. If the `malloc()` of space for `s1` or `s2` fails, we deliver an error message to the terminal and then call the `exit()` function.

`Exit()` and `malloc()` both reside in the `stdlib.h` header file. Typically, when a program ends prematurely because of an error condition, we return any integer value except zero. Zero is typically returned to the calling environment only upon a normal (error-free) termination of the program.

Once we've allocated memory and guarded against a memory failure, we call the `strswap()` function. Because we want the values of `s1` and `s2` to be changed in the function (so that they point at the other pointer's string), we must pass the address of `s1` and the address of `s2`—just as we must pass the address of any variable if it is to be changed in a function.

That's why the data types of the two parameters in the function's environment are `char **` (i.e., pointer-to-pointer-to-`char`). The following diagram shows the state of the pointers in `strswap()` before it does anything and then after each statement.

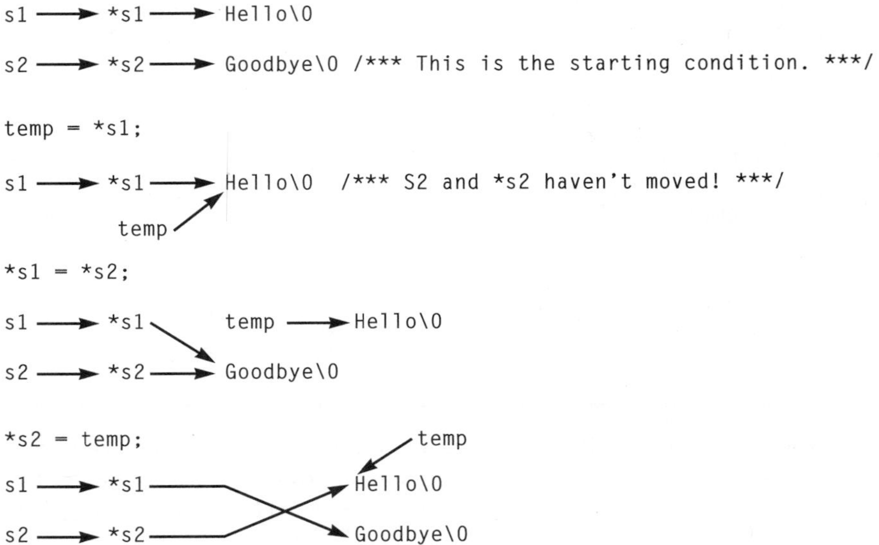

Just for fun, I want to pose another question here. When you are in `strswap` and have not yet swapped addresses, what are the values of `**s1` and `**s2`?

You can answer this question correctly by getting the correct data type. What is the data type of `s1` in `strswap()`? It's a `char **`. Then what is the type of `*s1`? It's a `char *`—you can see in the diagram that it is indeed pointing at the first character of a string. Therefore, the data type of `**s1` (same for `**s2`) is `char`. This reasoning leads you to the correct answer: `**s1` is the `"H"` in `"Hello"`, and `**s2` is the `"G"` in `"Goodbye"`. It is imperative that you not leave this chapter without understanding this last paragraph!

Facts About Functions

`<stdio.h>` Functions

Function: `int getchar (void);`

Fact: 1) Returns an `int` containing the ASCII value of one character received from the terminal.

Fact: 2) Because `EOF` is `-1` (an `int!`), you must remember to put the return value in an `int` variable.

Function: `int fgetc (FILE *fp);`

Fact: 1) Works the same as `getchar()` except that it reads the character from a file.

Function: `char *gets (char *string);`

Fact: 1) Reads from terminal until `'\n'` is encountered or `EOF` occurs, whichever comes first.

Fact: 2) If `'\n'` is encountered, it is overwritten by `'\0'`.

Fact: 3) If `EOF` occurs, a `NULL` pointer is returned.

Fact: 4) A pointer to the string obtained from the terminal is returned. The parameter string is filled up with the characters obtained from the terminal.

Fact: 5) You must be sure to allocate a space large enough to hold the user's input line! Better to waste a little space than risk a runtime memory error. A 500- or 1000-byte allocation should be quite safe.

Function: `char *fgets (char *string, int numchars, FILE *fp);`

Fact: 1) Same as `gets()` except that the `'\n'` is retained (if encountered) and `'\0'` is put after it.

Fact: 2) Stops after `numchars - 1` characters are read (to keep room for the `'\0'`).

Fact: 3) `Fgets()` may be safer for terminal input than `gets()` because you can specify the number of characters to read. When you use `gets()` to get terminal input, the `FILE *` parameter is `stdin`.

Function: `int putchar (int c);`

Fact: 1) Writes a single character (held in an `int` variable—you never know when it might be an `EOF`) to the screen.

Fact: 2) Returns a value that is identical to the character written.

Fact: 3) Returns `EOF` (which is usually `-1`) if the character could not be written.

Function: `int fputc (int c, FILE *fp);`

Fact: 1) Same as `putchar()` but writes the character (`c`) to a file.

Function: `int puts (char *string);`

Fact: 1) Writes `string` to the screen and then writes a `'\n'` as well.

Fact: 2) Returns `EOF` if the write cannot be done, and an unspecified positive (or zero) value if it succeeds.

Function: `int fputs (char *string, FILE *fp);`

Fact: 1) Same as `puts()` but writes to a file.

Fact: 2) Also, it does not append `'\n'` to the output as does `puts()`.

Function: `int ungetc (int c, FILE *fp);`

Fact: 1) Although not discussed in the chapter, this function is worth mentioning. It is *supposed* to put a character back onto the input stream (`fp`).

Fact: 2) It is one of the most unreliable and unpredictable `stdio.h` functions. *Do not use it!*

Function: `int printf (char *format_string, value-list);`

Fact: 1) Writes the list of values according to the specifications in the `format_string`.

Fact: 2) Returns the number of characters written (seldom used).

Fact: 3) `Printf()` is dangerous if any format specification represents a type of a larger byte size than the type in the value list corresponding to it. You must remember this!

Fact: 4) A failure leads to a negative return value.

Function: `int fprintf (FILE *fp, char *format_string, value-list);`

Fact: 1) Same as `printf()` but writes to a file.

`<string.h>` Functions

Function: `int strcmp (char *string1, char *string2);`

Fact: 1) Compares characters in `string1` and `string2` using the ASCII character set. Returns zero if the strings are identical, a positive value if the first string is greater than the second, and a negative value if the second string is greater than the first.

Fact: **2)** As with all `string.h` functions, it is imperative that (a) all strings be terminated with the `'\0'` character and, of course, (b) neither pointer parameter be `NULL`. You must remember these two rules!

Function: `char *strcat (char *string1, char *string2);`

Fact: **1)** Appends `string2` to the end of `string1`.

Fact: **2)** Return value is the same address as the first string parameter (`string1`).

Fact: **3)** When using `strcat()`, you must make sure that enough room is left in `string1` so that the append operation is safe.

Function: `char *strcpy (char *string1, char  *string2);`

Fact: **1)** Overwrites the characters in `string1` with the characters in `string2` (including `'\0'`).

Fact: **2)** As with `strcat()`, you must be sure that `string1` has room for the copy.

Fact: **3)** Returns `string1` just as `strcat()` did.

Function: `int memcmp (void *pointer1, void *pointer2, size_t numbytes);`

Fact: **1)** Compares `numbytes` bytes in the spaces pointed to by `pointer1` and `pointer2`.

Fact: **2)** Works just like `strcmp()` except that the comparison can be done on `int` or other array types. You must, however, remember that the comparison is done on a byte-by-byte basis.

Fact: **3)** Note the strange type of `numbytes (size_t)`. Don't worry. This type is compatible with a `short`, a `long`, or an `int`.

Function: `void *memcpy (void *pointer1, void *pointer2, size_t numbytes);`

Fact: **1)** Copies `numbytes` bytes from the space pointed to by `pointer2` to the space pointed to by `pointer1`.

Fact: 2) Value of `pointer1` is returned.

Fact: 3) The copy is done on a byte-by-byte basis. *The function is not guaranteed to work correctly if the bytes being copied overlap with the destination bytes.* Consult the `memmove()` function in the rare event that you must copy between overlapping areas.

`<stdlib.h>` Functions

Function: `void exit (int status);`

Fact: 1) Terminates the program (no matter where it is executing) and returns `status` to the calling environment of the program.

Fact: 2) A `return` in `main()` is functionally equivalent to `exit()`.

Fact: 3) A convention usually adopted is to exit with a zero `status` upon a "normal" termination and with a positive `status` when an unrecoverable error has occurred.

Function: `void *malloc (size_t numbytes);`

Fact: 1) Allocates `numbytes` bytes from the program's heap space and returns a pointer to the newly allocated space.

Fact: 2) Returns `NULL` if the allocation was not successful (in which case, you'd use `exit()`).

Fact: 3) Note the strange data type `size_t` again. Remember that this data type is compatible with any `long`, `short`, or `int` you may pass to `malloc()`.

Fact: 4) When you are using `malloc()`, it is always a good idea to cast the return value so that it is the same type as the pointer receiving the allocated space—for example,

```
char   *s;
s = (char  *) malloc (80);
```

Function: `void free (void *pointer);`

Fact: 1) Gives the space pointed to by `pointer` back to the system's dynamic memory space.

Fact: 2) A little-known fact about `free()` is that it will fail if the space being pointed to by `pointer` is not the starting location of a space allocated via `malloc()`. Thus the following code will fail.

```
char  *string = (char  *) malloc (30);
char  *mover = string + 3;
strcpy (string, "help");
free (mover);
```

This fails because `mover` is not the starting address of the `malloc`'ed space. The starting address is the address that contains the `"h"` from `"help"`, but `mover` is pointing at the `"p"`. Remember this to avoid a frustrating and hard-to-find bug. We'll look at `malloc()` and `free()` in greater detail in the next chapter.

Exercises

■ **1.** You have declared an array and a pointer as follows:

```
int a[] = {2, 4, 6, 8, 10, 12}, *b = &a[2];
```

Assume that your computer has four-byte `ints` and `int *`s and that `&a[0]` is 1000. Give the value of the following expressions.

a. `*(b + 2)` **b.** `b + 2`
c. `b[-2]` **d.** `b - a`
e. `&b[1]` **f.** `sizeof(a)`
g. `sizeof(a[1])` **h.** `sizeof(b)`
i. `*(a + 2) * (*b)` **j.** `*a * b[2]`

2. Write a function that will determine whether its `char *` argument is a palindrome. A palindrome is a string that looks the same way forwards and backwards (such as `"level"`). Your function should work even if the string passed has nothing but the `'\0'` character. It should not use any strings other than the one passed as a parameter!

3. Write a program that

a. Asks the user for the number of test scores in a class.
b. Allocates exactly the correct amount of space to hold that many scores.
c. Reads the scores into memory from the user at the terminal.

d. Sorts the scores if you know how to do that. If not, just enter the scores in ascending order.

e. Calculates the median score. If there are an odd number of scores, the median is the middle score. If there are an even number of scores, the median is an average of the two scores closest to the middle. For example, the third highest score is the median of five scores. The average of the third and fourth highest scores is the median of six scores.

f. Outputs the result of part e to the terminal.

■ **4.** State what, if anything, is wrong with the following code fragments. Assume that all necessary header files have been previously `#include`'d.

a.
```
int *pi;
*pi = 5;
```

b.
```
int i;
printf("%d\n", *i);
```

c.
```
int i;
printf("%ld\n", i);
```

d.
```
char c;
while ((c = getchar()) != EOF) putchar(c);
```

e.
```
int c;
while ( c = getchar() != EOF) putchar(c);
```

f.
```
char s[] = "hello", *p = &s[2], c;
c = toupper(p);
```

g.
```
char s[] = "hello";
printf("The string is %s\n", *s);
```

h.
```
char s[] = "hello", *p = &s[2];
printf("%c\n", toupper(*p));
```

i.
```
while ( i != 9, printf("%d\n", i)) ;
```

j.
```
char s[] = "hello", *p = &s[3];
printf("%c\n", p[3]);
```

■ **5.** You are given the following declarations and initializations:

```
char s1[] = "Able", s2[] = “Baker, *ps1 = &s1[1], *ps2 =
            &s2[1];
```

Given these declarations and that `s1` is 1000 and `s2` is 5000, find the value of the expressions below. Assume four-byte pointers.

a. `strcmp(s1, s2)` **b.** `ps1 - s1`

c. `&(*(s1 + 3))` **d.** `&s1[1]`

e. `*ps1 - *ps2 + 1` **f.** `sizeof(*ps2)`

g. `*s2` **h.** `*(ps1 + 1)`

i. `ps2[2]` **j.** `*ps1 + 1`

■ **6.** You are given the following declarations and statements. (See the individual parts for * markings.)

```
/*** Yes, pa and pb can be declared as pointer variables!! ***/
/*** They are allocated six ints apiece.                     ***/
int *pa = {1,2,3,4,5,6}, *pb = {7,8,9,10,11,12], *pc,*pd;
```

Write statement(s) that accomplish the following objectives. Assume that your answers to any part do not affect your answers to any other part. Use only the variables declared above in your answers.

■ **a.** Swap the contents of the two arrays without copying array element values.

b. Change the array pointed to by `pa` so that it contains 6, 5, 4, 3, 2, 1 in that order.

c. Copy the last three values of the array pointed to by `pb` so that they become `pa[2]`, `pa[3]`, and `pa[4]`. Do it in one statement, not three!

■ **d.** Allocate memory for `pc` so that it points at a space that may contain ten `int`s. Test `pc` for a `NULL` value after the attempted allocation, and leave the program if this happens. Initialize `pd` to point at the fourth slot in the `pc` array.

■ **e.** Write a loop that prints out the values of the array pointed to by `pa`. Do *not* use array indexing.

f. Do the same as in part e, but write the values backwards—the last first and so on. No indexing!

■ **g.** Assign the `pc` pointer so that it points at the third element of the array pointed to by `pb`.

h. Print the value of the element that is two elements after the one pointed to by `pb` from part g. Use indexing, *not* pointer arithmetic.

■ **7.** Write a function that accepts a single `int *` parameter representing an array of `int`. The function will assume that the value in the last array element is `-1`. The function will compute and return the number of elements in the passed array. Use pointers, not indices, and assume that `-1` can be only a sentinel value in the array. Don't count the `-1` as part of the array. Hint: `Sizeof()` will *not* do the job.

■ **8.** Write a function that accepts two parameters: an `int *` parameter representing an array of `int`, and an `int` parameter containing the number of elements in the array. The function will return a pointer to an `int` array containing the index numbers of all elements in the array parameter whose value is greater than 10. No array index brackets anywhere in your function! The returned array should have `-1` as a sentinel value. Allow for the possibility that all members of the passed array are greater than 10.

9. Write a function that accepts two parameters: an `int *` parameter representing an array of `int`, and an `int` parameter containing the number of elements in the array. The function will return a pointer to an `int` array containing the squares of the elements in the array parameter. No array index brackets anywhere in your function!

10. Write a function that accepts an `int *` parameter and the number of elements in the corresponding array. The function will transpose each pair of `int`s in the array—that is, the 0 and 1 element, the 2 and 3 element, the 4 and 5 element, and so on. Use indices when and if you feel they're appropriate.

Chapter 3

The Linear Dynamic Data Structures: Stacks, Queues, and Linked Lists

3.1 Why Do We Need Dynamic Data Structures?

Stacks, queues, and linked lists are made out of `structs`. However, unlike an array of `structs`, the "nodes" (i.e., `structs`) of these data structures are allocated (via `malloc()`) only when you need one. Arrays of `structs` are usually allocated at declaration time. Doesn't it therefore seem inefficient to `malloc()` space for one structure at a time? What is the advantage? The advantage is tremendous!

Think about the problem of maintaining a *sorted* array of `structs`. First, how many `structs` will you need? If you don't know the size of your data collection, you have to guess what the maximum size will be and allocate that. This is dangerous because you may exceed that number of `structs`. It is also wasteful, because the average number of `structs` that an average user of your program might need is likely to be far below your huge, compile-time allocation.

For example, suppose your program maintains student records for colleges and universities. It keeps the array sorted by the student_id field of the following `struct` type:

```
struct student
{
    long student_id;
    char student_address[200];
    char student_name[50];
    /*****  Lots more fields here!  *****/
};
```

Let's suppose that each `struct student` contains 500 bytes of information (not unreasonable). Further, let's make the reasonable assumption that the size of an average college is 15,000 students but the enrollment at the largest possible college is 60,000 students. Thus on an average campus site where our program is run, we will waste 45,000 times 500 bytes of memory—22.5 megabytes of waste!

We *still* have not touched on the most serious deficiency of using an array of `structs`: sorting them. Almost no real-world databases are static; they grow and shrink. Suppose we have all records of the student database loaded into an array of `struct` sorted in memory. What do we do about new insertions? If we just put them at the end of the array of existing records, then we lose our sorted order. If we want to keep the sorted order at all times, we have to create a "hole" in the middle of the array and then move the "greater than" elements to the right—a very expensive maneuver!

Deletion presents another problem. Whenever you delete a student record from the array of `struct students`, you have a hole in the array. After each batch of deletes, you have to run another function that removes holes by moving all records in higher indices of the array down to cover the holes. Clearly, this is also extremely inefficient.

As the reader can plainly see, fixed-allocation arrays of `structs` are inflexible, high-maintenance data structures. They are really not worth the trouble. Whenever we have data collections that can grow or shrink, we would like to receive or remove memory whenever we need it or are through with it.

The answer to our prayers is a *dynamic data structure.* A dynamic data structure in C is represented as a series of `structs` all with pointers in them to similar `structs`. Here is a graphical depiction of an *ordered linked list* data structure holding student records. Only the "key" of each structure (`student_id`) is shown, along with the pointer to the next structure.

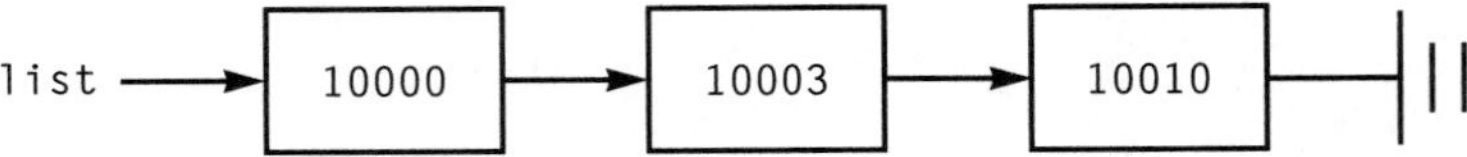

Note that there is a slight change to each `struct student` in this data structure. Each contains a pointer to another `struct student`. Thus each `struct student` would have a field in it that looks something like this:

```
struct student *next;     /**** It doesn't have to be called
                           "next"!  ****/
```

Note how easy it is to maintain this data structure. If we wished to add a new `struct student` to the database with `student_id` 10007, we would simply reassign the pointer in the 10003 record so that it points at the new record. The new `struct student` would then be made to point at the 10010 record. Of course, the record containing student 10007's data would have to be `malloc`'ed like this:

```
new_rec_ptr = (struct student *) malloc(sizeof(struct
                student));
```

Deletion is also easy. If we wished to delete the record of student 10003, we would only have to deallocate its space (we'll see how to do that later) and reassign the pointer coming out of the 10000 record we just inserted.

Consider why we refer to a structure such as a linked list as a linear dynamic data structure. It is dynamic because it grows or shrinks at runtime depending on how many records are inserted or deleted. It is linear because the "nodes" (we will use this term from now on to refer to the `struct`s in all dynamic data structures, linear and nonlinear), as can be seen in the foregoing diagram, are in a straight line.

3.2 The Stack and Queue Data Structures

We have just seen that linear dynamic data structures are far easier to maintain than arrays of `struct`s. Now we will examine the linear dynamic data structures in order of increasing complexity. The simplest of these data structures is called a *stack*. It is the simplest because all new nodes are placed at the top of the stack, and all nodes to be deleted are removed from the top of the stack. Examine the following diagram.

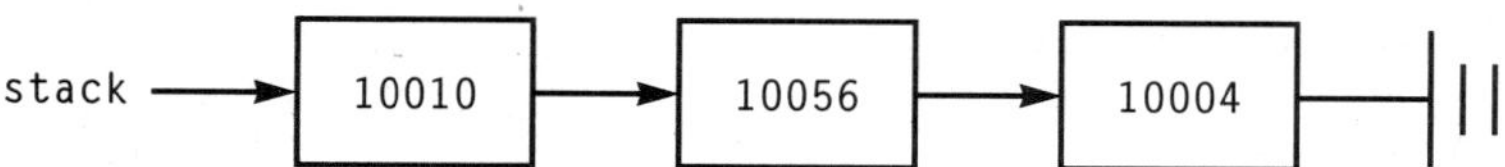

Note that although it looks just like a linked list, the nodes are not ordered. That's because they are always inserted in the same place, the top of the stack. The "top" of any stack is defined as the node pointed at by the stack pointer. Like many data structures books, we will use the electrical ground symbol (seen to the right of the last node) to indicate a NULL pointer. The pointer coming out of the last node should always be NULL.

The only difference between a stack and a queue is that a *queue* (pronounced "cue") receives new nodes at its rear. To do this easily, we must have a second pointer to refer to the last node. Thus a queue looks like this:

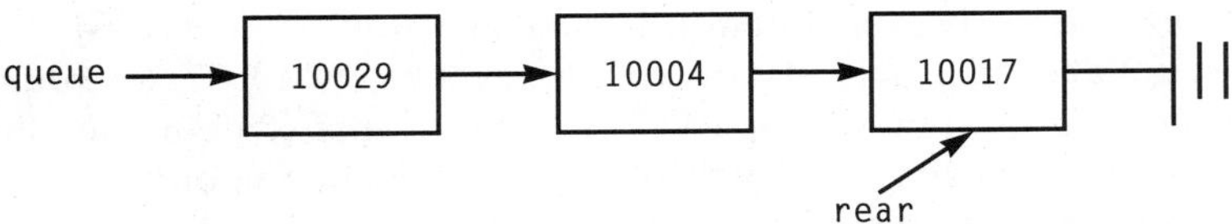

Let's look at some C code that demonstrates insertion into and deletion from stacks and queues.

Example 3.1 Preliminary Declarations for Stacks and Queues

```
/******   Demo of Stacks and Queues   ******/

#include <stdio.h>
#include <stdlib.h>   /*** For malloc and exit. ***/

#define EMPTY NULL
typedef struct node NODE;

struct node        /*****  Keep this struct simple for   *****/
{                  /*****  demonstration purposes.       *****/
    int i;
    struct node *next;
};
```

Here's the code to "push" a new node onto a stack.

Example 3.2 The Stack "Push" Function

```
/**********   "Push" new node on top of stack.   **********/
NODE *pushs(NODE *stack, int i)
{
    NODE *new;

    if ((new = (NODE *) malloc(sizeof(NODE))) == NULL)
    {
        printf("Fatal memory allocation error in pushs!\n");
        exit(1);
    }
    new->i = i;
```

```
    new->next = stack;
    stack = new;
    return stack;
}
```

Now, let's look at some calls to `pushs()`. I could have prototyped `pushs()` as

```
    void pushs(NODE  **stack, int i);
```

However, that would not be consistent with the philosophy of keeping code as simple as possible. It is harder to read code with double indirection (i.e., the two *'s) than code with single indirection. Therefore, I decided to use the return value of the function to pass back the new value of the stack pointer.

We will examine this in detail later, but let's look inside of `pushs()` first and analyze the code graphically while adding a node with key 3 to the stack.

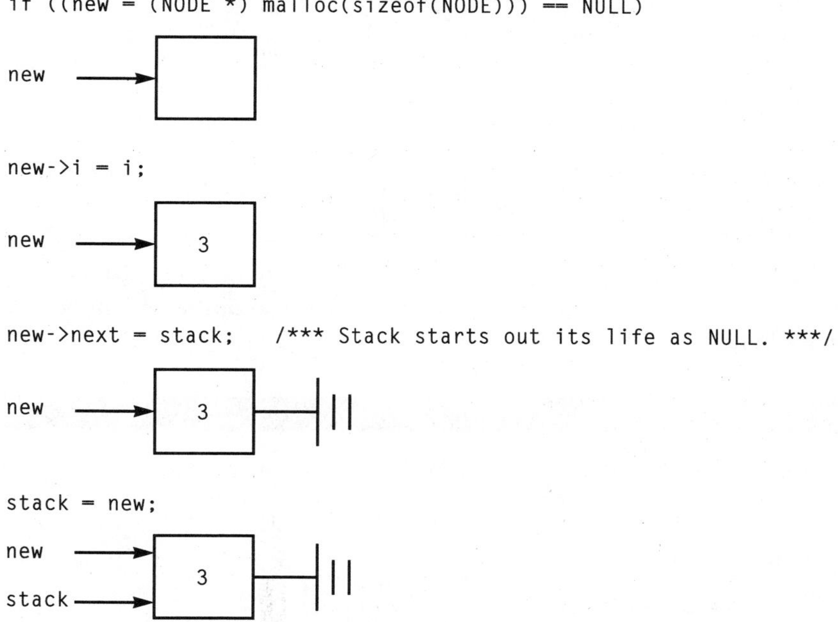

Then the function returns the `stack` pointer. Note the notation `new->i = i`. This could have been written `(*new).i = i`. However, the `->` notation was added to C to make it quite clear that `new` is a pointer. Thus `new->next` means "the component `next` in the node pointed at by `new`."

We saw this notation in Chapter 2, but it is so important that it is worth a quick review. Don't continue beyond this point without understanding this notation, because it will be used throughout the rest of the book. Now, say we add the node with 4 as its key value.

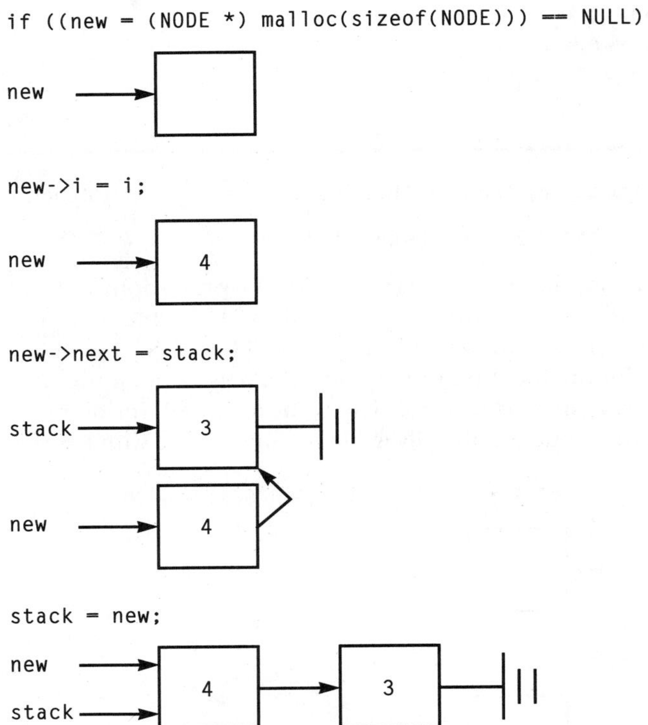

Nothing new here, so let's look at the `pops()` function, which *removes* a node from the stack. Let's assume that we have also pushed a 5 node onto the stack before entering `pops()`.

Example 3.3 The Stack "Pop" Function

```
/******  "Pop" a node off of the top of the stack.  ******/
NODE *pops(NODE **stack)
{
    NODE *first;

    if (*stack == NULL) return NULL;
    first = *stack;
    *stack = (*stack)->next;
    first->next = NULL;
    return first;
}
```

We have seen that a stack is a LIFO (**L**ast-**I**n, **F**irst-**O**ut) data structure. Thus the nodes that were inserted in 3-4-5 order will come off in 5-4-3 order. Look at this code. The `if` statement returns `NULL` if nothing is on the stack. `NULL` is generally regarded as a "failure" value in functions returning a pointer—we have failed to pop from the stack because nothing is there.

Let's remind ourselves of why `stack` is a `NODE **`. We cannot use the return value of `pops()` to return the `stack` pointer, because we are returning a pointer to the "popped-off" node. This is prudent: The person using our `pops()` function may want to do something with that node. Thus we must pass a pointer to the `stack` pointer so that, after a pop, the `stack` pointer comes back to the calling environment with a changed value.

We can also see why `*stack = *stack->next` is wrong. This says, "Look for a component `next` in a node pointed at by `stack` and then dereference that." But `stack` isn't pointing at the node; `*stack` is! To reinforce this concept, here's the state of the stack inside `pops()` before we have done anything.

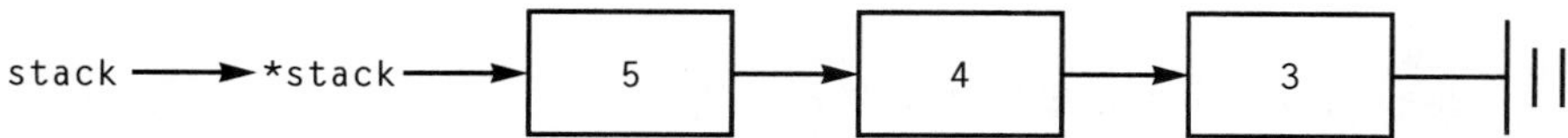

Now let's follow the statements in the `pops()` function graphically.

```
first = *stack;
*stack = (*stack)->next;
```

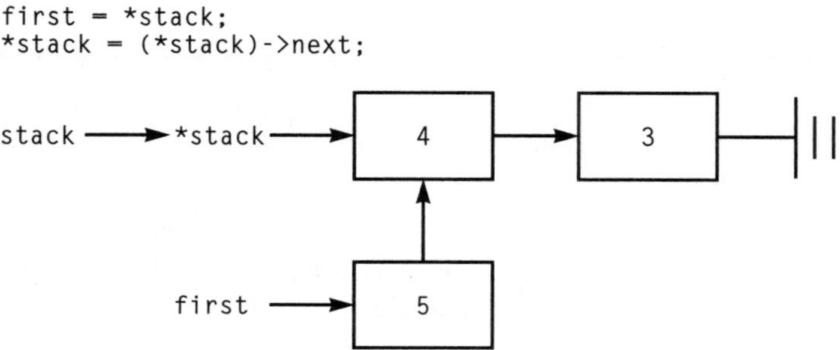

Now the last statement, `first->next = NULL`, detaches the node pointed at by `first` before returning `first` to the calling environment. Here's a picture of the state of our stack now:

```
first->next = NULL;
```

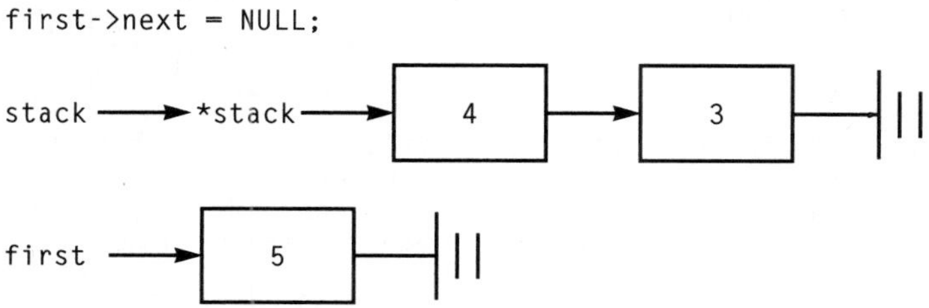

Now let's look at the code that pushes a node onto a queue. Note that this code maintains two pointers—a pointer to the front of the queue (because all popped nodes come off the front of the queue) and a pointer to the rear of the queue (because all new nodes are pushed onto the end of the queue).

Example 3.4 The Queue "Push" Function

```
/*********  Push a new node onto rear of queue.  *********/
void pushq(NODE **q, NODE **rear, int i)
{
    NODE *new;

    if ((new = (NODE *) malloc(sizeof(NODE))) == NULL)
    {
        printf("Fatal malloc error in pushq!\n");
        exit(1);
    }
    new->i = i;
    new->next = NULL;
    if (*q == NULL) *q = new;
    else (*rear)->next = new;
    *rear = new;
}
```

Let's follow this code graphically. First, if we have inserted a couple of nodes with keys 3 and 4, then the state of our queue inside of pushq() before anything has been done is

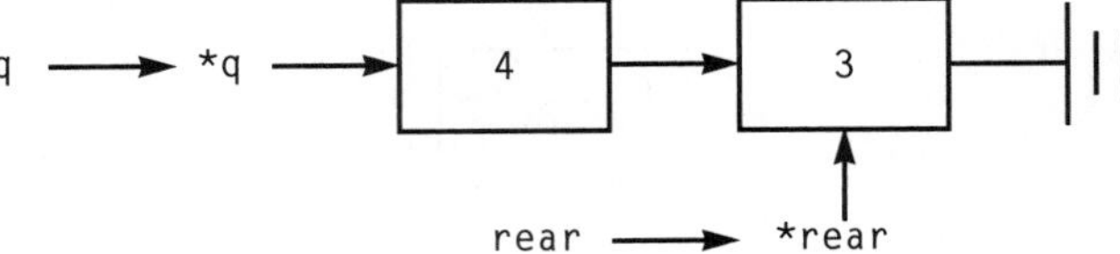

Now let's see how the code works to add a node with 2 onto the queue.

```
/* After a successful malloc.... */
new->i = i;
new->next = NULL;
```

```
if (*q == NULL) *q = new;     /*** False if queue not empty! ***/
else (*rear)->next = new;     /*** True on all other cases.  ***/
*rear = new;                  /*** Reassigns *rear to point  ***/
                              /*** at new rear of queue.     ***/
```

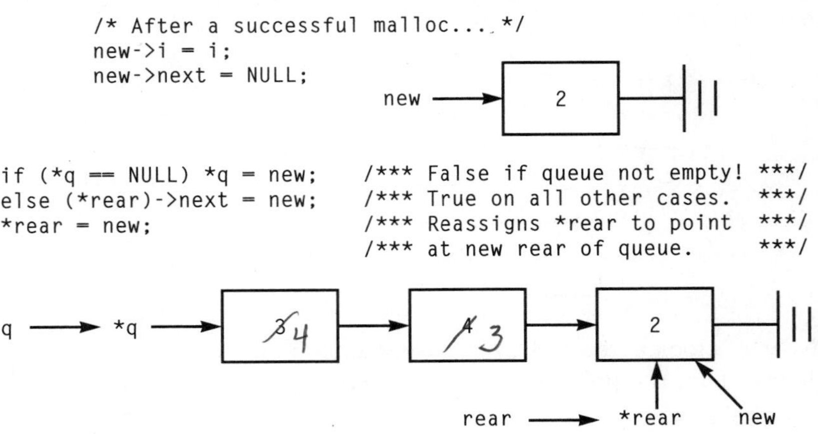

Now that we have seen that a new node is linked into a queue at its rear, let's examine the code to pop a node off a queue. Remember, queue nodes are always taken off the front of a queue, just as the first person in line at a movie theater is the first to get in. It's a FIFO (**F**irst-**I**n, **F**irst-**O**ut) data structure.

Example 3.5 The Queue "Pop" Function

```
/*****  "Pop" a node off the front of the queue.  *****/
NODE *popq(NODE **q, NODE **rear)
{
    NODE *first;

    first = *q;
    if (*q == NULL) return NULL;    /***  Nothing to pop!! ***/
    *q = (*q)->next;
    if (*q == NULL) *rear = NULL;   /*** Last node popped. ***/
    first->next = NULL;
    return first;  /*** Return pointer to popped off node. ***/
}
```

We won't be as helpful here as we were with `pushs()`, `pops()`, and `pushq()`. Try to follow the code of `popq()` on your own by drawing diagrams after each statement as we did with the other stack and queue functions. Use the queue we constructed above for convenience.

Example 3.6 Driver Program for Stack and Queue Functions with Output

```
main()
{
    NODE *stack = NULL, *q = NULL, *rear = NULL, *top;
    NODE *pushs(NODE *stack, int i), *pops(NODE **stack),
         *popq(NODE **q, NODE **rear);
    void pushq(NODE **q, NODE **rear, int i);

    /*****  Begin testing of stack functions.  *****/
    stack = pushs(stack, 3);
    stack = pushs(stack, 4);
    stack = pushs(stack, 5);
    top = pops(&stack);
    printf("Top node of stack is %d\n", top ? top->i : EMPTY);
    top = pops(&stack);
    printf("Top node of stack is %d\n", top ? top->i : EMPTY);
    top = pops(&stack);
    printf("Top node of stack is %d\n", top ? top->i : EMPTY);
```

```
    top = pops(&stack);
    printf("Top node of stack is %d\n", top ? top->i : EMPTY);
    putchar('\n');
    /*****  End test of stack functions.  *****/

    /*****  Begin test of queue functions.  *****/
    pushq(&q, &rear, 3);
    pushq(&q, &rear, 4);
    pushq(&q, &rear, 5);
    top = popq(&q, &rear);
    printf("Top node of queue is %d\n", top ? top->i : EMPTY);
    top = popq(&q, &rear);
    printf("Top node of queue is %d\n", top ? top->i : EMPTY);
    top = popq(&q, &rear);
    printf("Top node of queue is %d\n", top ? top->i : EMPTY);
    top = popq(&q, &rear);
    printf("Top node of queue is %d\n", top ? top->i : EMPTY);
    /*****  End test of queue functions.  *****/
}  /*** End of main().  ***/

/****************  Sample Program Session  ***************/

Top node of stack is 5      /****  Last in, first out!   ****/
Top node of stack is 4
Top node of stack is 3
Top node of stack is 0      /****  Stack is now empty!!  ****/

Top node of queue is 3      /****  First in, first out   ****/
Top node of queue is 4      /****  in a queue!!          ****/
Top node of queue is 5
Top node of queue is 0      /****  Queue is now empty!  ****/
```

Note that all functions to be called in `main()` are prototyped. Remember the style guideline in Chapter 1 that all functions should be prototyped in their caller(s). If you are programming in a team situation, some functions, such as utility functions needed by all team members, may have their prototypes grouped in a `.h` file. However, when we are talking about *your* code calling *your* code, it is much easier on the reader if you make his or her eyes move only a few inches to the top of the page rather than several pages back to some global area outside of all functions.

Stacks and queues have many obvious areas of applicability. Queues are used everywhere in operating systems: job queues, mail queues, print queues, and so on. Print jobs are queued because we want to provide print services in the order in which they are requested: *first come, first served!* Indeed, in any application demanding a "first come, first served" algorithm with a changing amount of data (e.g., print queues shrink and grow), a queue is indicated.

Stacks have somewhat fewer areas of applicability, because the need for a "last come, first served" algorithm is less common (though by no means rare). One very common use of stacks is in language compilers such as the C compiler you are using to do your homework.

Typically, if a function `A` calls a function `B` that calls a function `C`, the parameters of those functions are put on a stack, and so are the entry point addresses of the functions. Why? Because in the `A-B-C` calling sequence, we complete the entirety of `C`'s code before we finish the entirety of `B`'s code before we finish the entirety of `A`'s code. In other words, the last one called finishes before the second-to-last finishes, and so on. Last called, first finished!

Parameters of functions are also put on a stack by compilers. The order of processing of parameters is irrelevant (as long as we can refer to them in the function), so we should use the simplest dynamic structure possible: a stack. However, we do need a *dynamic* data structure, because the number of parameters in a function varies from one function to the next.

3.3 The Linked List Data Structure

At the beginning of this chapter, we saw why dynamic data structures are necessary when a program works with a data collection that grows or shrinks during program execution. Stacks and queues are useful when we have a variable amount of data that must be added or removed from the same place in the structure every time.

Sometimes, however, we may want to keep the nodes in *key order,* where a key is one component of a `struct`, such as an integer or a string. The list of college students discussed at the beginning of the chapter is a linked list in order of student id number.

We will now look at basic code for initializing, inserting into, deleting from, searching, and traversing linked lists. Read the code and the output from it carefully. We are using a very simple node type again, because we are interested mainly in the pointer operations.

Example 3.7 Preliminary Declarations for Linked Lists

```
#include <stdio.h>
#include <string.h>
#include <stdlib.h>   /* Has malloc and free. */

#define DUMMY_TRAILER '\177'
#define DUPLICATE 1
#define NEW_NODE  0
#define FOUND     1
#define NOT_FOUND 0
```

```
typedef struct node NODE;
struct node
{
    char string[20];
    NODE *next;
};
```

Given these declarations, let's follow some of the code. First, we will initialize our linked list with a dummy header node and a dummy trailer node. Here is the code that accomplishes this:

Example 3.8 Initialization of an Ordered Linked List

```
NODE *init_list(void)
{
    NODE *list;

    if ( (list = (NODE *) malloc(sizeof(NODE))) == NULL)
    {
        printf("Fatal malloc error in main!\n");
        exit(1);
    }
    list->string[0] = '\0';

    if ( (list->next = (NODE *) malloc(sizeof(NODE)))
        == NULL)
    {
        printf("Fatal malloc error in main!\n");
        exit(2);
    }
    list->next->string[0] = DUMMY_TRAILER;
    list->next->string[1] = '\0';
    list->next->next = NULL;
    return list;
}
```

After this list initialization, here is what our list looks like:

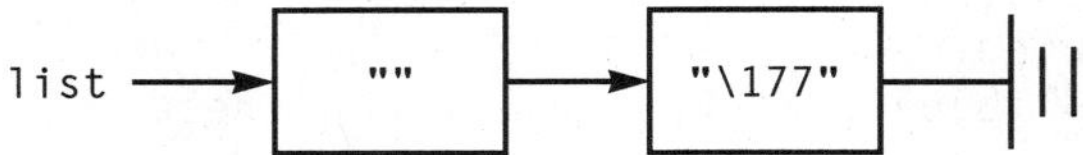

Why were two dummy nodes created in `main()`? Think about the difficulty of inserting into an ordered linked list *without* dummy nodes. You have three cases to consider—insertion at the front of the list, insertion at the end of the list, and insertion between two existing nodes.

Furthermore, if it is possible to insert at the front of the list, you must complicate matters more by passing a pointer to the list pointer in the `insert()` function. This leads to the greater complexity of double indirection (because `list` would be a `NODE **`), as with the queue insertion routines.

By wasting two `structs` to construct a dummy header node and a dummy trailer node before any *real* data are inserted, you are narrowing three insertion cases down to one. You must, however, be very careful to make the key value in the dummy header (the one pointed at by the list pointer) less than the key value of any actual data record. Similarly, you must be sure that the key value in the dummy trailer record is greater than the key value of any actual data record.

In addition to the obvious benefit of reducing three insertion cases to one, you need not pass the address of the list pointer to the `insert()` function, because the list pointer will always point at the dummy header node—no data record will ever have a key value less than the dummy header's key value.

We chose to make the key in the dummy header contain the empty string, one that has only the `'\0'` character. The dummy trailer record's key starts with the last character in the ASCII character sequence, the one with octal value 177. This is very safe if the key of actual data records consists of letters or numbers such as a name, address, or Social Security number.

In programming, you must often make trade-offs such as memory usage versus efficiency or code complexity versus efficiency. In this case the decision was easy. At a cost of a mere two `structs` of wasted storage, we have vastly simplified the insertion process and made it more efficient. Of course, evaluating such trade-offs is not always this easy.

Before we leave the list initialization code, let's look at the notation `list->next->next`. It is possible that you have never seen this form of double indirection before. Which pointer is this? It's the one coming out of the `"\177"` node (the `NULL` pointer). Read `list->next->next` as meaning "`List` points to a node that has a pointer component `next` that points to another node that also contains a component `next`."

Now we turn to the `insert()` and `delete()` functions, which use a method known as the "chasing pointers" method. If you read the code in these two functions, you will notice a pointer called `previous` that always lags one node behind a pointer called `current`. We say that `previous` is "chasing" `current`. Read the code for `insert()` and `delete()`, and then we will explain how it works via a diagram.

Example 3.9 The Linked List Insertion and Deletion Functions

```
/*****  Insert nodes into ordered linked list.  *****/
int insert(NODE *list, char *string)
{
    NODE *current = list->next;
    NODE *previous = list;
    NODE *new;
```

```
    while ( strcmp(string, current->string) > 0)
    {
        previous = current;
        current  = current->next;
    }
    if (strcmp(string, current->string) == 0)
    {
        return DUPLICATE;  /****  Disallow duplicates  ****/
    }
    else
    {
        if ( (new = (NODE *) malloc(sizeof(NODE))) == NULL)
        {
            printf("Fatal malloc error in insert!\n");
            exit(3);
        }
        /****  Fill up the new node and link it in.  ****/
        strcpy(new->string, string);
        new->next  = current;
        previous->next = new;
        return NEW_NODE;
    }
}


/******  Delete a node from ordered linked list.  ******/
int delete(NODE *list, char *string)
{
    NODE *current = list->next;
    NODE *previous = list;

    /****  Keep cycling in the loop until you pass the ****/
    /****  point where you expect to find "string".    ****/
    while(strcmp(string, current->string) > 0)
    {
        previous = current;
        current  = current->next;
    }
    if (strcmp(string, current->string) != 0)
    {
        return NOT_FOUND;
    }
    else
    {
        previous->next = current->next;
        free(current);
        return FOUND;
    }
}
```

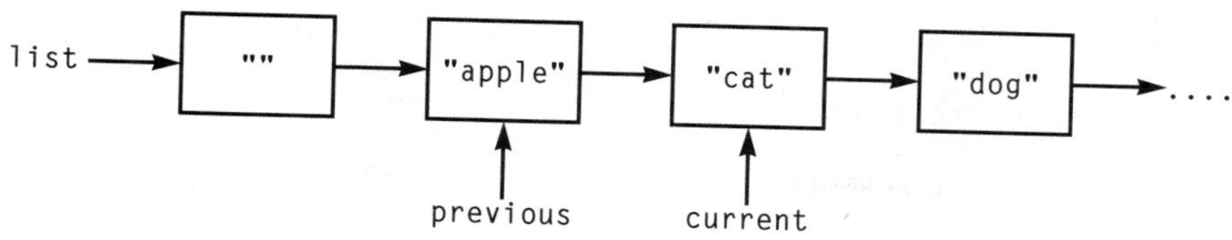

Suppose we want to insert a node with "banana" as its key. Obviously, the "banana" node must go between the "apple" node and the "cat" node to keep the list in alphabetical order. We need the current pointer so that the new "banana" node's pointer can be assigned to point at the "cat" node. This is done in insert() via the new->next = current statement.

In order to finish the job of linking the new "banana" node into the list, we must get the pointer coming out of the "apple" node to point at the new "banana" node. This is done via the statement previous->next = new. Just to crystallize this in your mind, we will diagram the effect of the two statements just mentioned.

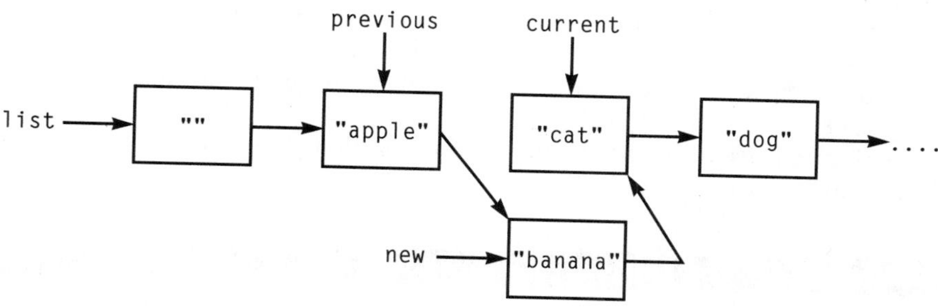

The delete() function also makes use of the "chasing pointers," but for a different reason. Looking at the diagram above (prior to insertion of the "banana" node), let us assume that we wish to delete the "cat" node. We need the previous pointer so that we can reassign the pointer previous->next so that it points to the "dog" node. We need the current pointer so that we can say free(current) and give the memory space used by the "cat" node back to the system.

How do you find a node in a linked list? You simply march across the list until you find a node with the desired key value. Then you return a pointer to the found node or NULL if it could not be found. Here is the code to find a node in a linked list:

Example 3.10 Finding a Node in an Ordered Linked List

```
/*****  Find a node in an ordered linked list.  *****/
NODE *find(NODE *list, char *string)
{
    list = list->next;    /***  Skip dummy header!  ***/
```

```
    while (strcmp(string, list->string) >=0)
    {
        if (strcmp(string, list->string) == 0)
        {
            return list;
        }
        list = list->next;
    }
    return NULL;
}
```

The statement `list = list->next` *above* the `while` loop skips over the dummy header node. We are not interested in that node—it merely makes insertions and deletions easier.

As the code states, we keep moving the `list` pointer from node to node until we either find the desired node or terminate the loop because we've gone past the point where the node was expected (i.e., the `strcmp()` returns a negative number). It does not matter that we are changing the value of `list` in the function. Because we did not pass a pointer to `list`, it will remain unchanged back in the calling environment, pointing at the dummy header node as usual.

Finally, we present the `traverse()` function that prints out the contents of all non-dummy nodes.

Example 3.11 The Linked List Traversal Function

```
/****  Print out contents of each node (except dummies).  ****/
void traverse(NODE *list)
{
    list = list->next;  /***  Skip over dummy header. ***/
    while(list->string[0] != DUMMY_TRAILER)
    {
        printf("%s\n",list->string);
        list = list->next;
    }
}
```

Because this function is a lot like the `find()` function, no commentary will be made on it. However, you should read the code; this is a stereotypical function.

Finally, we show you the `main()` function, which uses all of the linked list functions discussed thus far. A sample execution of the program is also included with `main()`.

Example 3.12 Driver Program for Linked List Functions with Output

```
/*****************************************************/
/*                                                   */
/*  This program initializes, inserts into, deletes  */
/*  from, searches, and traverses an ordered linked  */
/*  list with a string key.                          */
/*****************************************************/

main()
{
    NODE *list, *nodeptr;    /** Always prototype functions! **/
    char string[20];
    int found, duplicate;
    int insert(NODE *list, char *string);
    int delete(NODE *list, char *string);
    void traverse(NODE *list);
    NODE *find(NODE *list, char *string), *init_list(void);

    list = init_list();
    while (printf("Enter string (or quit): "), gets(string),
           strcmp(string,"quit"))
    {
        duplicate = insert(list, string);
        if (duplicate)
        {
            printf("That string already in the list.\n");
        }
    }

    traverse(list);    /* Print out strings in list nodes. */

    while (printf("Enter string (or quit): "), gets(string),
           strcmp(string,"quit"))
    {
        found = delete(list, string);
        if (!found)
        {
            printf("Couldn't find node with string: %s\n",
                   string);
        }
        else
        {
            printf("Deleted node with string %s\n", string);
        }
    }

    traverse(list);   /* Print out strings in list nodes. */
```

```
    while (printf("Enter string (or quit): "), gets(string),
           strcmp(string,"quit"))
    {
        nodeptr = find(list, string);
        if (!nodeptr)
        {
            printf("Couldn't find node with string: %s\n",
            string);
        }
        else
        {
            printf("Node with %s was found!\n",
            nodeptr->string);
        }
    }
}

/*****************  Sample Execution Below  *****************/

Enter string (or quit): dog    /* Start of list insertions. */
Enter string (or quit): zoo
Enter string (or quit): cat
Enter string (or quit): mouse
Enter string (or quit): turnip
Enter string (or quit): cat
That string already in the list.
Enter string (or quit): quit    /* End of list insertions. */

cat          /****  Ordered list contents. ****/
dog
mouse
turnip
zoo

Enter string (or quit): foobar  /* Start of node deletions. */
Couldn't find node with string: foobar
Enter string (or quit): mouse
Deleted node with string mouse
Enter string (or quit): quit     /* End of node deletions. */

cat    /****  New list contents after deletions.  ****/
dog
turnip
zoo

Enter string (or quit): foobar   /* Start node searching. */
Couldn't find node with string: foobar
Enter string (or quit): dog
```

```
Node with dog was found!
Enter string (or quit): quit      /* End of node searching. */
$   /*****  System prompt -- end of program execution.  *****/
```

3.4 The Doubly Linked List Data Structure

Occasionally, it pays to use a linked list structure with *two* pointers per node—one to the next node and one to the previous node. Although this data structure is not as frequently used as simple, singly linked lists, there are definitely applications where it is appropriate.

For example, suppose you wanted to write a simple text editor that keeps a "current line" indicator so that it is easy to manipulate lines before and after the current line. In such a case, you might want to put each text line into a list node and use the node's `forward` and/or `backward` pointers to access nearby lines efficiently.

Another interesting use of doubly linked lists is in the area of *simulation*. Suppose you are simulating message passing in a circular-shaped computer network. Messages can be passed to the left or right of any given computer in the network. In such a simulation, you would represent each computer as a node in a doubly linked ring (the last and first nodes of the list are joined), and the `forward` and `backward` pointers would allow the message to be passed to the computer (node) on the left or right of any given computer. This simulation is given as an exercise at the end of this chapter.

Now for the interesting stuff: the code to insert into, delete from, and "circularize" a doubly linked list. In contrast to our discussion of the singly linked listed functions, we will show only the insert, delete, and "circularize" functions, and we will not construct a `main()` to drive these functions to produce output. Try to do this as an exercise on your own.

Example 3.13 Doubly Linked List Insertion, Deletion, and "Circularization"

```
typedef struct node NODE;
struct node
{
    int i;
    NODE *forward, *backward;
};

/************************************************************/
/******************************************************/
/*******  Insert into a doubly linked list.    *******/
/*******  Assume that list header and trailer *******/
/*******  already exist. Assume no attempt     *******/
```

```
/*******  to insert duplicate nodes.           *******/
/*****************************************************/
void insert(NODE *list, int i)
{
    NODE *new, *previous = list, *current = list->forward;

    if ( (new = (NODE *) malloc(sizeof(NODE))) == NULL)
    {
        printf("Fatal malloc error in insert!\n");
        exit(1);
    }
    new->i = i;
    while (i > current->i)
    {
        previous = current;
        current  = current->forward;
    }
    new->forward = current;
    new->backward = previous;
    previous->forward = new;
    current->backward = new;
}


/***********************************************************/
/*******  Delete a node from a doubly linked list.  *******/
/*******  Assume that the node we want to delete is *******/
/*******  always found.                              *******/
/***********************************************************/
void delete(NODE *list, int i)
{
    NODE *current = list->forward, *previous = list;

    while (current->i != i)
    {
        previous = current;
        current  = current->forward;
    }
    previous->forward = current->forward;
    current->forward->backward = previous;
    free(current);
}


/*******  Making a ring out of a doubly linked list  ******/
void closering(NODE *list)
{
```

```
    NODE *mover = list->forward; /* Move past dummy header */

    while (mover->i != DUMMY_TRAILER_VALUE)
    {
        mover = mover->forward;
    }
    mover->forward = list;
    list->backward = mover;
}
```

The initialization of the doubly linked list with dummy header and trailer nodes is left as an exercise at the end of this chapter. Let's analyze this code in graphical fashion as we did for stacks, queues, and singly linked lists. First, here's a view of the doubly linked list with only a dummy header node and a dummy trailer node.

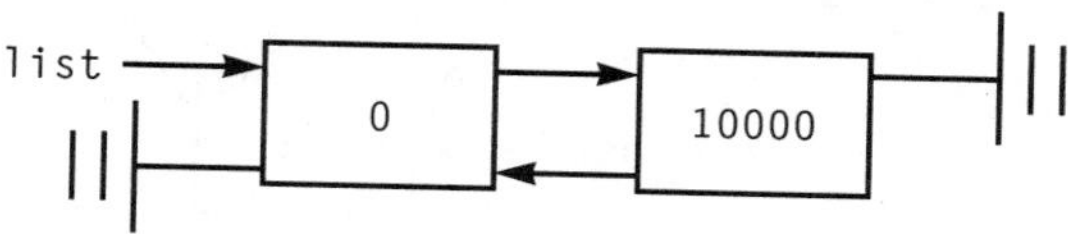

As you can see, the values in the dummy header and trailer nodes assume that no actual data value will be less than 1 or greater than 9999. The `forward` pointer coming out of the dummy trailer node is `NULL`, as is the `backward` pointer coming out of the dummy header node.

The method used to insert new nodes is still the "chasing pointers" method, just as it was for singly linked lists. The difference is that when we insert a new node, we have *four* pointer assignments to make instead of the two pointer assignments necessary in singly linked list insertion.

Let's assume that we have inserted a node with key value `250` into our doubly linked list. Here's what the data structure will look like:

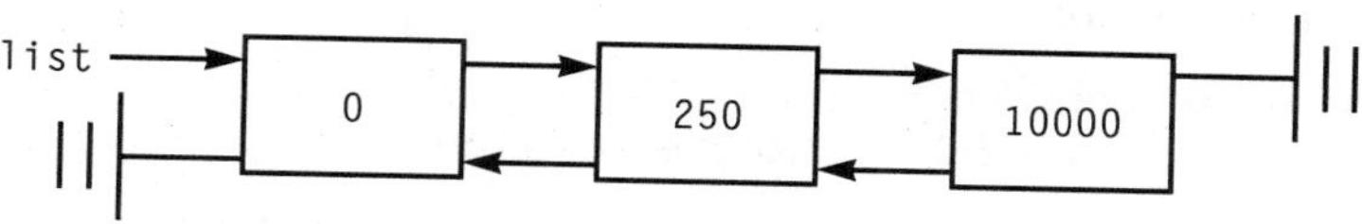

Let's follow the pointer assignments after the `insert()` function's `while` loop and insert a node with key value `500`. Remember that we are assuming that the new node will not be a duplicate of an existing node. You should think about how to alter the code in Example 3.13 to prohibit duplicates, as was done in singly linked list insertion.

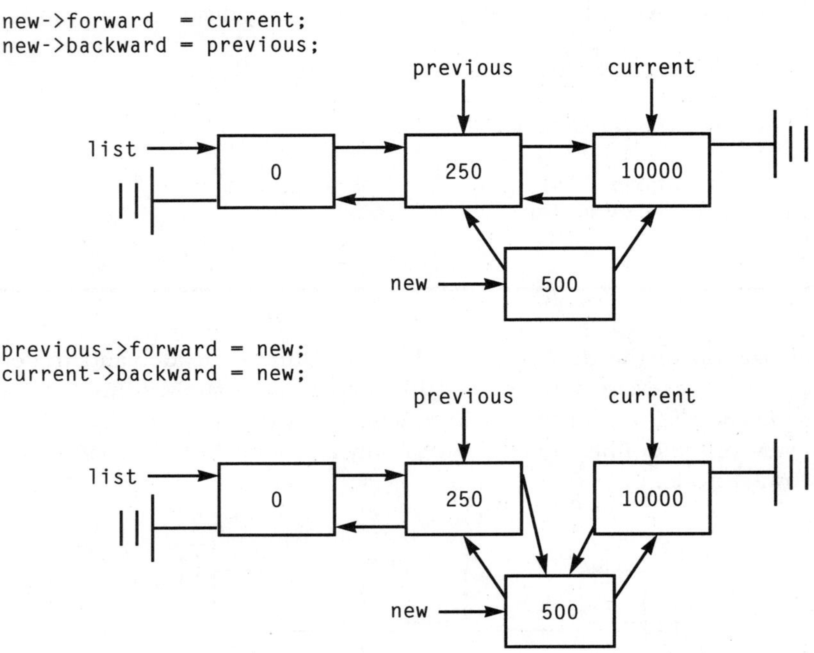

The `delete()` function uses the same old "chasing pointers" method but features a difficult pointer assignment. Therefore, we will assume that we are about to delete the record with key value 500 that we just inserted. Here's the state of the data structure in `delete()` just after the `while` loop:

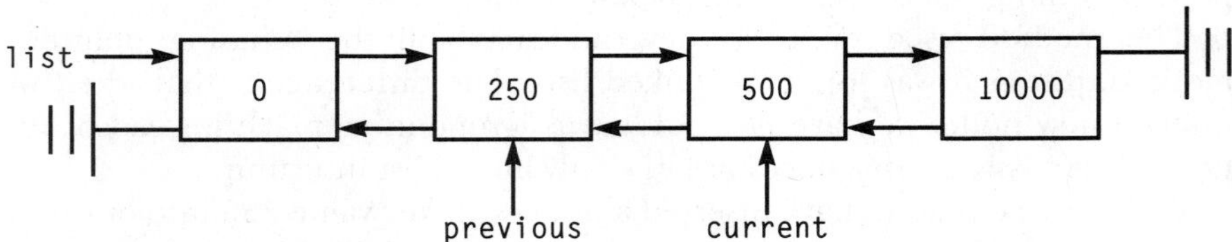

Now let's see the result of the following two statements after the `delete()` function's `while` loop.

```
previous->forward = current->forward;
current->forward->backward = previous;
```

Here's what the data structure looks like after these two statements:

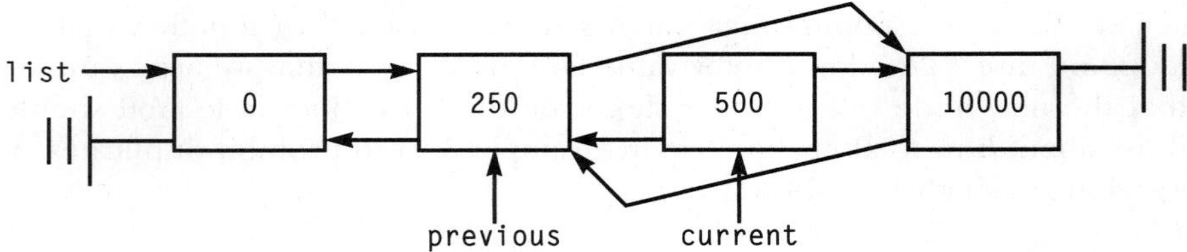

The first of these two statements makes the `forward` pointer coming out of the 250 node point to the 10000 (dummy) node. The second statement makes the `backward` pointer coming out of the 10000 node point to the 250 node. `Current->forward->backward` means "`Current` points at a node whose `forward` pointer points at a node with a `backward` pointer." (We saw such double indirection in the notation `list->next->next` from the singly linked list initialization code in Example 3.8.)

The `free(current)` statement gives the memory pointed at by `current` back to the system, and the pointer `current` is now unassigned! There is a tremendous difference between `NULL` and unassigned. A `NULL` pointer has a definite value, zero. An *unassigned* pointer has no value at all. Another crucial difference is that `free(some_pointer)` works on a `NULL` pointer but, if applied to an unassigned pointer, results in unpredictable (and possibly fatal) performance at runtime.

Now suppose we wish to close this doubly linked list and make a doubly linked *ring*. The `closering()` function moves a pointer out to the end of the list so that we have a way of referring to the `forward` pointer in the dummy trailer node. Now you know why pointers are often called *reference* variables—they give us a way of referring to a particular node. You are encouraged to review `closering()` on your own.

3.5 Programmer-Controlled Memory Management

Thus far, when constructing our dynamic data structures, we have asked `malloc()` for one `struct` of storage space when we needed it. Also, in the `delete()` functions in Examples 3.9 and 3.13, we used the `free()` function to give back one `struct` of space when we no longer needed it.

There are two problems with this approach: (1) It is inefficient with large data collections, and (2) the `malloc()` and `free()` functions are often poorly written. Indeed, sometimes the `free()` function gives back storage so that neither you nor anybody else can use the freed memory until your program terminates!

The new approach I am going to show you involves `malloc`'ing an array of `structs` all at once and, instead of using `free()`, putting deleted nodes on a free stack. When we need a new node for an insertion operation, we will check the free stack first and then the `malloc`'ed block. Only if both are empty will we then resort to `malloc()` to get a new array of `structs`.

Whenever you no longer need a node, you must *zero it out* before putting it on the free stack. Then, when you take a node off the free stack to put it into a list, stack, or queue, it doesn't have to be erased before it is overwritten. To assign zeroes to all bytes of a `struct`, you use the ANSI C function `memset()`. For illustration purposes, let's suppose we have a variable `sf` of type `struct foo`. Here's how to use `memset()` to zero it out.

```
memset (&sf, 0, sizeof(struct foo));     /**** Resides in
                                           string.h ****/
```

The ANSI prototype for memset() is

```
void memset (void *pointer, int value, size_t
                number_of_bytes);
```

The first parameter of memset() is a void *, which, as you will recall, is compatible with any pointer type. The second parameter is the value to be placed in number_of_bytes bytes, starting at the address given in the first parameter. Again, don't be confused by the size_t data type of the third parameter; it's compatible with any type from the int family.

In our call of the memset() function above, the first parameter is &sf. Remember that the first argument must be a pointer (in other words, an address). Because sf is a struct foo, and not a pointer to a struct foo, we must pass the address of sf to give memset() the proper data type. Do not forget this!

What follows is the code for the function get_node(). This function returns a pointer to a free node by first checking the free stack and then the malloc'ed block.

Example 3.14 Function to Perform Programmer-Controlled Memory Management

```
/*******************************************/
/*                                         */
/*  Gets a free node from the free stack (if not  */
/*  empty) or from a malloc'ed block of structs.  */
/*                                         */
/*******************************************/

#define BLOCKSIZE 100

NODE *get_node(NODE **stack)
{
    static NODE *block = NULL, *blockrear;
    NODE *first;

    if (*stack != NULL)  /***  Pop node off of free stack. ***/
    {
        first = *stack;
        *stack = (*stack)->next;
        first->next = NULL;    /***  Detach from stack!  ***/
    }
    else if (block != NULL)  /***  Get node from block.  ***/
    {
        first = block;
        if (block == blockrear) block = NULL;
        else block++;    /****  Move to next struct!  ****/
    }
```

```
    else    /*****  Stack and block are NULL!!  *****/
    {
        if ((block = (NODE *) malloc(BLOCKSIZE * sizeof(NODE)))
            == NULL)
        {
            printf("Fatal malloc error in get_node!\n");
            exit(1);
        }
        memset(block, 0, BLOCKSIZE * sizeof(NODE));
        blockrear = block + BLOCKSIZE - 1;
        first = block;
        block++;
    }
    return first;
}
```

Note that the stack pointer is passed in—it is not a local variable. This is because a node to be deleted from a list, stack, or queue will not be freed by a call to free(). It will be deleted by a function we will write that will *push a node onto the free stack.* Thus, this variable must be manipulable outside of get_node() and passed in as a parameter to this deleting function.

Otherwise, the logic of get_node() is fairly straightforward. If there is a NODE on the free stack, we pop it off, update the value of the stack pointer, and pass back the pointer to the popped NODE.

If the free stack is empty, we look at the block of malloc'ed nodes. If we have not yet exhausted all nodes in the block, we pass back a pointer to the current struct in the block and then move the block pointer to the next struct. Remember that this block is an array of struct, not a linked list, so we move block along the array via block++. Block = block->next would be a horrible blunder because the component next in the struct pointed at by block is zero—that is, NULL. Why? Read the next paragraph!

Finally, if both the free stack and the block are exhausted, we create a new block (the malloc() call), initialize block and blockrear, zero out all nodes in the block via memset() (now you know why all the next components are zero or NULL), give the calling environment the address of the first struct in the new block, and once again move the block pointer to the next struct in the block of structs.

Note that block and blockrear are declared as static NODE pointers. A static local variable in a function has a value that *persists between calls.* It is essential that the current position of block and blockrear be preserved between calls to getnode().

Another mystery that needs to be cleared up is the NULL initialization of block in its declaration. Won't every call to getnode() result in this initialization? No. A static local variable in a function is initialized on the first call only. Thus, from the second call of `get_node()` to the final call, this initialization will not occur.

The code for a `delete()` function, as shown for lists in Examples 3.9 and 3.13, is not shown in Example 3.14. (It appears as an exercise at the end of this chapter.) However, it will clearly be different from the `delete()` functions already shown in this chapter, because it will not call `free()`. It will push the unneeded node onto the free stack.

Now that we see how the code works, let's see what its advantages are. First, `free()` is never called, so we don't care whether it is written well or poorly! Second, `malloc()` is called very infrequently, which leads to enhanced program performance. Still don't understand how the code works? Let's look at a few situations graphically.

stack   block

The situation in the diagram above would occur if the free stack *and* the block were exhausted and we were in the code of Example 3.14 just before the `malloc()`.

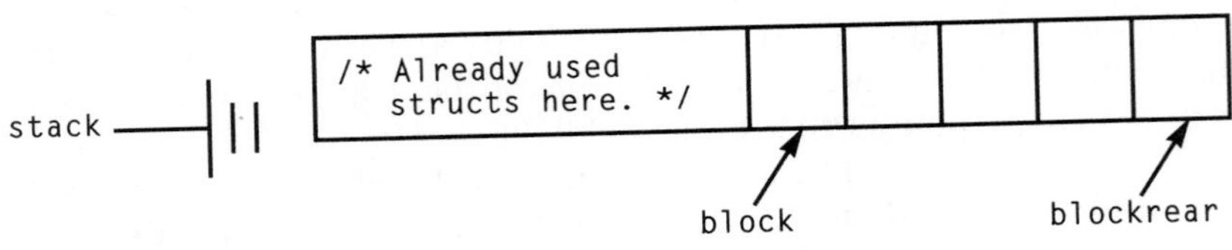

The situation shown in this diagram would occur if the free stack were empty (because no deleted nodes were pushed onto it) and many `structs` were taken from the `malloc`'ed block of `structs`. The `structs` before the `struct` pointed at by `block` have already been used to build a list, stack, or queue. In this case, when one needs a new `struct` to use as a new node for a list, stack, or queue, it would come from the block of `structs`, and the `block` pointer would move forward by one `struct`.

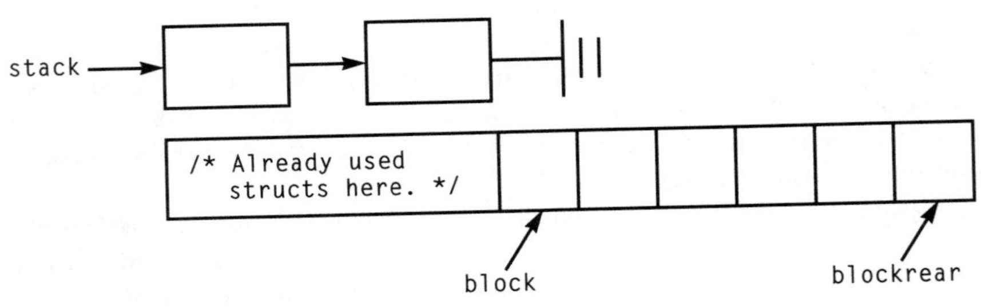

The previous diagram shows a case where many nodes have been inserted into, and many deleted from, some kind of dynamic data structure. The free stack must have been empty many times; otherwise the `block` pointer would never have moved from its original position. Remember, new nodes are always taken off the free stack until it is empty.

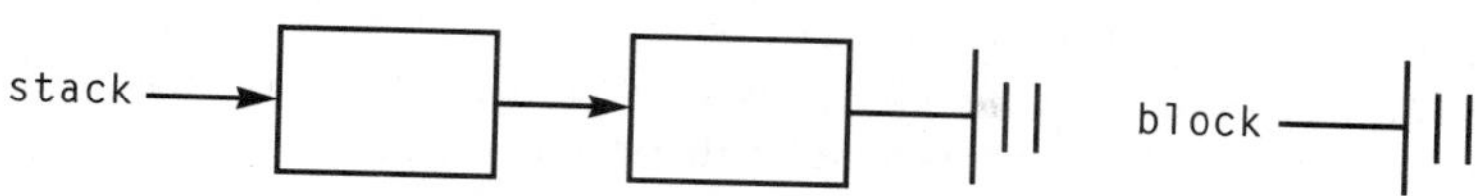

This diagram shows a situation that looks impossible but is actually quite possible! However, a couple of things have to fall in place for this to happen. If several insertions were done consecutively when the free stack was empty, this could exhaust the `malloc`'ed block of `structs`. If two nodes were then deleted immediately after exhaustion of the block, they would be placed where deleted nodes are always placed—on the free stack. Thus, this situation can only arise if several deletions immediately follow the exhaustion of the `malloc`'ed block of `structs`.

As you can see, many states are possible: stack-empty/block-not-empty, stack-not-empty/block-not-empty, stack-not-empty/block-empty, and stack-empty/block-empty. It is useful to think about which insertion/deletion permutations give rise to these four possibilities. When you write such code, *all* possibilities must be accounted for, even if some of them are highly unlikely.

Students often ask this perfectly reasonable question: "Can't I do everything with just one data structure?" They mean with just a free stack or just a `malloc`'ed block. A free stack alone is a possibility, but without the aid of a preallocated block, all `malloc`s needed for insertions when the free stack is empty will be one-node-at-a-time `malloc`s—just the kind of inefficiency our approach avoids.

It *seems* feasible to do everything with a `malloc`'ed block. If you want to delete a node from a list, stack, or queue, you simply move the `block` pointer backwards (i.e., toward the beginning of the original block). Here's the situation that spoils this plan: Suppose you have just exhausted a block (because of insertions), `malloc`'ed a new block, and then performed several node deletions from your data structure(s). You risk moving the `block` pointer *backwards past the beginning of the original block.* Needless to say, this will lead to a serious runtime problem when you try to get a new node from this (illegal) location.

I hope that these analyses have given you an appreciation for the attention to detail demanded of all programmers who want to call themselves experts. This code will enable you to "roll your own" memory management code so that you don't have to rely on good operating system memory management. If you want something done right, do it yourself!

3.6 Hashing to Memory with Arrays of Lists

The major shortcoming of ordered linked lists is slow search times in large data collections. For example, if a linked list has 10,000 nodes, an average search will look at 5000 nodes (half of the total nodes). That is why linked lists are generally not used for pure searching algorithms on large data volumes. We will look at better dynamic data structures for searching later in this book—namely, binary trees. The major *advantage* of linked lists is that the data are ordered and can therefore be displayed sequentially.

For pure searching, however, nothing beats the technique known as *hashing*. Let us explain what hashing is by returning to our college student record database from the beginning of the chapter.

Suppose we needed to organize student records to retrieve them as quickly as possible. Let's suppose that the key of each student's record is the Social Security number. Because a Social Security number consists of nine digits, even a `long int` may not be big enough to hold it, so we will put the nine digits in a string. The key of each `struct student` will be

```
char  student_id[10];
```

Of course, we allocate ten characters so that each id number string has room for the `'\0'` character. Now let's suppose that we are going to put all entered student records into some data structure in memory. How will we do it? We will create an array of pointers. Then we will invent a hashing function to turn the `student_id` string into a number between zero and the maximum index of the array of pointers.

Once the hash of the Social Security number has been performed, the node will be placed in the linked list indexed by the hash value just computed. If we declare our *array of lists* as

```
struct student  *student_body[5];
```

and a given student's id hashes to a value of 2, then that student's node will go into the linked list pointed at by `student_body[2]`. Obviously, any hash function in this application must produce a value between 0 and 4 for every record, because those are the minimum and maximum indices of the `student_body` array. This is the essence of hashing.

However, there are two pertinent questions here: (1) How many linked lists should you have in your hash table? and (2) What constitutes a good hashing formula? Entire books have been written to answer these questions! However, without going into the mind-numbing mathematical theory behind hashing, we can suggest two rules of thumb.

First, the number of linked lists should roughly equal the number of data records you expect. If you have, say, 40,000 records and only 100 linked lists, then each list will be so large that you will lose the benefits of hashing. Second, the hashing formula should distribute data records relatively evenly among all the lists.

Therefore, a decent hashing function for our student records would be to sum the cubes of the ASCII values of the characters in the student id number and then modulo by the number of linked lists (we will only use five lists in our example so that we don't need to enter too many data to test our code). It turns out that the sum of the cubes will range from 995,328 (Social Security number 000-00-0000) to 1,666,737 (Social Security number 999-99-9999). That's a pretty decent range of possibilities and should distribute records among the lists relatively randomly.

Without further ado, then, here are two functions. The first will be preliminary data types and constants needed for our hashing-to-array-of-lists battery of functions. The next will be the hashing function itself.

Example 3.15 Preliminary Declarations for Hashing to Array of Linked Lists

```
/*********************************************************/
/*                                                       */
/*  Demonstration of array storage/retrieval via hashing */
/*  to an array of linked lists.                         */
/*********************************************************/

#define NUMPOINTERS 5
#include <stdio.h>
#include <stdlib.h>
#include <string.h>

typedef struct student STUDENTREC;

struct student
{
   char ss[10];
   struct student *next;
};
```

These declarations will be used for the hashing formula and for other functions in this section.

Example 3.16 Function to Hash Social Security Number

```
/*******************************************************/
/*                                                     */
/*  Hash Social Security number by summing the cubes   */
/*  of the ASCII value of characters and then take     */
/*  the modulo of this sum.  Return result (hashval).  */
/*******************************************************/
```

```
int hash(char ss[])
{
    long hashval = 0;

    for (; *ss != '\0'; ss++)
    {
        hashval += (*ss) * (*ss) * (*ss);
    }
    return hashval % NUMPOINTERS;
}
```

Hold on a second, you say! What if two or more records' `student_id` fields hash to the same value. No problem. Because each pointer in the array of pointers points to a list, we simply add the new record to the end of that list (provided it is not a duplicate entry). When the keys of two or more records produce the same hash value, then we say a *collision* has taken place. Lists can hold limitless numbers of records, so collisions don't present any problem here—collidees simply occupy the same list.

Are these lists really stacks? No. Because we must check all entries to avoid inserting a duplicate record, we cannot just add the node to the front of the list. Are they queues? Again, the answer is no. We can't add to the end of each list straight away, because it might be a duplicate entry.

Should we have dummy headers and trailers such as we had with ordered linked lists? No, the records in each list are not ordered by key. Also, in a real-world application with 1000 lists, you'll waste 2000 `structs`! And because each list will have a very short size in a real-world application, the "chasing pointers" method simply won't work well if the average size of a list is 1.3 nodes per list—a realistic occurrence!

So how do we insert into these lists? Look at the code that follows.

Example 3.17 Inserting Nodes into an Array-of-Lists Hash Table

```
/******************************************************/
/*  Put hashed record in list indicated by hash value.  */
/*  Demonstrate use of pointing to pointers as a method */
/*  of list traversal.                                  */
/******************************************************/
STUDENTREC *insert(char ss[],
                   STUDENTREC *student_body[], int hashval)
{
    STUDENTREC **mover;

    mover= &student_body[hashval];
    while (*mover)
    {
        if (strcmp(ss,(*mover)->ss) == 0) return (*mover);
```

```
        mover = &((*mover)->next);
    }
    if ((*mover = (STUDENTREC *) malloc(sizeof(STUDENTREC)))
        == NULL)
    {
        printf("Malloc error in insert!\n");
        exit(1);
    }
    strcpy((*mover)->ss,ss);
    printf("Person with ss number %s placed in list %d.\n",
            ss, hashval);
    return NULL;
}
```

The real magic of this code is that it uses a pointer (mover) to follow the *pointers* coming out of the nodes in each list, instead of following the nodes themselves as we did with regular linked lists.

Here's a graphical demonstration wherein a student with Social Security number 888-88-8888 is about to be added to the list pointed at by student_body[4], which already has the record for student 333-33-3333. Each code line from this insert() function is followed by a picture of the list.

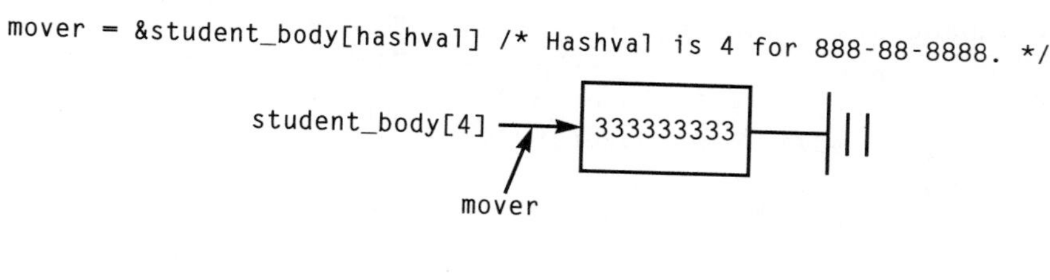
mover = &student_body[hashval] /* Hashval is 4 for 888-88-8888. */
student_body[4]
333333333
mover

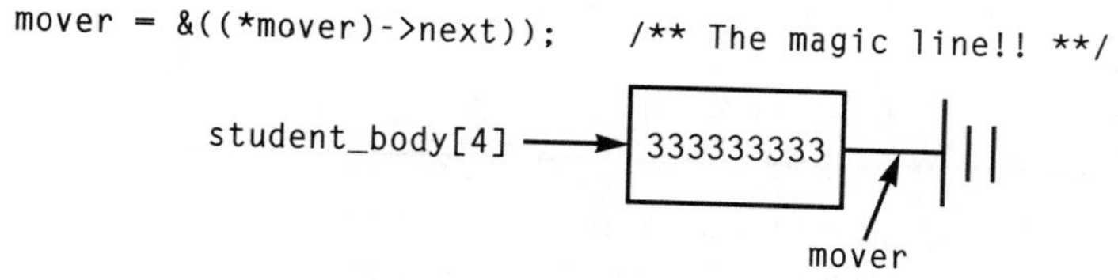
mover = &((*mover)->next)); /** The magic line!! **/
student_body[4]
333333333
mover

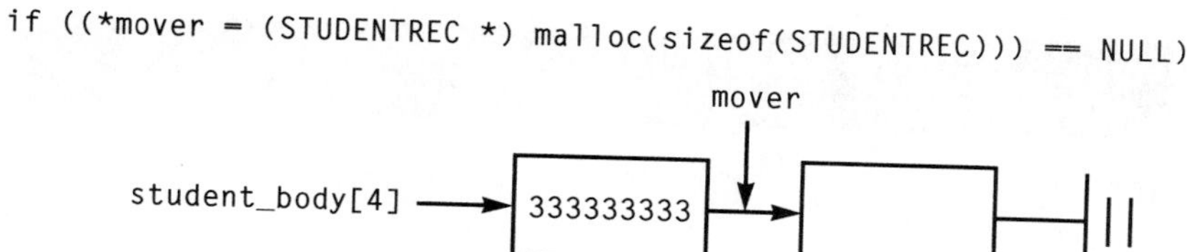
if ((*mover = (STUDENTREC *) malloc(sizeof(STUDENTREC))) == NULL)
mover
student_body[4]
333333333

Notice that mover is of type STUDENTREC **. That's right—it's a pointer to a pointer to a STUDENTREC. And the diagram bears this out. The advantage of this approach is that when mover encounters the NULL pointer coming out of the "333333333" node, it has a reference to that pointer. In fact, that pointer has a name, `*mover`. We simply `malloc` space for this pointer. The code after the call to `malloc()` simply fills up the node with "888888888."

This same logic is used in the `traverse()` function, which simply prints out the contents of each list. Like `insert()`, it follows pointers instead of nodes. True, `traverse()` can be written to bounce from node to node instead of from pointer to pointer. However, we wanted to give you as much practice as possible reading this type of code, because certain problems, such as `insert()`, can't be solved easily without this logic and its associated syntax.

This code represents a very powerful kind of C "magic" that we will revisit when we look at binary trees.

Example 3.18 Traversing the Lists in a Hash Table

```
/**********  Output contents of lists.  **********/
void traverse(STUDENTREC *student_body[]);
{
    int i;
    STUDENTREC **mover;

    for (i = 0; i < NUMPOINTERS; i++)
    {
        printf("Contents of list %d:\n", i);
        printf("-------------------\n");
        for (mover = &student_body[i]; *mover;
             mover = &(*mover)->next)
        {
             printf("%s\n", (*mover)->ss);
        }
        printf("\n");
    }
}
```

And now finally, after all the preliminaries, here is a `main()` function that utilizes all of these functions and produces output.

Example 3.19 Driver Program to Demonstrate Hashing-to-Lists Functions

```
main()
{
    char ss[10];
    STUDENTREC *student_body[NUMPOINTERS] = {NULL};
    STUDENTREC *person;
    STUDENTREC *insert(char ss[], STUDENTREC *student_body[],
                             int hashval);
```

```
    int hashval, hash(char ss[]);
    void traverse(STUDENTREC *student_body);

    while(printf("Enter Social Security Number: "),
          strcmp(gets(ss),"quit"))
    {
        hashval = hash(ss);
        person = insert(ss,student_body, hashval);
        if (person)   /***  NULL if it is a duplicate.  ***/
        {
            printf("You have attempted to enter\
                    a duplicate record!\n");
        }
    }
    traverse(student_body);
}
/****************  Sample Execution Below  *****************/

Enter Social Security Number: 111111111
Person with ss number 111111111 placed in list 1.
Enter Social Security Number: 333333333
Person with ss number 333333333 placed in list 4.
Enter Social Security Number: 666666666
Person with ss number 666666666 placed in list 1.
Enter Social Security Number: 666666666
You have attempted to enter a duplicate record!
Enter Social Security Number: 555555555
Person with ss number 555555555 placed in list 3.
Enter Social Security Number: 888888888
Person with ss number 888888888 placed in list 4.
Enter Social Security Number: 444444444
Person with ss number 444444444 placed in list 2.
Enter Social Security Number: quit

Contents of list 0:
--------------------

Contents of list 1:
--------------------
111111111
666666666

Contents of list 2:
--------------------
444444444

Contents of list 3:
--------------------
555555555
```

```
Contents of list 4:
--------------------
333333333
888888888
```

As you can see from this sample output, list 0 (pointed at by `student_body[0]`) is empty, and the other four lists (pointed at by `student_body[1]` through `student_body[4]`) have one or two nodes apiece. Before we finish this section, let's take a closer at one more little detail, the line in `main()` that says

```
STUDENTREC   *student_body[NUMPOINTERS] = {NULL};
```

We discussed this point in Chapter 2, but it is important enough to reiterate here. If there are fewer initializing values in the declaration than there are array elements, the remaining elements are automatically initialized to zero. This is very convenient, because zero just happens to be the value of a `NULL` pointer—the desired starting value for each pointer in `student_body`. Thus, by using a "trick," we have initialized each list pointer to `NULL`.

3.7 Totally Dynamic Nodes in Dynamic Data Structures

So far in this chapter, we have dealt with allocating, freeing, and managing memory. We have illustrated techniques that waste no memory at some cost in efficiency and control. We have also illustrated techniques that risk wasting a small amount of memory to gain efficiency and control. However, there is one last issue to deal with: wasting memory *within* nodes. For example, suppose you have nodes with many arrays such as this:

```
struct foo
{
    char  name[40];
    char  address[80];
    /***  Many more components here.  ***/
};
```

When `structs` have many arrays, as this one does, you have to allocate space for the largest possible size for each array component. Thousands or hundreds of thousands of bytes are wasted this way. A better way to declare `struct foo` is

```
struct foo
{
    char  *name;
    char  *address;
    /***  Many more components here.  ***/
};
```

When you are ready to fill up the name and address components, you can use temporary string buffers with a large declaration (say, 200 bytes) to fill up the struct components. For example, let's say that a pointer fooptr is pointing at a struct foo that is to be filled up with the values stored in local variables name and address. Here's how you would do it:

```
fooptr->name = (char  *) malloc(strlen(name) + 1);
strcpy(fooptr->name, name);
fooptr->address = (char  *) malloc(strlen(address) + 1);
strcpy(fooptr->address, address);
```

When we malloc space for fooptr->name, we allocate just enough room for the name plus the terminating '\0' character. Not a byte is wasted! From now on, your nodes within your data structures should be as dynamic as the data structures themselves.

3.8 Multi-lists and Hybrid Dynamic Data Structures

Some applications require a data structure that is not purely list-, stack-, or queue-oriented. One example is an operating system (OS) simulation where we wish to keep track of all possible queues on the system (printer, mail, job, and so on) in one data structure. A linked list will hold the queue name and pointers to the front and rear of a queue of requests for a service.

Here's a picture of an example of such a data structure:

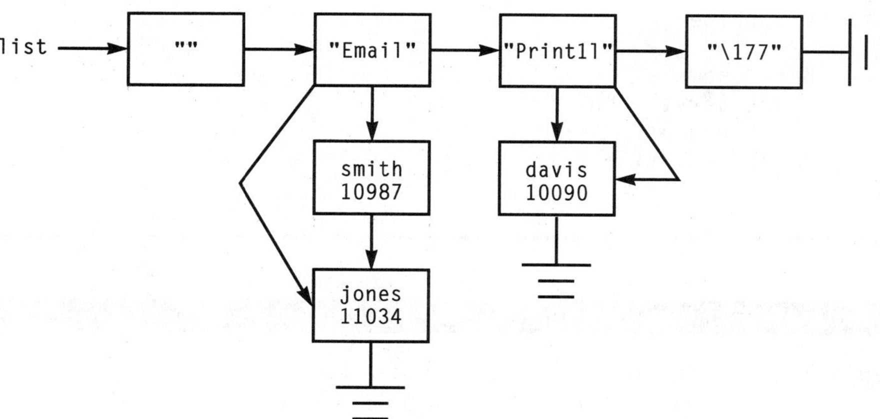

In this diagram, each queue node holds the job-id and username of a user requesting mail service, printer service, etc.—whatever type of service is named in the main list node. This flexible data structure allows for a limitless number of operating system services, and each service can accommodate a limitless number of user requests for that service.

The data structure in this example is a *list of queues.* Clearly, you could also find applications for lists of lists (often called *multi-lists*), lists of stacks, stacks of lists, queues of stacks, and so on. The number of permutations is very large! The hard part, as usual, is designing the node structures and pointer assignments to implement initialization, insertion, deletion, and traversal algorithms for these complex, hybrid structures.

We'll show you the insertion, traversal, and initialization algorithms for this application. The deletion algorithm is left as a chapter exercise.

Example 3.20 Preliminary Declarations for the OS Queues Program

```
#include <stdio.h>
#include <stdlib.h>
#include <string.h>

#define DUMMY_TRAILER '\177'

typedef struct request REQUEST;
struct request
{
    char *username;
    long job_id;
    struct request *next;
};

typedef struct service SERVICE;
struct service
{
    char *qname;
    struct service *next;
    struct request *front;
    struct request *rear;
};
```

Example 3.21 Insertion Code for the OS Queues Program

```
void insert(SERVICE *serv_ptr, char *qname,
            char *username, long job_id)
{
    SERVICE *current = serv_ptr->next;
    SERVICE *previous = serv_ptr;
    SERVICE *newserv;
    REQUEST *newreq;

    while ( strcmp(qname, current->qname) > 0)
    {
```

```
            previous = current;
            current  = current->next;
        }
        if (strcmp(qname, current->qname) != 0) /* New service! */
        {
                if ((newserv = (SERVICE *) malloc(sizeof(SERVICE)))
                    == NULL)
                {
                    printf("Fatal malloc error!\n");
                    exit(1);
                }
                if ((newserv->qname =
                    (char *) malloc(strlen(qname) + 1)) == NULL)
                {
                    printf("Fatal malloc error!\n");
                    exit(2);
                }
                strcpy(newserv->qname, qname);
                newserv->next  = current;
                previous->next = newserv;
                newserv->front = NULL;
        }
        if ((newreq = (REQUEST *) malloc(sizeof(REQUEST)))
            == NULL)
        {
            printf("Fatal malloc error!\n");
            exit(3);
        }
        if ((newreq->username =
            (char *) malloc(strlen(username) + 1)) == NULL)
        {
            printf("Fatal malloc error!\n");
            exit(4);
        }

        strcpy(newreq->username, username);
        newreq->job_id = job_id;
        newreq->next   = NULL;

        if (newserv->front == NULL)
        {
            newserv->rear = newserv->front = newreq;
        }
        else
        {
            current->rear->next = newreq;
            current->rear = current->rear->next;
        }
}
```

This code can be quite confusing to the uninitiated. Let's see how it words graphically. Let's assume that username `smith` is entering job-id 22222 as a request for queue `Print1`. Assume that our data structure looks just like the diagram at the beginning of this section.

Here's what the data structure looks like when `Print1` is found, a new `REQUEST` node is allocated and filled up, and the new `REQUEST` node is linked into the proper queue.

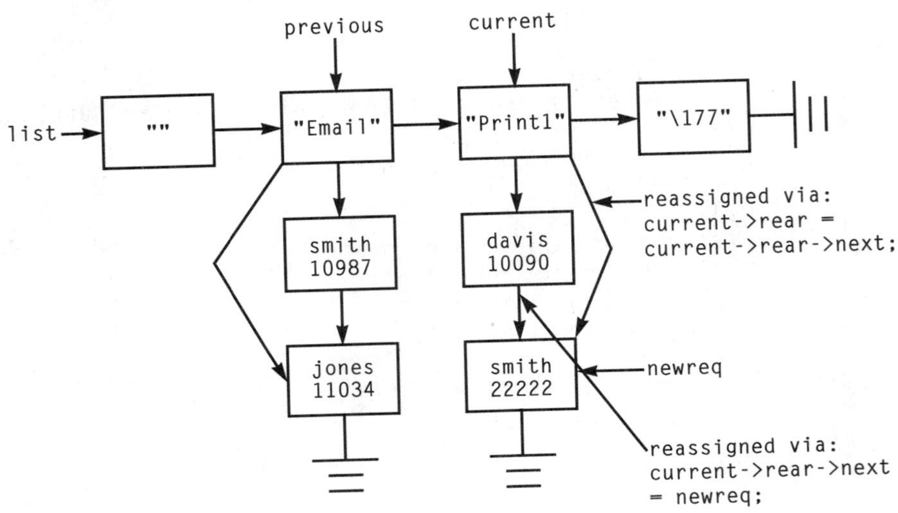

Now let's look at the traversal program that prints out all the list and queue contents.

Example 3.22 Traversal Code for the OS Queues Program

```
void traverse(SERVICE *serv_ptr)
{
    REQUEST *reqptr;

    serv_ptr = serv_ptr->next;  /* Skip dummy header */
    while (*serv_ptr->qname != DUMMY_TRAILER)
    {
        printf("Service name: %s\n", serv_ptr->qname);
        printf("--------------------\n");
        for (reqptr = serv_ptr->front; reqptr != NULL;
             reqptr = reqptr->next)
        {
            printf("%-15s %ld\n", reqptr->username,
                   reqptr->job_id);
        }
```

```
            printf("\n");
            serv_ptr = serv_ptr->next;
        }
}
```

This code goes to each SERVICE node, prints out the service name in a heading, and then prints out the contents of the queue associated with that service—that is, the usernames and job-ids of the service requesters. The for loop processes all the REQUEST nodes in a queue. The while loop processes the SERVICE nodes.

Now let's look at the rest of the code associated with this program and at its output.

Example 3.23 Remaining Code and Output for the OS Queues Program

```
main()
{
    SERVICE *serv_ptr, *init_list(void);
    void getinfo(char *qname, char *username, long *job_id);
    void insert(SERVICE *serv_ptr, char *qname,
                char *username, long job_id);
    void traverse(SERVICE *serv_ptr);
    char qname[30], username[20];
    long job_id;

    serv_ptr = init_list();
    while (getinfo(qname, username, &job_id),
           strcmp(qname, "quit") != 0)
    {
        insert(serv_ptr, qname, username, job_id);
    }
    traverse(serv_ptr);
}


/******  Create dummy header/trailer for SERVICE list. ******/
SERVICE *init_list(void)
{
    SERVICE *serv_ptr;

    if ((serv_ptr =
        (SERVICE *) malloc(sizeof(SERVICE))) == NULL)
    {
        printf("Fatal malloc error in init_serv_ptr!\n");
        exit(1);
```

```
    }
    if ((serv_ptr->qname = (char *) malloc(1)) == NULL)
    {
        printf("Fatal malloc error in init_serv_ptr!\n");
        exit(1);
    }
    *serv_ptr->qname = '\0';  /**** Dummy header value. ****/
    if ((serv_ptr->next =
        (SERVICE *) malloc(sizeof(SERVICE))) == NULL)
    {
        printf("Fatal malloc error in init_serv_ptr!\n");
        exit(1);
    }
    if ((serv_ptr->next->qname = (char *) malloc(2)) == NULL)
    {
        printf("Fatal malloc error in init_serv_ptr!\n");
        exit(1);
    }
    *serv_ptr->next->qname = DUMMY_TRAILER;
    serv_ptr->next->qname[1] = '\0';
    serv_ptr->next->next = NULL;
    return serv_ptr;
}
/*****  Get input from user at the terminal.  *****/
void getinfo(char *qname, char *username, long *job_id)
{
    char line[512];

    printf("Enter qname username job-id: ");
    gets(line);

    if (strcmp(line, "quit") == 0) strcpy(qname, "quit");
    else sscanf(line, "%s %s %ld", qname, username, job_id);
}
/******************  Sample Execution Below  ****************/

Enter qname username job-id: print1 jones 22222
Enter qname username job-id: mail1 thomas 12343
Enter qname username job-id: print1 smith 23232
Enter qname username job-id: print2 edwards 44444
Enter qname username job-id: mail1 james 25432
Enter qname username job-id: batch snell 11111
Enter qname username job-id: mail1 james 25433
Enter qname username job-id: quit  /* Now print out queues. */

Service name: batch
--------------------------
snell          11111
```

```
Service name: mail1
-------------------------
thomas            12343
james             25432
james             25433

Service name: print1
-------------------------
jones             22222
smith             23232

Service name: print2
-------------------------
edwards           44444
```

As you can see, the service names are printed out in ASCII order, which is correct because the `SERVICE` nodes are in an ordered linked list. The `REQUEST` nodes are printed out in the order in which they were entered into the request queue. This also is as it should be; a queue is a "first-in, first-out" (FIFO) data structure.

Facts About Functions

`<string.h>` Functions

Function: `void *memset(void *pointer, int value, size_t number_of_bytes);`

Fact: 1) Copies the value in `value` to all bytes, starting at address `pointer`, and continues this for `number_of_bytes` bytes.

Fact: 2) `Size_t` third parameter is compatible with all `int` types.

Fact: 3) First parameter can be a pointer of any type, but it must be a pointer (i.e., an address).

Fact: 4) It is imperative that `value` be a value between –256 and +255, because only this range of values can fit inside one byte. To disregard this is to court disaster!

Fact: **5)** Although this function can be used to fill up arrays of any type, it is generally used for arrays of `char`. It is also used to zero out arrays of other types.

Fact: **6)** The return value is equal to the first parameter. Make sure this first parameter is not `NULL`, or your program will behave strangely at runtime.

Fact: **7)** This function will be visited again later in this book.

Function: `int strlen(char  *string);`

Fact: **1)** Returns the length of `string`, not including the terminating `'/0'` character.

Fact: **2)** Is often used to assist in calculating space needed for an unassigned pointer in a list, stack, or queue node, as in

```
list->string = (char  *)
                    malloc(strlen(string) + 1);
```

This mechanism ensures that no space is wasted in the `string` component of the node pointed at by `list`.

Fact: **3)** As with all `<string.h>` functions, you must make sure that the `char *` parameters are not `NULL`.

Exercises

1. You have a file that contains the names of computers in a ring network (i.e., a network in a circle shape) and whether they are up or down (down, of course, means not functioning). The file looks like this:

```
tiger 1
slowpoke 0
foobar 1
/****  More data here ****/
```

As can be seen, 1 means the computer is functioning ("up"), and 0 means it is "down." The order of the names in the file determines the order of computers in the ring network. Of course, the last computer is joined to the first. Put these computer names in a doubly linked ring. After you do so, your program will

a. Repeatedly prompt the user for a computer name (until user says "quit").

b. If the computer name exists, the program will return the nearest up computer to the left and right of the user-supplied computer.

c. If the user-supplied computer does not exist, the program will supply an appropriate "Not found" error message.

d. If the computer has only one up neighbor, this fact should also be reported.

e. Do not try to calculate "nearest." Follow the left (or backward, whatever you call them) pointers first to find the left neighbor.

■ 2. Write a function that takes a stack pointer of type `NODE *` as its only parameter and returns a pointer to the stack *turned backwards.* Assume that the pointer component of stack nodes is called `next`. Your answer should have no `malloc()` calls!

3. Write a function that will initialize a doubly linked list with nodes that look like this:

```
struct node
{
    char  *key;
    struct node  *next;
};
```

■ 4. Assume you have a program that has constructed a linked list and that is supposed to put deleted nodes onto a free stack. Rewrite the linked list `delete()` function given this information. *Hint:* It should have three parameters.

5. Create a file with lines that look like this:

```
MULLIN, CHRIS 23
ROBINSON, DAVID 32
JABBAR, KAREEM 25
BIRD, LARRY 22
MULLIN, CHRIS 30
... etc. ...
```

As you can see, each line contains the name of a basketball player followed by the number of points he scored in a game played within the last month. Obviously, a player will have multiple entries (as Chris Mullin does above) if he played in more than one game in the last month. Write a program that will

a. Create a linked list ordered by player name. Each list node will have a stack of point nodes attached to it. See the following data structures:

```
struct points
{
    int points;
    struct points *next;
};

struct player
{
    char name[30];
    struct player  *next;
    struct points  *stack;
};
```

b. After the linked list is created, prompt a user for a player name. If the player is in the list, display the average points per game for that player.

c. Give an error message if the player is not in the player list.

d. Prompt the user repeatedly until he or she says `"quit"`.

e. When the user quits, create an output file that looks like the following. As can be seen, the output file should be in alphabetical order, and the numbers represent individual game totals followed by the average points for these games.

```
BIRD, LARRY 22 23 25 23.2
MULLIN, CHRIS 23 30 20 24.3
ROBINSON, DAVID  17 17 17 17 21 21 21 21 19.0
```
... etc. ...

f. Remove all whitespace from the user's entries, but otherwise assume that these entries are correct.

■ **6.** You have a file (accounts) with lines consisting of two fields: a four-digit bank account number, and the balance in the user's account—for example,

```
1111 2343.90
1001 2500.00
1058 24.34
```
... etc. ...

Write a program that will do the following:

a. The records in this file are in random order, but you will put them into a linked list in order of account number. Assume correct input, and assume that no account number will occur more than once in the file.

b. Then you will put the program user in an input loop (until the user types "quit"). The user will enter transactions as follows: account-number transaction-amount. Thus if account 1111 has two entries, such as

```
1111 -100.00          /***  A withdrawal!    ***/
1111  95.00           /***  A  deposit!  ***/
```

then account 1111 will end up in an ordered "transactions" list with a net transaction amount of –5.00. You may assume correct user input. Thus each account number will be associated with one "net transactions record" that is updated each time the user enters more information.

c. After the user enters "quit", update the list created in part a by adding the transaction amount to each account's balance (if it had any transactions). You may assume that every account number from the list made in part b is represented in the list made in part a.

d. Create three output files: one to contain the transaction records, one to contain all the net balance records (after updating), and one to contain just the records of the people with negative net balances.

e. Use the block allocation technique discussed in Section 3.5.

7. Write a function that will join all the `student_body` linked lists discussed in Section 3.6 into one big linked list and return a pointer to that list. You will be very surprised how short this function is if you code it properly!

■ **8.** Write a function that will go through a doubly linked list of nodes and transpose each pair of nodes. Nodes are of type `NODE` and have components `char *key` and a `next` pointer. The header is the empty string, and the trailer node contains "ZZZZ". Do not move the list header or trailer nodes. Pointers in nodes are called `forward` and `backward`.

9. Rewrite the `else` clause code from the `insert()` function in Example 3.9 if the `string` component of each `NODE` is declared as a `char *`.

■ **10.** Write a deletion function for the operating system (OS) queue program shown in this chapter. This function should remove a request from the front of a service queue, symbolically indicating that a user has been processed.

11. Do the same as in Exercise 10, but assume that the deleted node goes on a free stack.

12. Write a program that:

a. Reads a data file that contains a city name followed by an arbitrarily long list of space-separated computer names belonging to that city's local area ring-shaped network.

b. Separates the city name from its computer names with a colon.

c. Shows a pound sign after the last computer name belonging to a city.

d. Puts the cities into an ordered linked list. Each node in this list will have a pointer pointing to that city's ring network.

e. Has the ring of computers belonging to each city's network as a doubly linked ring.

f. After all list or ring construction, prompts users for a city name and a computer name.

g. Displays on the screen the computer's left and right neighbors in the ring if the city and computer name are found. Otherwise, an appropriate city or computer `"Not found"` message will be sent to the screen.

h. Allows users to continue to enter city or computer requests until they enter `"quit"` in response to your prompt.

i. Following the `"quit"`, allows users to request a full display of all cities and the computers they contain.

This is a very challenging project but one whose successful completion will indicate true mastery of pointer manipulation in linear dynamic structures.

■**13.** Redo Exercise 8 for a *singly linked* list. This is much harder, because the list nodes have no `backward` pointer. Your function should have no calls to `malloc()`. You may assume that the number of (non-dummy) `NODE`s is even (0, 2, 4, 6, and so on).

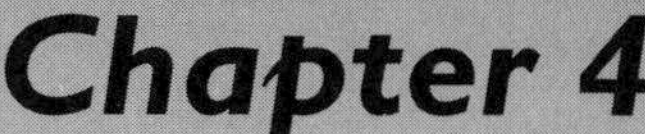

Chapter 4

Advanced String Handling

4.1 Passing Address Expressions as Arguments to String.h Functions

Almost everybody at the beginning and intermediate levels has learned how to pass simple string variables to functions like `strcmp()`, `strcat()`, `strlen()`, and `strcpy()`. In fact, many people at these levels have never passed anything but simple variable names to these functions. However, like all C functions, the `string.h` functions can take any *expression* as a parameter so long as it agrees with the parameter data type. Look at the following code.

```
strcpy(string, "Hello");
printf("%d\n", strlen(string + 2));
```

What number will the `printf()` print on the screen? Many, knowing that the length of "`Hello`" is 5, would answer 7. However, 7 is the value of

```
strlen(string) + 2;
```

As usual, if you draw a picture, you can figure out the correct answer very rapidly.

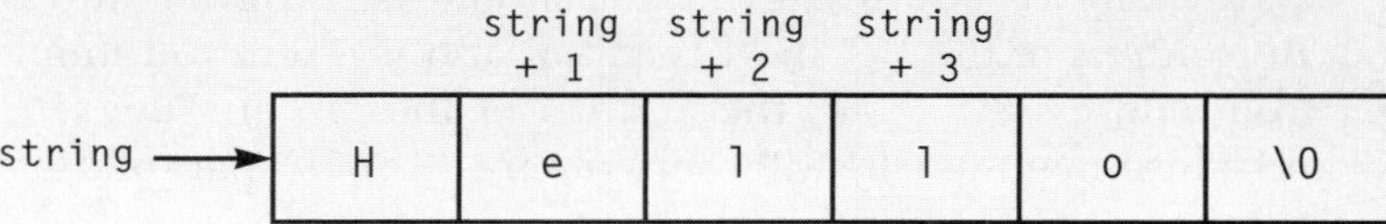

The length of `string` starting at address `string + 2` is 3. That's the value the `printf()` will print on the screen. Another situation not encountered by most beginning and intermediate C programs can be depicted in the following diagram.

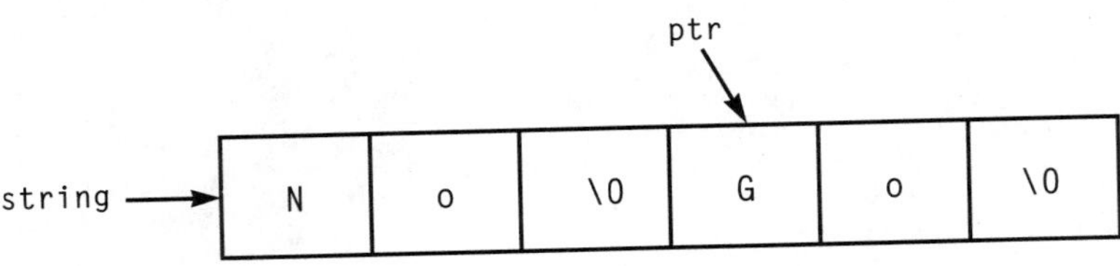

What will the following `printf()` print?

```
printf("%s\n", ptr);
```

Because `ptr` points to a character after the first `'\0'`, many would contend that this `printf()` should lead to a runtime error or print nothing at all. However, this contention would be incorrect, because `printf()` simply starts printing the characters from the given address (i.e., `ptr`) and keeps printing until a `'\0'` is encountered. Thus `"Go"` will appear on the screen. Given the previously diagrammed string, what will the following `printf()` print?

```
printf("%s\n", string + 3);
```

This `printf()` will also make `"Go"` appear on the screen, because the address `string + 3` is the same as `ptr`. Later in this chapter, we will look at a very special and powerful `string.h` function called `strtok()` that cuts a long string up into tokens all separated by the `'\0'` character. This last example was not merely an academic exercise!

Thus we can state a rule of thumb: *When a string-handling function is given an address, it starts the manipulation of the string at that address and continues until it encounters the* `'\0'` *character.*

Before we leave this section, let's look at two more situations where address expressions are passed to `string.h` functions. Here's one:

```
char  s1[10] = "Go Lions!",  s2[10] = "Mad Dogs!";
strcpy(s1 + 3, s2 + 4);
printf("%s\n", s1);
```

What will this `printf()` print? Don't look at the answer just yet—this is a preparation for some of the exercises at the end of this chapter.

If your answer is that "`Go Dogs!`" (quotes not included) will be printed, you are correct. The `strcpy()` says that you should start copying into address `s1 + 3`, the address of the `"L"` in `"Lions"`. It also says that you should start copying from address `s2 + 4`, the address of the `"D"` in `"Dogs!"`. Thus `"Dogs"` and a terminating `'\0'` will overwrite the `"Lions"` part of `s1`.

What will the `printf()` in this code print?

```
char  s1[30] = "A Stitch in Time Saves Nine",
      s2[20] = "I need itch powder!";
printf("%d"\n",  strncmp(s1 + 4, s2 + 7, 4));
```

It will print a zero on the screen. Remember that `strncmp()` is just like `strcmp()` except that the third parameter says to compare only that many characters, starting at the two addresses given as the first and second parameters. Indeed, at the two addresses given, both strings are `"itch"` for the next four characters. Remember that many `string.h` functions have "n" partners (e.g., `strncat()`) that take a third parameter.

4.2 The `Strchr` and `Strrchr` Functions

These two functions look for a particular character, starting from the left end of the string (`strchr`) or from the right end of the string (`strrchr`). Their prototypes are identical, so we will save the prototype of `strrchr()` for the "Facts About Functions" section.

```
char  *strchr(char  *string, int c);
```

Here's some sample code using `strchr()` and `strrchr()`, followed by the output generated by that sample code.

Example 4.1 A Sample of Code Using `Strchr` and `Strrchr`

```
#include <stdio.h>
#include <string.h>
main()
{
    char s1[] = "I am the one, the only one.";
    char *ptr1, *ptr2;

    ptr1 = strchr(s1, 'o');
    ptr2 = strrchr(s1, 'o');
    printf("String starting at leftmost  'o' is: %s\n", ptr1);
    printf("String starting at rightmost 'o' is: %s\n", ptr2);

   /****  Find all the o's in s1. Print their addresses.  ****/

    printf("Address of beginning of s1 is: %p\n", s1);
    for (ptr1=s1; (ptr1=strchr(ptr1,'o')) != NULL;  ptr1++)
    {
        printf("Address of current 'o' is %p\n", ptr1);
    }
}
/****************  Sample Execution Below.  ****************/

String starting at leftmost  'o' is: one, the only one.
String starting at rightmost 'o' is: one.
Address of beginning of s1 is: 0063FDE4
```

```
Address of current 'o' is 0063FDED
Address of current 'o' is 0063FDF6
Address of current 'o' is 0063FDFB
```

Let's analyze this code and output. The first calls to `strchr()` and `strrchr()` produce predictable results. They return the addresses of the first and last `'o'` in `s1`. When these addresses are given to the `printf()` function using the `%s` format descriptor, it prints from the address given to the `'\0'` character. Clearly, both functions worked correctly.

The `for` loop appears to do a few mysterious things. First, what is the `%p` format descriptor in the `printf()`? This is the format descriptor you should use to print out addresses. As you can see, these addresses are printed in hexadecimal (base 16). The biggest mystery in the `for` loop involves the use of `ptr1`. How does this loop work?

After `strchr()` finds an `'o'`, it assigns the address of it to `ptr1`. But then you want to start the search for the next `'o'` in the part of the string after the `'o'` just found! That's why we increment `ptr1` in the increment section of the `for` and then use `ptr1` as the first parameter to `strchr()`. Thus, every `strchr()` call from the second call to the last call is given the address of the character that immediately follows an `'o'`. When no `'o'` characters remain, `strchr()` returns `NULL`, which ends the loop.

Here's a diagram indicating `ptr1`'s position after the `ptr++` in each iteration of the `for` loop. The characters that make up the string are spaced out for readability.

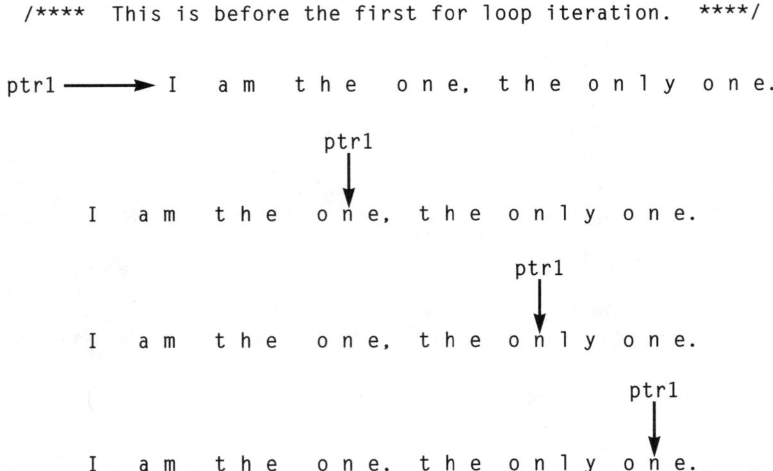

Finding all instances of a particular character in a string is a commonly required task and should be in your arsenal of programming tricks. And we did it by processing *partial* strings after each `'o'` in the original string.

4.3 Looking for Strings Within Other Strings: The `Strstr` Function

The `strstr()` function allows you to look for substrings within strings. The ANSI prototype for `strstr()` is

```
char  *strstr(char  *string, char  *substring);
```

Like `strchr()` and `strrchr()`, `strstr()` returns an address if it succeeds and returns `NULL` if it does not succeed. "Success" means that `substring` is found within `string`. The address returned (if not `NULL`) is the address where `substring` starts within `string`. Here is a code fragment with output to demonstrate how `strstr()` works.

Example 4.2 A Demonstration of `Strstr`

```
#include <string.h>    /***  This program looks for   ***/
#include <stdio.h>     /***  string a in b, c, and d. ***/
main()
{
     char a[] = "cat", b[] = "cattle",
          c[] = "concatenate", d[] = "foobar";

     printf("Address of b = %p\n\
             Address of c = %p\n\
             Address of d = %p\n\
             Address of a in b = %p\n\
             Address of a in c = %p\n\
             Address of a in d = %p\n", b,c,d,
                                 strstr(b,a), strstr(c,a),
                                 strstr(d,a));
}
/*****************  SAMPLE EXECUTION  *******************/
Address of b = 7fffaf24
Address of c = 7fffaf18
Address of d = 7fffaf10
Address of a in b = 7fffaf24    /* Points at "c" in cattle */
Address of a in c = 7fffaf1b    /* Points at second "c"    */
                                /* in concatentate         */
Address of a in d = 0  /**** NULL! No "cat" in "foobar"! ****/
```

Let's analyze the results. Because `"cat"` is at the very beginning of `"cattle"`, `strstr(b, a)` should return an address that is identical to the starting address of `"cattle"`—that is, the `'c'` in `"cattle"`. Indeed, the output bears this out.

`"Cat"` is also found in `"concatenate"` starting at the fourth character. Thus `strstr(c, a)` should produce an address that is 3 higher than the address of the beginning of "concatenate". "Concatenate" starts at address 7fffaf18. Strstr(c, a) returns 7fffaf1b. Remember that in hexadecimal, the digit 'b' is equivalent to the decimal value 11. Thus, 7fffaf1b - 7fffaf18 equals 11 – 8, which equals the predicted 3.

Finally, "cat" is nowhere to be found in the string "foobar". Therefore, strstr(d, a) should produce a NULL return (integer value zero). Indeed, the output is zero.

Let's give strstr() a problem similar to the one we gave strchr() in Example 4.1. Let's write a function that will find all instances of a string within another string, returning the number of instances. This isn't as easy as the strchr() problem.

Here's an example illustrating the pitfalls inherent in this problem: How many times does the string "aa" occur in "aaaaaa"? Given the ambiguity in the wording of the problem, your answer could be 3 (there are 3 consecutive "aa") or 5 (an "aa" starts at every character except the last).

Such a simple task, yet we must be very clear about what we really want. If we stipulate that no two substrings should overlap, then the answer to how many "aa" there are in "aaaaaa" is 3. We will write our function with this in mind. The function is driven by a main() function, and output is shown.

Example 4.3 Using Strstr to Find All Instances of a Substring Within a String

```
#include <stdio.h>
#include <string.h>
main()
{
    char a[] = "Mississippi is my sister state",
         b[] = "Nonsense",
         c[] = "banana anatomy",
         d[] = "Andy Andrews";
    int find_num_substrings(char *string, char *substring);
    int numfound;

    numfound = find_num_substrings(a, "is");
    printf("The string \"is\" is in \"%s\" %d times.\n",
            a, numfound);
    numfound = find_num_substrings(b, "is");
    printf("The string \"is\" is in \"%s\" %d times.\n",
            b, numfound);
    numfound = find_num_substrings(c, "an");
    printf("The string \"an\" is in \"%s\" %d times.\n",
            c, numfound);
    numfound = find_num_substrings(d, "an");
    printf("The string \"an\" is in \"%s\" %d times.\n",
            d, numfound);
}
```

```
int find_num_substrings(char *string, char *substring)
{
    int count = 0;

    while (string = strstr(string, substring))
    {
        count++;
        string += strlen(substring);
    }
    return count;
}
/***************  Program Output Below  ****************/

The string "is" is in "Mississippi is my sister state" 4 times.
The string "is" is in "Nonsense" 0 times.
The string "an" is in "banana anatomy" 3 times.
The string "an" is in "Andy Andrews" 0 times.
```

Let's analyze the `find_num_substrings()` function. It takes a minimalist approach with no extra variables. You may have noticed that I'm writing some functions in a "wordier" fashion than others. This is no accident! It's to give you practice reading different coding styles.

First, the `while` loop has an assignment only with no relational test (such as == or != or the like). Remember from beginning C that the value of an assignment statement is the value of the left side of the = after the assignment. When there are no more `substrings` in `string`, `strstr()` will return `NULL`, which is zero, which terminates a loop.

Second, we are using no local string variables to move along `string`. Remember call-by-value! Because we did not pass a pointer to `string` (which would have made the parameter a `char **`), no matter what we do to `string` in the function, it will contain the same address *after* the call to `find_num_strings()` as it did before.

Because of the "non-overlapping substrings" assumption, every time we find `substring` within `string`, we want to start the search for the *next* `substring` within `string` by skipping over the number of characters in the `substring`. Still confused? Look at following the series of diagrams for finding `"is"` in `"Mississippi is my sister state"`. The first diagram shows the situation before the first `while` iteration in `find_num_substrings()`. Each diagram thereafter shows where `string` points after it is reassigned (last statement in the body of the `while`). Characters are spaced for easy reading.

```
string ——►m i s s i s s i p p i  i s  m y  s i s t e r  s t a t e \0

     m i s s i s s i p p i  i s  m y  s i s t e r  s t a t e \0
         ▲
         |
       string
```

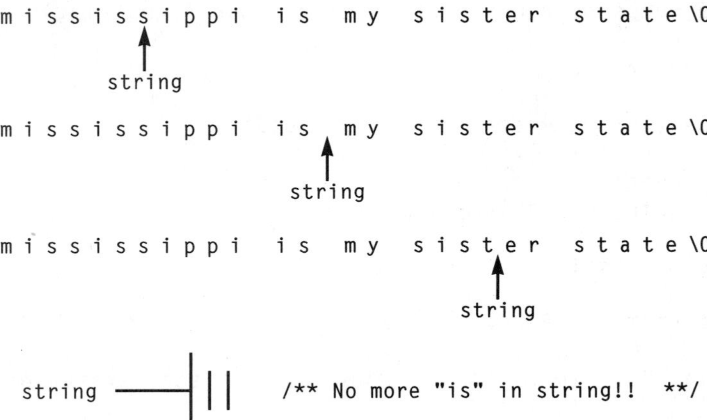

Thus in each `while` iteration, `string` moves from its current position to the `"i"` in the next `"is"` in `string`. The `count` variable is then incremented, and `string` skips over `strlen("is")` characters to reposition itself for the next search. See—it really is as easy as it looks!

Later, after we learn about *arrays of strings*, we will rewrite `find_num_substrings()` so that, instead of returning the number of `substrings` in `string`, it will return an array of all the addresses in `string` where `substring` occurs—that is, an array of `long`.

Let's continue our investigation of the more advanced `string.h` functions.

4.4 Spanning Strings: The `Strspn` and `Strcspn` Functions

These functions are used to answer the questions "Are there any characters from a given character set in string S?" and "Are there any characters in string S that are *not* in a given character set?" For example, here's a use of `strspn()` that attempts to see whether a string has any non-digit characters in it:

```
char  *digits = "0123456789";
if (strspn(string, digits) != strlen(string))
{
    printf("A non-digit character is contained in the
         string!\n");
}
```

In this example, `strspn()` returns the number of characters in `string` that are skipped over until a character is found that is not a member of `digits`. If they aren't *all* skipped over, then the return value of `strspn()` won't equal the length of `string`. In this case, the `printf()` will not be executed, because there is no non-digit character in `digits`. The prototype of `strspn()` is

```
size_t strspn(char  *string,  char  *set_to_skip_over);
```

Remember, a `size_t` is compatible with any kind of `int` (provided your `int` is large enough to hold the return value). `Strcspn()` is the complement of `strspn()`. It returns the number of characters in `string` that are skipped over until a character is found that *is* in `set_to_skip_over`. Its prototype is identical to `strspn()`. Here's a bit of code with output to give you a more concrete idea of how these functions work.

Example 4.4 A Demonstration of Strspn **and** Strcspn

```
#include <stdio.h>
#include <string.h>
main()
{
    char sentence[] = "Hello, I am John!";
    char nonsense[] = "~*%#";
    char letters[] = "ABCDEFGHIJKLMNOPQRSTUVWXYZ\
                      abcdefghijklmnopqrstuvwxyz";
    int numskipped;

    numskipped = strcspn(sentence, letters);
    printf("%d chars skipped over until a letter was found.\n",
           numskipped);
    numskipped = strspn(sentence, letters);
    printf("%d chars skipped over until a non-letter\
           was found.\n", numskipped);
    numskipped = strcspn(sentence, nonsense);
    printf("%d chars skipped over until a nonsense\
           character was found.\n", numskipped);
}
/******************  Program Output Below  ****************/

0 chars skipped over until a letter was found.
5 chars skipped over until a non-letter was found.
17 chars skipped over until a nonsense character was found.
```

`Strspn()` can be used quite effectively to see whether all characters of a string meet a certain requirement (e.g., all digits, all letters, and so on). However, I have yet to use `strcspn()` in a practical application. That's because a fabulous cousin of `strcspn()`, the `strpbrk()` function, has a tremendous variety of uses. We will visit this function next and examine a case study where `strpbrk()` is used to do a study of a text file.

4.5 Finding a Member of a Set in a String: The Strpbrk Function

The prototype for strpbrk() is

```
char  *strpbrk(char  *string, char  *set_to_find);
```

Like strcspn(), strpbrk() skips over characters in string until it finds a character that is in set_to_find. However, instead of returning the number of characters skipped over (a number that is seldom useful), it returns the *address* in string where the member of set_to_find was found.

This function's many uses include finding the location of delimiters between tokens on a user input line. Such a search, which is a form of *parsing* (chopping a line into tokens and delimiters), can be found in applications ranging from compilers to user interfaces to calculator expression evaluators.

We will put this function to work immediately in an example: counting sentences in a text file. As always seems to be the case with programming, there are a few subtleties you must deal with. One is that sentences may end with two or more '?' or '!' characters. Another is that a period (.) might be in a floating point number.

We will therefore make the following assumptions: (1) A period not followed by a digit is an end-of-sentence marker. (2) Sentences may end with more than one '?', '!', or a combination of the two. (3) The '?' and '!' characters are used only to end sentences, not for other purposes. (4) Sentences are always followed by at least one space character. With these assumptions in mind, take a look at the following code.

Example 4.5 Counting the Number of Sentences in a File with Strpbrk

```
#include <stdio.h>
#include <string.h>
#include <stdlib.h>  /***  For exit function.  ***/

#define BIGLINE 1024
main()
{
    int num_sentences;
    int count_sentences(char *filename);

    num_sentences = count_sentences("strpbrk.dat");
    printf("Your file had %d sentences in it!\n",
            num_sentences);
}
```

```
/******  Counts the number of sentences in a file.  ******/
int count_sentences(char *filename)
{
    char line[BIGLINE];  /*** Allow for very long lines.  ***/
    char *mover, ;
    FILE *fp;
    int  num_sentences = 0;

    if ((fp = fopen(filename, "r")) == NULL)
    {
        printf("Failure to open input file!  Aborting!\n");
        exit(1);
    }
    while (fgets(line, BIGLINE - 1, fp))
    {
        for (mover = line; mover = strpbrk(mover, "?!.");
             mover++)
        {
            if (!isdigit(mover[1])) num_sentences++;
            for ( ; mover[1] == '?' || mover[1] == '!';
                    mover++) ;
        }
    }
    return num_sentences;
}

/**********  Contents of Input File (strpbrk.dat)  **********/

This is a sentence.  I am John!!!  This sentence has the
number 3.5 in it and it also runs along for more than one
line until it comes to an untimely end.  Do you know what
I mean, Jelly Bean??  That's all I've got to say!

/***************  Output from Program Below  ***************/

Your file had 5 sentences in it!
```

Note that strchr() would not be an appropriate choice for our sentence counter, because it can look for only one kind of character per search. Strpbrk() can look for any one of a set of characters.

The code in count_sentences() is very minimalist. Fgets() returns NULL when EOF is encountered. Because NULL is zero, this terminates the while. Otherwise, fgets() puts a line from the file into its first argument (line) including the line terminator ('\n').

The outer for loop keeps looping if strpbrk() finds one of the end-of-sentence markers. It terminates when strpbrk() returns NULL (which means it couldn't find any more `'?'`, `'!'`, or `'.'`). If a digit follows an end-of-sentence marker, it does not increment `num_sentences`. That's because, given our assumptions, it means that the end-of-sentence marker found was a period that was part of a number (such as 3.5) rather than a real end-of-sentence marker.

Finally, the inner `for` loop keeps cycling if the next character is a `'?'` or `'!'`. This accounts for sentences that end with two or more `'?'` or `'!'` or both. We don't want to double- or triple-count these sentences. The notation `mover[1]` seen in `count_sentences()` means "the character after the one currently pointed at by `mover`." Remember that array indices are always relative to the current pointer location.

Now that we have explained how `count_sentences()` works with words, let's explain it with pictures. We will show the mysterious movements of the `mover` pointer as it hops along each line of text. Characters in the diagrams are spread out so that you can see where `mover` is pointing without difficulty.

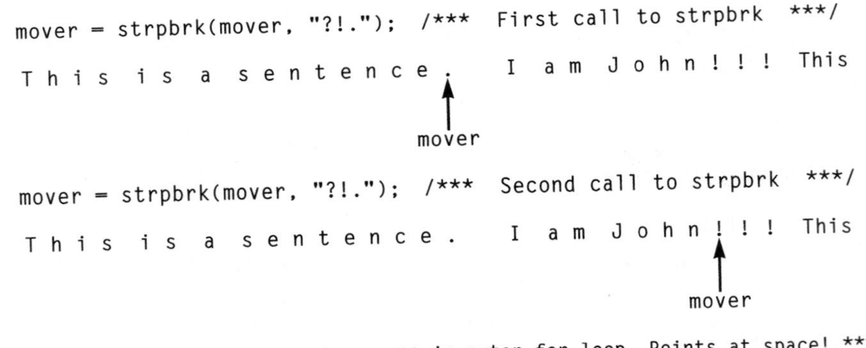


```
/*** After inner for loop and mover++ in outer for loop. Points at space! ***/
  T h i s   i s   a   s e n t e n c e .   I  a m  J o h n ! ! !  This
                                                                 ↑
                                                               mover
```

The next call to `strpbrk()` from this point results in a `NULL` return, terminating the outer `for` loop. Now we get the next line in the input file:

```
mover = strpbrk(mover, "?!.");
n u m b e r  3 . 5  i n  i t  a n d  i t  a l s o  r u n s  a l o n g
                ↑
              mover
```

Because `mover[1]` is the `5` (thus, `!isdigit(mover[1])` is false), this period is not counted as an end-of-sentence marker. The outer `for` then does `mover++`, making `mover` point at the 5. The next `strpbrk()` produces a `NULL` return, and we move on to the next line in the input file.

At this point we will stop, because the last two lines of the file contain nothing extraordinary. When testing the validity of your program, you must always be sure to test extreme cases. In this program, the "extreme cases" are lines ending with more than one '?' or '!' and lines containing a period in a number. It's just such cases that normally make programs bomb if they are not accounted for!

4.6 Tricky String Parsing with the String.h Functions

Before we look at the trickiest string.h function, strtok(), let me show you how you can solve some thorny problems with the functions we have examined thus far in this chapter. Suppose someone told you that she wanted to print the part of a string between the first and second '#' characters. Furthermore, you want to do nothing with the string if it doesn't have at least two '#' characters. Try to solve the problem on your own before you look at the answer code in Example 4.6. You'll get lots of practice with such trickery in the exercises as well.

Example 4.6 Printing Text Between Two '#' Characters in an Unknown String

```
#include <stdio.h>
#include <string.h>
main()
{
    char line[80], *ptr1, *ptr2;

    /****  Get input from the user at the terminal.  ****/
    while (gets(line), strcmp(line, "quit"))
    {
        ptr1 = strchr(line, '#');
        if (ptr1)
        {
            ptr1++;  /***  Move to char after '#'.  ***/
            ptr2 = strchr(ptr1, '#');
        }
        if (!ptr1 || !ptr2)
        {
            printf("Line doesn't have two '#' characters!\n");
            continue;
        }
        printf("%.*s\n\n", ptr2 - ptr1, ptr1);
    }
}
```

If the line entered by the user does not have two '#' characters, the rest of the loop body is skipped via a `continue` instruction. The real "trick" here is the use of *variable formatting* in the `printf()`. An asterisk (*) in the format spec tells `printf()` to look in the expression list for the size of the string—in this case, `ptr2 - ptr1`. We will examine such variable formatting in detail later in Chapter 5 on advanced input and output.

Here's a sample string with the positions of `ptr1` and `ptr2` just prior to the `printf()`. Again, the characters in the diagram are spaced out for visibility. There are no actual spaces in the string.

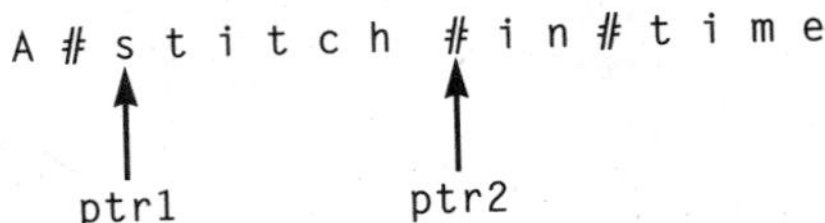

Now let's change the wording of the problem slightly. Suppose you are asked to print out the part of the string *between the first two digit characters*. As it turns out, the only change to the code in Example 4.6 would be to change the two `strchr()` calls to `strpbrk()` calls, because the digits are a set of characters and not just one character. The two `strchr()` calls would be replaced by

```
ptr1 = strpbrk(line, "0123456789");
```

and

```
ptr2 = strpbrk(ptr1, "0123456789");
```

I hope Examples 4.5 and 4.6 have opened your eyes to the vast problem-solving power of the C string-handling functions. And the best is yet to come!

4.7 Parsing Strings with Strtok

When users enter input in response to a program prompt, the program usually has to "chop" the input into "tokens" and "delimiters." For example, suppose you wanted a user to enter two numbers separated by a comma and (optional) whitespace:

```
10 , 25
```

A computer scientist would say that `10` and `25` are the *tokens* (the stuff you are interested in processing) and that the comma and the whitespace are the *delimiters* (the stuff you are not interested in processing).

Virtually every user interface of every program sold in the world has to deal with separating tokens and delimiters. ANSI C helps us with this task via the remarkable (and very dangerous) `strtok()` function. Here's the ANSI C prototype for this function:

```
char *strtok(char *string, char *delimiters);
```

This function's workings are much easier to show (via example) than to explain. Suppose a user entered the following input line:

```
10  ,        35,   40
```

Let's assume that we have this entire input line in string variable `line`. Let's also assume that we have four `char *` variables—`ptr1`, `ptr2`, `ptr3`, and `ptr4`. Then we have the following four lines of code:

```
ptr1 = strtok(line, ",\040\t");
ptr2 = strtok(NULL, ",\040\t");
ptr3 = strtok(NULL, ",\040\t");
ptr4 = strtok(NULL, ",\040\t");
```

Here's a diagram depicting the effect of the four `strtok()` calls on `line` and the values of the four pointer variables.

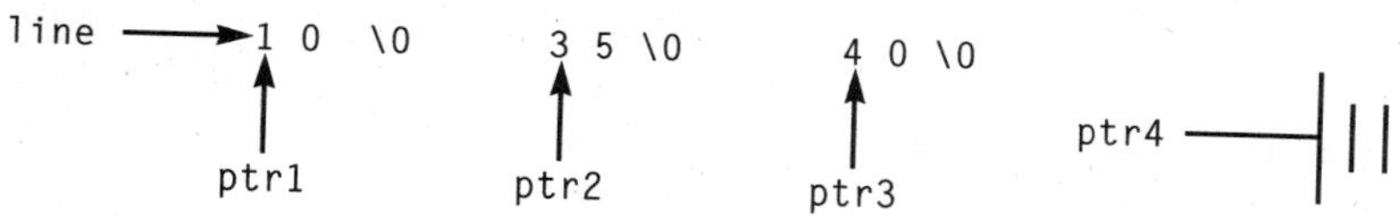

Now for the "official" explanation of how `strtok()` works.

1. On the first call to `strtok()`, you pass the string variable to be parsed (`line`). On the second through last calls, you pass `NULL` as the first parameter. This tells `strtok()` to continue parsing the same string.
2. The second parameter to `strtok()` is a string containing the delimiter list.
3. `Strtok()` skips leading delimiters, overwrites the first trailing delimiter with a `'\0'` character, and returns the address of the first character of the token.
4. `Strtok()` returns `NULL` if the remainder of the string contains only delimiter characters or only the `'\0'` character.

A quick look at the diagram will tell you why I have referred to `strtok()` as a dangerous function—it mangles the original string by overwriting the first delimiter after a token with `'\0'`.

You may be wondering how `strtok()` knows where to start parsing when you give a `NULL` first parameter. It does so through the use of `static` variables. The values of `static` variables persist between calls to a function. (Remember our memory manager in Chapter 3?) Thus `strtok()` maintains a `static` local pointer to the current place in the string.

As you can see in the foregoing diagram, `ptr1`, `ptr2`, and `ptr3` point to the first character of the three tokens. `Ptr4` is `NULL` because there are no more tokens after the `40` token.

Note that I have indicated the ASCII space character in the delimiter list as `'\040'` —the octal value of the space character. I did this because I want to make the space visible to the reader of my program. Many unprintable characters show up on printers and/or terminals as whitespace, so you are doing the reader a favor by making it obvious that it is a space. Of course, the `'\t'` is ANSI C's escape sequence for the tab character.

The beauty of `strtok()` is that it delivers "clean" tokens to our program, free of any "junk" characters that we are not interested in. Quite often, these tokens are supposed to denote numeric strings. Therefore, wherever `strtok()` appears, you usually find one of its three cousins—`strtol()`, `strtoul()`, and `strtod()`. These three functions attempt to convert a string into a `signed long`, an `unsigned long`, and a `double`, respectively. They also have valuable error detection facilities not present in their outmoded (and terrible!) brethren, the `atoi()` and `atof()` functions.

In the next section, you will see `strtok()` work together with these three crucial functions.

4.8 Converting Numeric Strings to Numbers

The three string-to-numeric conversion functions `strtol()`, `strtoul()`, and `strtod()` convert strings to `long ints`, `unsigned long ints`, and `doubles`, respectively. They are superior in every way to the old C conversion functions such as `atoi()` and `atof()`. But the main reason they are superior is that they do error detection, whereas the older functions essentially do none.

These conversion functions are often seen in the same section of code as `strtok()`. `Strtok()` gets nice, clean tokens from a user input line. If these clean tokens are supposed to be numbers, they are then fed to one of the three conversion functions, as appropriate. Unlike the other functions in this chapter, these three conversion functions are in the `stdlib.h` header file, not `string.h`.

Let's look at the ANSI C prototypes for these three functions.

```
long strtol(char  *string, char  **endp, int base);
unsigned long strtoul(char  *string, char  **endp, int
                      base);
double strtod(char  *string, char  **endp);
```

We will not discuss `strtoul()`, which ignores a sign, if one is present, rather than reporting it as an error. The key to understanding `strtol()` and `strtod()` lies in the second parameter: the `char **` I have called `endp`.

Usually, you pass the address of an unassigned `char *` into these conversion functions, and they come out pointing at the first character in `string` that could not be converted into a number. If `string` is a clean token collected by `strtok()`, the character pointed at ought to be the `'\0'` character unless the `string` does not represent a correct `long` or `double`, depending on which conversion function you've called.

Example 4.7 demonstrates the use of `strtok()` and `strtol()` together.

Example 4.7 Conversion of User Input to Integer

```
/**********  Parse tokens.  Convert to int.  ***********/

#include <stdlib.h>    /* Library where strtol is located. */
#include <string.h>    /* Library where strtok is located. */
#include <stdio.h>     /* Library for gets, printf, etc.   */

main()
{
    int tokennum, num;
    char line[256], *lineptr, *tokenptr, *endp;

while (printf("\nEnter some integers: "), gets(line),
       strcmp(line, "quit"))
{

    /*****************************************************/
    /*                                                   */
    /*  Lineptr == line for first iteration of for loop  */
    /*  only.  It is set to NULL after that.             */
    /*****************************************************/

    lineptr = line;
    for (tokennum = 1; tokenptr = strtok(lineptr, "\040\t");
         lineptr = NULL, tokennum++)
    {
        num = (int) strtol(tokenptr, &endp, 10);
        if (*endp != '\0')
        {
            printf("   Token number %d is not a valid\
                    integer!\n", tokennum);
        }
        else
        {
            printf("   Token number %d is = %d\n", tokennum,
                    num);
        }
    }
}
}


/**********  Sample Execution of Code Above  **********/

Enter some integers:   /*** Reprompt on empty response. ***/

Enter some integers: 4 5 x
    Token number 1 is = 4
```

```
        Token number 2 is = 5
        Token number 3 is not a valid integer!

    Enter some integers: 3 x4 5
        Token number 1 is = 3
        Token number 2 is not a valid integer!
        Token number 3 is = 5

    Enter some integers: x
        Token number 1 is not a valid integer!

    Enter some integers:      10             12x5   3
        Token number 1 is = 10
        Token number 2 is not a valid integer!
        Token number 3 is = 3

    Enter some integers: x23
        Token number 1 is not a valid integer!

    Enter some integers: 23
        Token number 1 is = 23

    Enter some integers: 10   20                             66
        Token number 1 is = 10
        Token number 2 is = 20
        Token number 3 is = 66

    Enter some integers: quit
$   /****  System prompt.  Program has terminated!!  ****/
```

As you can see from an examination of the code and output in Example 4.7, the value of `*endp` coming out of the call to `strtol()` is very important. If the value of `*endp` is the `'\0'` character, then the string was a good `long`. If `*endp` points at anything else, it is not a good `long`. If a character can't be converted properly, its value is contained in `*endp`. Thus, if a user entered `3z4` as a number, `*endp` would emerge from `strtol()` with the erroneous `'z'` as its value.

Another feature of the code in Example 4.7 that should be mentioned is the assignment

```
lineptr = line;
```

This is important, because from the second call through the final call of `strtok()`, we want the first parameter to be `NULL`. On the first call of `strtok()` we want the first parameter to point at the line to be parsed. Because `line` is a pointer constant, its value cannot be changed. Thus we used `lineptr`, which is a pointer variable. Oh, those nagging little details!

We have seen how the second parameter of all three conversion functions gives us vital information about the success or failure of the conversion. If there's a failure, it will be reflected in the value of `*endp`. However, something else can go wrong that you must know about. It is possible that a token contains all digit characters, but the number is *too big to be represented on your computer!* In this event, the following behavior occurs:

1. The value of `*endp` is set equal to the first character of the first parameter.
2. The built-in variable `errno` is set to `ERANGE`. If `errno` is used, you must include the `errno.h` header file in your program.
3. The return value of the function is `HUGE_VAL`.

`HUGE_VAL` is generally the largest `long` representable on your machine. Now that you know what happens when a user types in a number that is too large, must you always guard against it? Usually not. In many cases, the number you are seeking from the user is a menu choice number, a line number in a file, or some other number that is likely to be small.

All you care about is whether the number is in a certain range (less than the highest menu choice, the last line number in a file, etc.). If it is above that range, you don't care how much larger it is. Thus it is seldom important to look at `errno`. But if you do, you must remember to reset `errno` to zero before each call of the conversion function. Why? Sometimes functions in C set `errno` when something goes wrong but do nothing to `errno` when things go right.

Thus, if something goes wrong on one call to `strtol()` and you don't set `errno` to zero before the next call to `strtol()`, your program may assume that something went wrong on the second call, because `errno` still has the (unchanged) `ERANGE` value. Be careful! To summarize this, look at the pseudo-C code that follows.

Example 4.8 Correct and Incorrect Ways to Use `Errno` with `Strtol`

```
#include <errno.h>
while (some-condition)  /****  This loop is incorrect!! ****/
{
    num = strtol(string, &endp, 10);
    if (errno == ERANGE) { do something }
}
```

versus,

```
#include <errno.h>
while (some-condition)  /****  This loop is correct!!  ****/
{
```

```
    errno = 0;
    num = strtol(string, &endp, 10);
    if (errno == ERANGE) { do something }
}
```

Strtod() sets errno to ERANGE on both overflow (number too large) and underflow (number too small). Because strtod() usually returns zero on underflow, checking for ERANGE with doubles may be more important than it is for long returns from strtol(). However, I think it's safe to say that you'll be using strtol() dozens or hundreds of times more often than strtod().

Because strtok() and strtol() are such vital functions, this is probably a good time to gather what we know about them in two lists of "Key Facts."

Example 4.9 Key Facts to Remember About `Strtok`

1. `Strtok` needs the name of the string variable to parse the first token from the string. To collect all other tokens from the same string, give `NULL` as the first parameter.
2. You may change the delimiter list from one call of `strtok()` to the next if you find it necessary.
3. `Strtok` returns `NULL` if it cannot find any more tokens in the string starting from the current point out to the `'\0'`.
4. `Strtok` overwrites the first delimiter character after a token with `'\0'`. This means that it mangles the original string! If you need the original string in its original form, make a copy of it before you `strtok()` it!
5. The string pointer returned by `strtok()` points to a string with no delimiter characters. This is what we have referred to as a "clean" string.

Example 4.10 Key Facts to Remember About `Strtol`

1. `Strtol` returns a `long int` if it can find one. Thus, if the string parameter points to `"56X"`, `strtol()` will return a `56` but `endp` will point at the (unconvertible) `X`.
2. If a "clean" token (no whitespace) containing a valid `long int` is given to `strtol()`, `endp` should point at the `'\0'` character at the end of the token string.
3. If the first character of a token is not convertible, `strtol()` returns zero, and `endp` points at the "offending" character. For example, if token = `X56`, then `*endp` will be the `X`.

4. If the token given to strtol() is all digits but is too large (in the positive or negative direction), strtol() will return HUGE_VAL and set the errno variable to ERANGE.
5. If you use errno, don't forget to include errno.h, and don't forget to set errno to zero before each strtol() call.

Before moving to the last topic of this chapter, arrays of strings, I want to encourage you to do as many exercises at the end of this chapter as you can. Aside from dynamic data structures, there isn't a more important topic in this book than string manipulation. If you intend to write compilers, user interfaces, point-of-sale systems, text file analysis programs, or Web browsers, you are going to work with strings until you are blue in the face!

To re-emphasize this importance, I am going to present a short case study—a program that counts the frequency of each word in a text file. All programs must make assumptions about the nature of the data they encounter. So will this one. Those assumptions follow.

1. Punctuation will always occur immediately after the end of a word and will never be preceded by a space.
2. A "word" can contain letters, digits, periods (as in 3.5), and hyphens. However, no word will be all hyphens, and a period at the end of a word will be considered an end of a sentence and not as part of a word.
3. All sentences will be separated from one another by at least one whitespace character.

The program will read from a text file whose name is entered by the user. It will output the list of words (all lowercased) in ASCII order. Thus you should keep an *ordered linked list* of nodes containing a word and its frequency count. We're going to use everything discussed in the book thus far!

Hints? Use fgets() to read the lines of the file and strtok() to parse the tokens. Good luck!

4.9 Case Study of String Handling: The Word Counter Program

Example 4.11 Source Code for the Word Frequency Counting Program

```
/*****************************************************/
/*                                                   */
/*  This program counts the frequency of words in a  */
/*  file.  Words are defined as any combination of   */
```

```
/*  letters, digits, hyphens, or periods.  However,    */
/*  a word cannot be ALL hyphens.  Also, a period at   */
/*  the end of a word will be considered an end-of-    */
/*  sentence marker and NOT as part of a word.         */
/*                                                     */
/******************************************************/

/****************  Start include files.  *************/
#include <stdio.h>
#include <string.h>
#include <stdlib.h>   /****  For malloc and exit.  ****/
/****************  End include files.  ***************/

/**********  Start constant declarations.  ************/
#define DUPLICATE 1
#define NEW_WORDNODE  0
#define DUMMY_TRAILER '\177'
#define PERIOD '.'
#define DELIMS  "\001\
\002\003\004\005\006\007\010\011\012\013\014\015\016\017\020\
\021\022\023\024\025\026\027\030\031\032\033\034\035\036\
\037\040!\"#$%&()|'*+',!?/:;<=>?@[\092]^_{}~\177"
/**********  End constant declarations.  **************/

typedef struct node WORDNODE;
struct node
{
   char *word;
   int  count;
   WORDNODE *next;
};
main()
{
    WORDNODE *list, *nodeptr;
    char word[40], *filename;
    FILE *wordfile;
    void traverse(WORDNODE *list);
    char *get_filename(void);
    WORDNODE *find(WORDNODE *list, char *word);
    WORDNODE *init_list(void);
    FILE *open_file(char *filename);
    void read_file_into_list(WORDNODE *list, FILE *wordfile);

    list = init_list();
    filename = get_filename();
    wordfile = open_file(filename);
    read_file_into_list(list, wordfile);
    fclose(wordfile);
    traverse(list);
}
```

```
/********************************************/
/*                                          */
/*  Initialize list with dummy header and   */
/*  trailer node.  Header node has an empty */
/*  string.  Trailer node is "\177".        */
/*                                          */
/********************************************/
WORDNODE *init_list(void)
{
    WORDNODE *list;

    if ((list = (WORDNODE *)malloc(sizeof(WORDNODE))) == NULL)
    {
        printf("Fatal malloc error in init_list!\n");
        exit(1);
    }
    if ((list->word = (char *) malloc(1)) == NULL)
    {
        printf("Fatal malloc error in init_list!\n");
        exit(1);
    }
    if ((list->next = (WORDNODE *) malloc(sizeof(WORDNODE)))
        == NULL)
    {
        printf("Fatal malloc error in init_list!\n");
        exit(1);
    }
    if ((list->next->word = (char *) malloc(2)) == NULL)
    {
        printf("Fatal malloc error in init_list!\n");
        exit(1);
    }
    *list->next->word = DUMMY_TRAILER;
    list->next->word[1] = '\0';
    list->next->next = NULL;
    return list;
}


/********************************************/
/*                                          */
/*  Obtain input filename from user.        */
/*  User's entered filename has whitespace  */
/*  removed and all chars are lowercased.   */
/*                                          */
/********************************************/
char *get_filename(void)
{
```

```
   static char filename[512];
   char *slow, *fast;

   printf("Please enter a filename: ");
   gets(filename);
   /******  Remove whitespace and lowercase the name.  ******/
   slow = fast = filename;
   while (*fast)
   {
      if (!isspace(*fast)) *slow++ = tolower(*fast);
      fast++;
   }
   *slow = '\0';
   return filename;
}
/****************************************/
/*                                      */
/*  Open user-specified input file.  Abort */
/*  if unsuccessful.  Pass FILE pointer  */
/*  back if open is successful.          */
/*                                      */
/****************************************/
FILE *open_file(char *filename)
{
    FILE *wordfile;

    if ((wordfile = fopen(filename, "r")) == NULL)
    {
        printf("Fatal error opening input file!\n");
        exit(2);
    }
    return wordfile;
}


/****************************************/
/*                                      */
/*  Insert a word into an ordered linked  */
/*  list.  If the word is already in the  */
/*  list, increase the frequency count by */
/*  one and do NOT insert a new node.     */
/*                                      */
/****************************************/
void insert(WORDNODE *list, char *word)
{
    WORDNODE *current = list->next;
    WORDNODE *previous = list;
    WORDNODE *new;
```

```
    while ( strcmp(word, current->word) > 0)
    {
        previous = current;
        current  = current->next;
    }
    if (strcmp(word, current->word) == 0)
    {
        current->count++;
    }
    else   /****  New node -- add to list.  ****/
    {
        if ((new = (WORDNODE *) malloc(sizeof(WORDNODE)))i
            == NULL)
        {
            printf("Fatal malloc error in insert!\n");
            exit(3);
        }
        if ((new->word = (char *) malloc(strlen(word) + 1))
            == NULL)
        {
            printf("Fatal malloc error in insert!\n");
            exit(3);
        }
        strcpy(new->word, word);
        new->next  = current;
        new->count = 1;
        previous->next = new;
    }  /*** End else ***/
}


/*********************************************/
/*                                           */
/*  Get lines from input file.  Fetch all word  */
/*  tokens from each line.  Put words and their */
/*  frequency count into a linked list with     */
/*  nodes in ASCII order.                       */
/*                                           */
/*********************************************/
void read_file_into_list(WORDNODE *list, FILE *wordfile)
{
    char line[1024], *word, *mover, *ptr;
    char *period_ptr, *left_period, *right_period;
    void insert(WORDNODE *list, char *word);

    while (fgets(line, 1024, wordfile))
    {
```

```
        for (ptr = line; word = strtok(ptr, DELIMS); ptr = NULL)
        {
            if (strspn(word, "-") == strlen(word)) continue;
            if (word[strlen(word) - 1] == PERIOD)
            {
                word[strlen(word) - 1] = '\0';
            }
            for (mover = word; *mover != '\0'; mover++)
            {
                *mover = tolower(*mover);
            }
            insert(list, word);
        }  /**** End for ****/
    }   /**** End while ****/
}


/*******************************************/
/*                                         */
/*  Move across the word list.  Print the  */
/*  words and their frequency counts in    */
/*  ASCII order to file freq.out.          */
/*                                         */
/*******************************************/
void traverse(WORDNODE *list)
{
    FILE *freq_file;

    if ((freq_file = fopen("freq.out", "w")) == NULL)
    {
        printf("Could not open output file!\n");
        exit(4);
    }
    list = list->next;
    while(*list->word != DUMMY_TRAILER)
    {
        fprintf(freq_file, "%-20s %-5d\n",
                list->word, list->count);
        list = list->next;
    }
    fclose(freq_file);
}
```

If you comprehend this program completely, congratulations! It is at least as important to be able to read complex code as to write it. If you managed to write this program, well done indeed! You've mastered all of the material presented thus far in this book.

The text file used as input and the program output follow.

Example 4.12 Input File for the Word Frequency Counter Program

```
The average American has 2.3 children. Children are a
joy in their lives. However, due to the increased
stress in the workplace, parents find that they have
less time for their attention-starved children.To
combat this, some companies are allowing telecommuting,
paid leave to take care of pressing family matters,
or on-site counseling for stressed-out parents.

Companies which have volunteered to take these steps find
that employee morale is higher, as is productivity. Due to
increasing global competition and profit margin pressure,
companies have been reluctant to take this course even when
they know, objectively, that it would be best for them and
their employees and families.

However, when matters get out of hand in the workplace, you
can usually look to bad morale caused by overwrought employees
whose nerves are frayed due to the lack of time to deal with
non-work issues. The bottom line is: Companies must take care
of their employees like family or else face the politics of
the family!

To find out more about this issue, visit our Web site --
www.foobar.foo.
```

Example 4.13 Output from the Word Frequency Counter Program

```
2.3                 1
a                   1
about               1
allowing            1
american            1
and                 3
are                 3
as                  1
attention-starved   1
average             1
bad                 1
be                  1
been                1
best                1
```

```
bottom          1
by              1
can             1
care            2
caused          1
children        3
combat          1
companies       4
competition     1
counseling      1
course          1
deal            1
due             3
else            1
employee        1
employees       3
even            1
face            1
families        1
family          3
find            3
for             3
frayed          1
get             1
global          1
hand            1
has             1
have            3
higher          1
however         2
in              3
increased       1
increasing      1
is              3
issue           1
issues          1
it              1
joy             1
know            1
lack            1
leave           1
less            1
like            1
line            1
lives           1
look            1
margin          1
matters         2
morale          2
```

```
more                1
must                1
nerves              1
non-work            1
objectively         1
of                  5
on-site             1
or                  2
our                 1
out                 2
overwrought         1
parents             2
paid                1
politics            1
pressing            1
pressure            1
productivity        1
profit              1
reluctant           1
site                1
some                1
steps               1
stress              1
stressed-out        1
take                4
telecommuting       1
that                3
the                 8
their               4
them                1
these               1
they                2
this                3
time                2
to                  10
usually             1
visit               1
volunteered         1
web                 1
when                2
which               1
whose               1
with                1
workplace           2
would               1
www.foobar.foo      1
you                 1
```

This program uses virtually all of the C idioms discussed so far in this book. You used your knowledge of lists to create the list initialization, insertion, and traversal functions. You used `strtok()` with an exceptionally long delimiter list (all characters except letters, digits, hyphens, and period!) to parse each input line in the file, given the rules for word parsing. You used your pointer skills to clear whitespace from the user's input. If you have completed this lengthy exercise, congratulations; you've come a long way!

I hope you noticed that the input file, as it always should, tested the extreme cases—words with periods at the end, words with periods in the middle, words that are all hyphens, and so on. Everybody loves to code, but few delight in constructing a proper test of their code. It will serve you well to develop this habit.

Now you're ready to make the final leap—the leap that will complete your study of strings.

4.10 Arrays of Strings (Arrays of Pointer to `Char`)

The following is a typical declaration for an array of strings, more formally known in C as an array of pointer to `char`.

```
char  *strings[5] = {"hello", "cat", "dog", "mouse", NULL};
```

Arrays of strings are extremely versatile and are commonly used. Compilers may put *reserved words* in an array of strings and then do a "table lookup" to see whether a token parsed from a program is one of the reserved words.

An array of strings might be used to hold the lines of a text file in memory, especially when the file is known to be of short or intermediate size. Another use might be in a user interface to hold user input tokens, especially when the number of these tokens is unknown. This data structure, like queues and lists, has an endless variety of application domains.

Let's start with the most important array of strings in a C program—the command line argument list. Up to this point in the text, we have given the `main()` function no arguments. Up to this point, if we wished to pass values into the program, we have had to prompt the user for the value of these arguments, one by one. Now we'll show you the correct way to do it!

Example 4.14 Using Command Line Arguments

```
/********************************************************/
/*                                                      */
/*  A demonstration of using and traversing command line */
/*  arguments.  These arguments are held in an array of  */
/*  pointer to char.                                     */
/*                                                      */
/********************************************************/
```

```
#include <stdio.h>

main(int argc, char *argv[])  /* argc = number of arguments */
{
   int i;
   char **mover;

   for (i = 0; i < argc; i++)
   {
      printf("Argument %d is %s\n", i, argv[i]);
   }
   printf("\n");
   for (mover = argv; *mover != NULL; mover++)
   {
      printf("Argument pointed at by mover is %s\n", *mover);
   }
}
/*****************  SAMPLE EXECUTION  *******************/

$argv eye ear nose  /*** MS-DOS command line. ***/

Argument 0 is C:\ADVC\ARGV.EXE
Argument 1 is eye
Argument 2 is ear
Argument 3 is nose

Argument pointed at by mover is C:\ADVC\ARGV.EXE
Argument pointed at by mover is eye
Argument pointed at by mover is ear
Argument pointed at by mover is nose
```

As you can see, we traversed the command line argument list in two different ways. We did it the first way to show that the argument count, represented by the variable `argc`, equals the number of tokens on the command line, including the filename of the program executable itself. The program name, and all of the arguments on the command line invoking the program, make up the `argv` array.

Then we traversed the list another way, by traversing the array of pointers with a `char **` variable (`mover`) until the pointer it pointed at became `NULL`. The second `for` loop is the correct way to traverse the array, because it uses all pointer arithmetic and shows you that operating systems always terminate the `argv` list with a `NULL` pointer. This is a convention that you should adopt when building your own arrays of strings.

Still don't get it? Let's look at a graph showing the state of this data structure before the first `for` iteration.

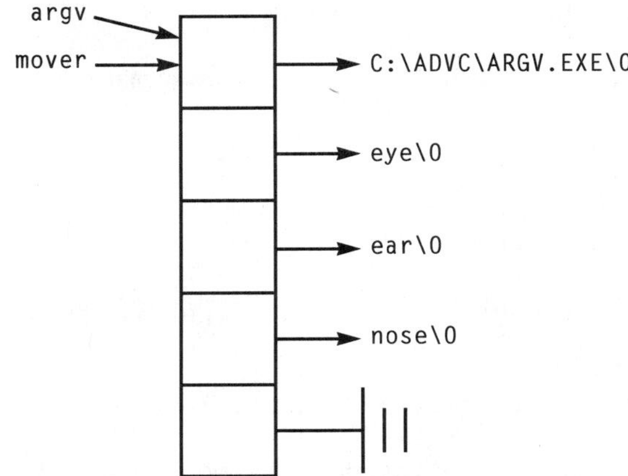

Once you look at this diagram, it is obvious that `mover` is a `char **`. But so is `argv`! Remember that the name of a one-dimensional array is a pointer to its first element. If that first element is a pointer, then we must conclude that `argv` is a *pointer to a pointer.*

What is the notation for the pointer that `mover` points at? It's `*mover`. If `mover` is pointing at the pointer that points at `"eye"`, what is the notation for the first `"e"` in that `"eye"`? You guessed it, it's `**mover`. If you understood pointers to pointers in Chapter 3, this should present no difficulty except that the data here are strings instead of nodes in a list, stack, or queue.

If you've read the code in Example 4.14 then you know that `mover++` moves the pointer to the next element in the array of pointers. This continues until `mover` points at the `NULL` pointer in the last element of the array. At this point, `*mover` is `NULL` and the `for` terminates.

Here's some more demo code to show that you can manipulate your own array of strings just like the built-in `argv` array.

Example 4.15 Traversing an Initialized Array of Character Pointers

```
#include <stdio.h>
main()
{
    char *commands[] = { "copy",
                         "delete",
                         "print",
                         "move",
                         "display",
                         "rename",
                         "quit",
                          NULL };
    char **mover = commands;

    while (*mover)
```

```
    {
        puts(*mover);
        mover++;
    }
}
/****************  Program Output Below  ****************/

copy
delete
print
move
display
rename
quit
```

Just to mix things up, we used the terse form of the loop conditional, `*mover`. If `mover` is pointing at a `NULL` pointer, then `*mover` is `NULL` (zero), which terminates the loop. The longer conditional is slightly, but not markedly, more readable.

We've been working with strings for a while now, but I want to remind you of something you should have learned in beginning C: A constant string (such as `"hello"`) is a character pointer because the compiler replaces it with the address of the string's first character.

Also, you should know that the declaration of `commands` could have been these two as well:

```
char    **commands    = { /* strings in here. */ };
char    *commands[8]  = { /* strings in here. */ };
```

Now I'm going to stop and give you some really tricky notational questions based on the following diagram.

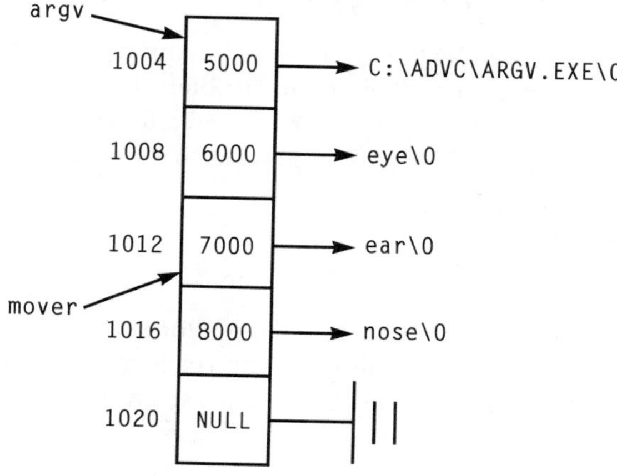

Assume that (1) The values *inside* the boxes are the starting addresses for the strings, and (2) the values *outside* the boxes are the addresses holding the string pointers.

Question: What is the value of `mover - ptr`?
Answer: The value is 2. Why? Two `char *` units separate `mover` from `ptr`.

Question: What is the value of `mover`?
Answer: The value is 1012. `Mover` has the address of the pointer to `"ear"`. The address of that pointer is clearly 1012.

Question: What is the value of `mover[-1]`?
Answer: The value is 6000. `Mover[-1]` is the same as `*(mover - 1)`. We know that `mover - 1` is 1008, and dereferencing gives us what's in that address: 6000.

Question: What is the value of `**mover`?
Answer: The value is the `'e'` in `"ear"`. If `*mover` points at the `'e'` in `"ear"`, then clearly `**mover` must be the `'e'` itself!

Question: What is the value of `*(*(mover + 1))`?
Answer: The value is the `'n'` in `"nose"`. Why? Because `*(mover + 1)` is the pointer to `"nose"`. Dereferencing that address gives us that `'n'`!

I hope you enjoyed this little pop quiz. You're going to get a lot more of it in the exercises at the end of this chapter. The payoff from mastering this notation is that if you find yourself in the unenviable position of having to read obscure code, nothing will cause you anxiety!

At the risk of stressing something I've already stressed, I want to emphasize that you'll read far more C code in your programming lifetime than you'll write. Poorly written code won't be pleasant to read, but your boss will be oh-so-appreciative if you can decipher it!

4.11 Growing and Shrinking Arrays of Strings with `Realloc`

Up to this point, we have dealt with arrays of many types: `int` types, `struct` types, `char` types, and so on. Their main problem is that once we make an array declaration, we are stuck with the declared allocation size until the program terminates. However, if you use a pointer to `malloc()` the first batch of array elements, you can then grow or shrink the array with `realloc()`.

`Realloc`'s ANSI prototype is

```
void *realloc(void *pointer, size_t number_of_bytes);
```

The `pointer` parameter is the pointer whose allocation size you are trying to change. The return value is a pointer to the reallocated space. The variable receiving the return value is usually the one passed as the first parameter, but this is by no means a requirement.

`Realloc()` contains a very serious trap for the unwary. The `realloc`'ed space may be *nowhere near the original space.* Suppose you have a situation like that shown in the next diagram.

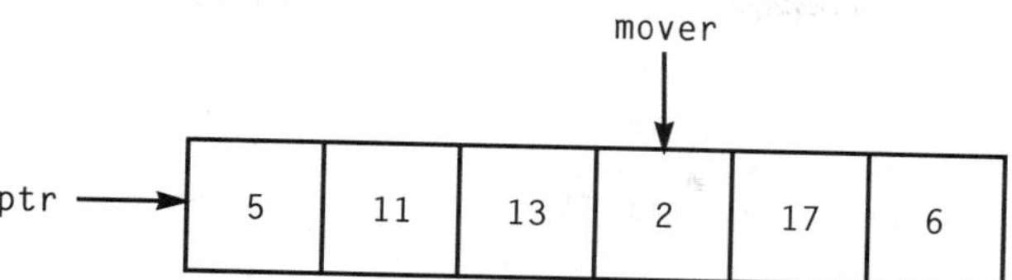

If you `realloc(ptr)`, the `realloc`'ed space may be moved far away, which means that `mover` would be pointing into thin air! The lesson? If you `realloc()` a pointer, be sure to update any pointers that were pointing to places within the pre-`realloc`'ed space. You do not have to worry about the values in the original space; they are maintained.

Now you're ready for some sample code. This code will create an array of pointer to `char` from the ground up using `realloc()`.

Example 4.16 Creation of an Array of Strings from Nothing!

```
/**********************************************/
/*                                            */
/*  Reads lines from a file whose name is passed */
/*  on the command line.  These lines are placed */
/*  into an array that grows dynamically via  */
/*  realloc().                                */
/*                                            */
/**********************************************/

#include <stdlib.h>    /* Has malloc, realloc */
#include <stdio.h>

#define POINTERS  5
#define MAXLINE   1024

main(int argc, char *argv[])
{
    char **line_ptrs, **mover, line[MAXLINE];
    FILE *fp;
    int arr_size = 0, i;

    if ((fp = fopen(argv[1], "r")) == NULL)
    {
        printf("File %s could not be opened!\n\n", argv[1]);
        exit(1);
    }
```

```
   if ((line_ptrs = (char **)malloc(POINTERS * sizeof(char *)))
        == NULL)
   {
        printf("Fatal malloc error!\n");
        exit(1);
   }

   mover = line_ptrs;
   while (fgets(line, MAXLINE - 1, fp))
   {
        if ((*mover = (char *)malloc(strlen(line) + 1) == NULL)
        {
             printf("Fatal malloc error!\n");
             exit(2);
        }
        strcpy(*mover, line);

        if (++arr_size % POINTERS == 0) /** Need more ptrs!! **/
        {
             if ((line_ptrs = (char **) realloc(line_ptrs,
                 (arr_size + POINTERS) * sizeof(char *))) == NULL)
             {
                  printf("Fatal realloc error!\n");
                  exit(3);
             }
             mover = line_ptrs + arr_size - 1; /* Essential!!! */
        }

        mover++;
    }  /****  End while  ****/

    *mover = NULL; /*** Sentinel. Signals "end of array." ***/

    for (mover = line_ptrs; *mover; mover++)
    {
         printf("%s", *mover);  /** Look Mom, no indexing! **/
    }
}
/**********************  Execution Below  *****************/

$realloc  realloc.dat   /*** Invoking the code above!!  ***/
line 1  /*** These lines are the contents of realloc.dat. ***/
line 2
line 3
line 4
line 5
line 6
```

```
line 7
line 8
line 9
line 10
```

This is some of the most difficult code I've asked you to read. I hope you tried. The following diagram illustrates how the code works. It shows you the position of the `mover` pointer just prior to the `realloc()` call (whose return should be tested for `NULL` just like `malloc()`).

Note that after the `realloc()` call and the `mover = line_ptrs + arr_size - 1` reassignment, `mover` is pointing at the last element of the old allocation, not at the first element of the new allocation. This trick allows us to assign `*mover = NULL` immediately after the loop ends. Remember always to make the last pointer in an array of pointers `NULL`. That way, another programmer using your array can use the `NULL` as a *sentinel* value—no more data follows.

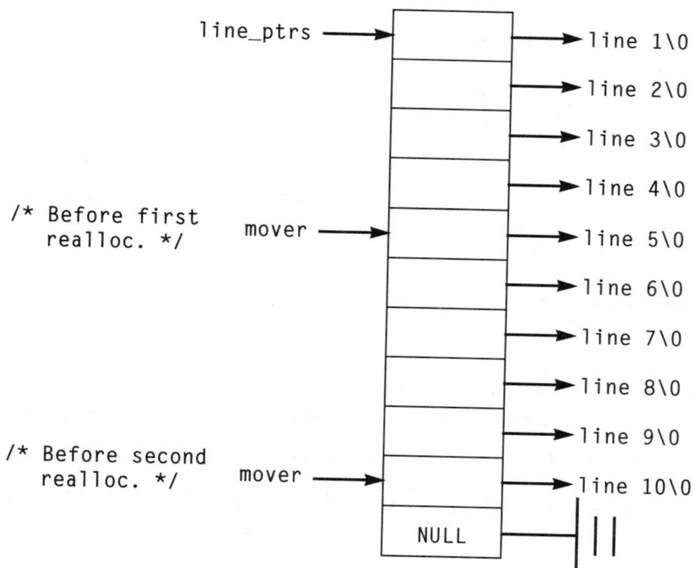

I hope this little picture helped. The most crucial thing in this code, because it is the easiest part to forget, is the reassignment of `mover` immediately after the `realloc()`. Remember, above all, that `realloc()` may pick the whole array up and move it to a different location in memory!

Even though our example used `realloc` "buckets" of only 5 pointers, this was merely to demonstrate that `realloc()` does what it is supposed to do. In a "real-world" application, you should use more reasonable bucket sizes, such as 1000 or more pointers. Realloc(), like malloc(), is expensive and gives too much memory control to the operating system and the designers of realloc(). Therefore, it should be called *as seldom as possible.*

You've now completed the two "meatiest" chapters in this book. The rest should be clear sailing. But don't skip the exercises at the end of this chapter!

Facts About Functions

<stdio.h> Functions

Function: `int printf(char *format_string, value-list);`

Fact: 1) Strings can be variably formatted as seen in this chapter via

```
printf(".*s", number_to_print, address);
```

You will learn more about variable formatting and other advanced uses of printf() in Chapter 5 on advanced input and output.

Function: `char *fgets(char *string, int num_of_chars, FILE *fp);`

Fact: 1) Reads num_of_chars - 1 characters into string or until '\n' is encountered, whichever comes first.

Fact: 2) Unlike gets(), it keeps the '\n' if it is captured.

Fact: 3) Returns the value of string unless EOF is the only character read. In this case, it returns NULL.

Fact: 4) Make sure that your string has at least num_of_chars bytes allocated.

Fact: 5) If a read error on fp occurs, NULL is returned and the contents of string are not predictable!

Fact: 6) In order not to cause trouble, most operating systems put a '\n' at the end of the last line so that EOF will be the only character read after the last line of the file has been captured. Make sure *your* operating system does this.

<string.h> Functions

Function: `char *strchr(char *string, int c);`

Fact: 1) Searches for character `c` starting at the address in `string`.

Fact: 2) Returns the address in the string where `c` is found or `NULL` if `c` is not found.

Fact: 3) The second parameter is an `int` just in case `EOF` is passed in `c`.

Fact: 4) Like virtually all `string.h` functions, this will blow up at runtime if `string` is `NULL`.

Function: `char *strrchr(char *string, int c);`

Fact: 1) Works the same way as `strchr()` except that it looks for the rightmost `c` in `string`. The definition of *rightmost* is "starting at the first `'\0'` character after address `string`".

Function: `size_t strspn(char *string, char *charset);`

Fact: 1) Returns the number of characters in `string` skipped over until a character that is not in `charset` is found.

Fact: 2) `Size_t` return type is compatible with the `int` family.

Fact: 3) If every character in `string` is also in `charset`, the return value will equal `strlen(string)`.

Fact: 4) If either `charset` or `string` or both are empty strings, `strspn()` returns zero.

Function: `size_t strcspn(char *string, char *charset);`

Fact: 1) Identical to `strspn()` except that it returns the number of characters skipped over until a character that *is* in `charset` is found.

Function: `char *strpbrk(char *string, char *charset);`

Fact: 1) Returns the address of the first character in `string` that is also in `charset`.

Fact: 2) Returns `NULL` if no character in `string` is in the `charset`.

Fact: 3) Returns `NULL` if either or both strings are the empty string.

Function: `char *strtok(char *string, char *delims);`

Fact: 1) Searches for a token in `string`, where *token* is defined as "a string of characters containing no member of `delims`".

Fact: 2) To get the second through the final tokens from `string`, you need to pass `NULL` as the first parameter to the `strtok()` call. This is a signal that you wish to continue parsing `string`.

Fact: 3) `Strtok()` skips leading delimiters and overwrites the first trailing delimiter after a token with the `'\0'` character.

Fact: 4) `Strtok()` returns the address of the first character of the token just acquired or `NULL` if only delimiters (or nothing at all) remain between the current place in `string` and the terminating `'\0'` character.

Fact: 5) It is OK to change the `delims` set from one call of `strtok()` to the next.

Fact: 6) If `delims` is an empty string, all characters are part of tokens and no characters are considered delimiters.

Function: `char *strstr(char *string, char *substring);`

Fact: 1) Starts searching for `substring` at address `string`.

Fact: 2) If `substring` is in `string`, the address in `string` where the `substring` starts is returned.

Fact: 3) If `substring` cannot be found in `string`, `NULL` is returned.

Fact: 4) If `substring` is an empty string, the return value will always be that of the first character of `string`. Thus the empty string is a subset of *any kind of string!*

`<stdlib.h>` **Functions**

Function: `long strtol(char *string, char **endp, int base);`

Fact: 1) Attempts to convert a `string` with characters from radix `base` into a `long int`.

Fact: 2) Returns a `long int` if it found legal characters from `base` before it found a character not legal in radix `base`.

Fact: 3) Returns zero if it encounters an illegal (according to base) character before it finds a legal one.

Fact: 4) Whether the first character is a legal or an illegal according to `base`, `*endp` points at the first character found in `string` that could not be converted to a legal number in `base`.

Fact: 5) Returns `HUGE_VAL` and sets the `errno.h` built-in variable `errno` to `ERANGE` if it could obtain a `long int` but the number is too large for the user's computer.

Fact: 6) If using `errno`, be sure to reset its value to zero before each call to `strtol()`.

Fact: 7) Here are some samples of all variable states after `strtol()` calls to obtain a number in base 10 (decimal):

```
string is: X23  **endp is: X    returns: 0
string is: 23X  **endp is: X    returns: 23
string is: 23   **endp is: '\0' returns: 23
string is: 2X3  **endp is: X    returns: 2
```

Function: `double strtod(char *string, char **endp);`

Fact: 1) Works the same way as `strtol()` but returns a `double` and converts only base-ten floating-point strings.

Fact: 2) Overflows and underflows cause a zero return, and the `errno.h` variable `errno` is set to `ERANGE`.

Function: `void *realloc(void *pointer, size_t newsize);`

Fact: 1) Reallocates the space pointed at by `pointer` so that it has `newsize` bytes.

Fact: 2) Returns the starting address of the reallocated space.

Fact: 3) Returns `NULL` on failure to reallocate.

Fact: 4) Retains values of assigned array elements (unless `newsize` is smaller than the original size—then truncated elements are gone!).

Fact: 5) May create the reallocated space in an area of memory that does not overlap with the space pointed at by `pointer`. This means that any pointers pointing inside the original space must be reassigned.

Exercises

■ **1.** Write a function that

a. Returns all the starting addresses in a string where a substring starts.

b. Assumes you do not want substrings that overlap within the string.

c. Returns `NULL` as a sentinel value in the array of addresses and assumes that no string will have more than 100 instances of the substring.

d. *Hint:* The return type is `char **`.

■ **2.** In each of the following parts, indicate what each `printf()` will print on the screen.

a.
```
char *p1 = "mississippi";
printf("%s", strtok(p1, "ism"));
```

b.
```
char *p1 = "abracadabra";
printf("%s", strtok(p1, "abr"));
```

c.
```
char *p1 = "A dingbat is an animal", *p2;
p2 = strchr(p1, 'b');
printf("%c %s", *p1, p2);
```

d.
```
char *p1 = "Bullwinkle is a moose", *p2 = "A taxi is a
cab", *p3, *p4;
p3  = strchr(p1, 'm');
*p3 = '\0';
p4  = strchr(p2, 'c');
printf("%s%s%s", p1, p4, p3 + 1);
```

e.
```
char *p1 = "Hello, I am John!  What's up?", *p2;
p2 = strpbrk(p1, "?.!");
printf("%s", p2 + 1);
```

f.
```
char *p1 = "www.foobar.com", *p2, *p3;
p2   = strrchr(p1, '.');
*p2  = '\0';
p3   =  strtok(p1, ".w");
printf("%s", p3);
```

g.
```
char *p1 = "www.foobar.com";
int i;
i  =  strcspn(p1 + 4, ".");
printf("%.*s, i, p1 + 4);
```

h.
```
char *p1 = "banana band and me!";
printf("%d", strlen(strtok(p1, "\040band")));
```

i.
```
char *p1 = "Where oh where is there a tree?", *p2[3];
int i;
for (i = 0; p1 = strstr(p1, "here"); p1++)
{
```

```
        p2[i] = p1;
        p1 += strlen("here");
        *p1 = '\0';
    }
    printf("%s %s %s!", *p2, p2[1], *(p2 + 2));
```

j. `printf("%s", "abcdefg" + 2);`

■ **3.** Write code fragments to do the following tasks. Declare all variables used except string `s`.

a. Print the portion of a string `s` between the last two periods in it. If the string has fewer than two periods, print `"Not enough periods"`.

b. Print all the strings of non-digit characters in string `s`. Print one string per line, and make no assumption about the number of non-digit strings in `s`.

c. Print all the digit strings in `s`. Make no assumption about the number of digit strings in `s`.

d. String `s` is supposed to be a binary number (all ones and zeroes). Print the decimal value of the number in `s` if it is a valid binary number. Print `"Error"` if it is not a valid binary number. Assume that whitespace is already removed from `s`.

e. Overwrite all the '#' characters in `s` with a period. Do not visit every character in `s` to see whether it is a period! Use a `string.h` function.

4. Write a function that

a. Is given one string parameter.

b. Assumes that the string should contain an arithmetic expression with a variable number of operators and operands such as `"45 + 6 - 2 / 4 * 8"`.

c. Assumes that the only legal operators are `'*'`, `'+'`, `'/'`, and `'-'`.

d. Assumes that a correct expression has no parentheses.

e. Assumes that operands and operators must be whitespace-separated.

f. Assumes that all operators are binary operators.

g. Assumes that legal operands are signed or unsigned `long int`s in base 10 (decimal).

h. Evaluates the value of the expression from left to right.

i. Returns the expression value as a `long`.

j. Returns `HUGE_VAL` if there is an error in the expression or the result cannot be represented in the computer.

5. Write a program that

a. Reads a file whose name is passed to the program on the command line.

b. Reads the file in such a way that each line is put into one element of an array of pointer to `char`.
c. Prompts the user for one or two line numbers.
d. Prints the line or line range of the file determined by the number(s) input by the user.
e. Allows users to do this repeatedly until they enter `"quit"`.
f. Detects and reports all errors in user input. You must decide for yourself what an "error" in the user's input is. Good luck!

■ **6.** Write a function that

a. Takes the name of a file as its only parameter.
b. Opens the file.
c. Puts the line numbers of all lines containing no digits into an array of `long`.
d. Closes the file.
e. Puts a zero in the last element of the array of `long` as a sentinel value.
f. Returns the array to the calling environment.
g. *Makes no assumption about the number of lines in the file.* Good luck!

■ **7.** You are given the following declarations:

```
char   *strs[] = {"mouse", "cat", "dog", "loose", NULL};
char   **ptr = strs + 2;
```

You may assume that the starting addresses of the strings are 5000, 6000, 7000, and 8000, respectively. The `&strs[0]` is 1000, and your computer has four-byte pointers. Given all of these assumptions, find the value of the following expressions. Assume that no expression affects any string in later parts of the problem.

a. `strtok(*strs, "om")`
b. `strlen(*(strs + 2))`
c. `**strs`
d. `*(ptr[-1])`
e. `strlen(*strs + 2)`
f. `**ptr + 1`
g. `*(*ptr + 1)`
h. `strs + 3`
i. `strpbrk(*(ptr - 1) + 1, "c")`
j. `ptr[1]`

■ **8.** You are a psychologist studying the role of punctuation in the English language. Your goal is to determine whether people can still read a text file if all the punctuation characters are replaced by spaces. Write a program that reads an input text file and writes an output text file with all the punctuation marks replaced by spaces. The user is expected to enter the input and output filenames *on the command line invoking your program.*

■ **9.** You work for the Central Intelligence Agency. The CIA is giving you an input file with text and numbers interspersed. The text is irrelevant, but you are supposed to total all the numbers embedded in the text. For example, if the text file consists of

```
Hello, John 45. You are going56 to be on the next
    airplane 40 to Brazil. Good luck and say hello to 100.
```

then the total of the numbers is 45 + 56 + 40 + 100, which equals 241. Write a program that accepts an input filename on the command line and outputs the numeric total in the file to the screen. Assume that the total will fit into an `int` on your machine and that all numbers that start on a line are completed on that line.

10. A language expert is doing a study that counts the frequency of certain words in an ordinary text file. Write a program that accepts three command line arguments: (1) a list of words, one per line in UPPERCASE, (2) the name of an input text file, and (3) the name of an output text file. The output text file will consist of a listing of all words in the wordlist file (argument 1) and the frequency of their occurrence in the input text file. *Hint:* Read the words in the wordlist file into a `malloc`'ed or `realloc`'ed array of strings. You must figure out the rest! Assume that the input text file is all UPPERCASE.

Chapter 5

Advanced Input and Output

If C is relatively new to you, it is quite possible that you have used only the "magnetic tape" model to read or write disk files. That is, you have read or written them from start to finish without backing up or randomly jumping to some other place in the file. Although it is true that many C applications don't demand greater sophistication than this, many very important applications, especially database management systems, do.

Therefore, one of the main thrusts of this chapter is in the area of *random access input and output.* Included in this discussion is the idea of *hashing to disk.* Because Chapter 3 introduced the idea of hashing, we will concentrate less on the hashing formula and focus on the more difficult task of hashing with disks rather than with memory.

At the end of the chapter, we will also deal with advanced aspects of the `printf()` and `scanf()` families. We will offer a more thorough discussion of *variable formatting* (a topic we have introduced before). Other issues that will be discussed are: non-decimal input and output, assignment suppression on input, output field justification, string output, scan sets, and escape sequences.

5.1 Random Access Binary Files

You may wonder at the title of this section. What about random access *text* files? Don't they exist? Of course. However, they will be discussed in another (smaller) section.

Most random access files are binary and have fixed-length records. However, before we get into record-oriented input/output, let's introduce binary files and random access in a simplified example. We will construct a file that consists only of the integers 1 through 5. We will move around it, overwrite certain values in it, and demonstrate all of the relevant C library functions for relocating the file pointer, finding its offset, and reading/writing.

Example 5.1 Demonstration of Functions to Manipulate Random Access Files

```
#include <stdio.h>
main(int argc, char *argv[])
{
    FILE *fp;
    int i[] = {1, 2, 3, 4, 5}, j[5], k, *moverj;
    long pos;

/**********  End of declarations.  *********/
    if ((fp = fopen(argv[1], "w+b")) == NULL)
    {
        printf("Could not open %s.\n", argv[1]);
        exit(1);
    }
    fwrite(i, sizeof(int), 5, fp);
    rewind(fp);  /*** Back to first byte of file!  ***/
    fread(j, sizeof(int), 5, fp);
    for (moverj = j, k = 0; k < 5; k++)
    {
        printf("j[%d] = %d\n", k, *moverj);
        moverj++;
    }
    fseek(fp, 2 * sizeof(int), SEEK_SET);  /* Points at 3 */
    k = 6;
    fwrite(&k, sizeof(int), 1, fp);  /* Overwrites 3 with 6 */
    fseek(fp, -1 * sizeof(int), SEEK_CUR); /* Is 6 there? */
    fread(&k, sizeof(int), 1, fp);
    printf("Integer obtained is %d.\n", k);
    k = 13;
    fseek(fp, -1 * sizeof(int), SEEK_END);  /* Points at 5 */
    fwrite(&k, sizeof(int), 1, fp); /* Overwrites 5 with 13 */
    fseek(fp, -1 * sizeof(int), SEEK_CUR);
    fread(&k, sizeof(int), 1, fp);  /* Is 13 there?? */
    printf("Integer obtained is %d.\n", k);
    pos = ftell(fp);  /* Byte offset from beginning of file.*/
    printf("We are %ld bytes from beginning of file.\n", pos);
}
```

```
/*****************  Program Output Below  *****************/

$binio binio.dat    /** Invokes program from command line. **/

j[0] = 1
j[1] = 2
j[2] = 3
j[3] = 4
j[4] = 5
Integer obtained is 6.   /*** 3 successfully overwritten! ***/
Integer obtained is 13.  /*** 4 successfully overwritten! ***/
We are 20 bytes from beginning of file.
```

Although it is not included in the code, the function `fflush()` is very important and deserves mention. `Fflush()` must be called when you are shifting from writing to reading, or vice versa, in a file in *update* mode (i.e., a "+" in the `fopen()` mode) unless you do an intervening `fseek()` or `rewind()`. See Section 5.2 for a lengthy discussion of `fopen()` modes.

The operations in Example 5.1 are sufficiently important to warrant a diagram showing the file pointer's changes and the changes in the file after each statement.

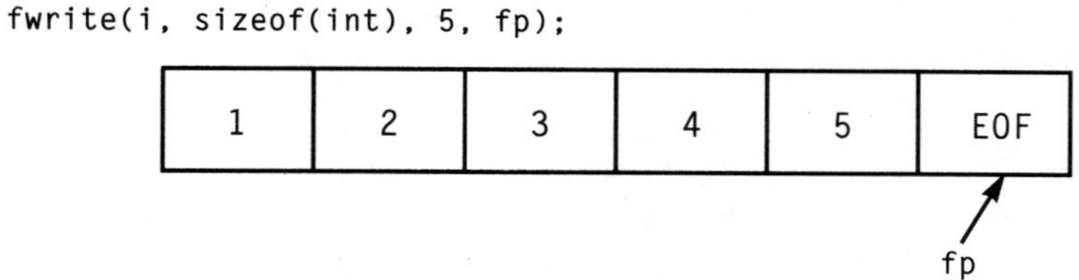

The `fwrite()` function's prototype is

```
size_t fwrite(void  *pointer, size_t element_size, size_t
              num_elements, FILE  *fp);
```

The `size_t` parameters and return type are almost always implemented as `long int`, but of course, they are compatible with any member of the `int` family. Although `fp` is depicted as a pointer, you should know that you cannot manipulate this pointer directly. Only the file reading/writing functions can do that. In this respect, `FILE *`'s differ from any other pointer type.

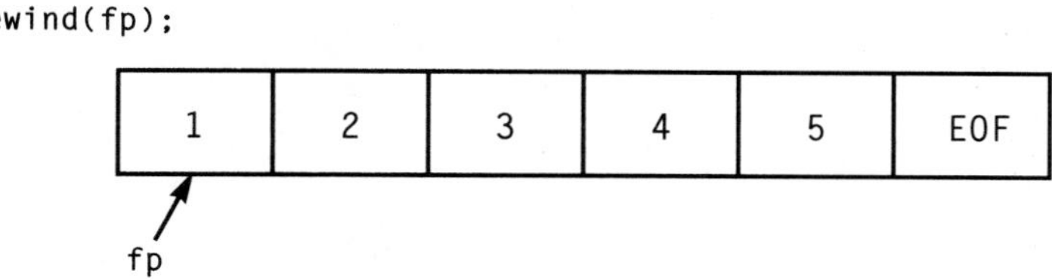

The `rewind()` function positions the file pointer to the first byte of the file. Thus, in this diagram, `fp` is actually pointing at the first byte of an integer 1 that occupies `sizeof(int)` bytes. We will not show a diagram for the statement

```
fread(j, sizeof(int), 5, fp);
```

It reads the five integers that have been placed in the file. The prototype for `fread()` is identical to that of `fwrite()`. The `for` loop following the `fread()` simply prints out the integers obtained by the `fread()` as proof that our program is working.

```
fseek(fp, 2 * sizeof(int), SEEK_SET);
```

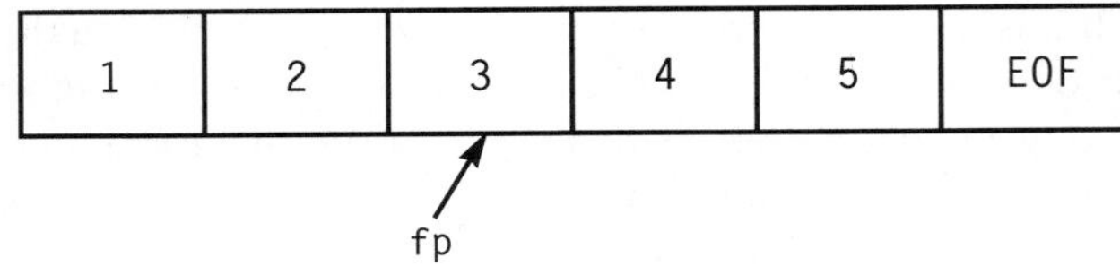

The ANSI C prototype for the `fseek()` function is

```
int fseek(FILE  *fp, long offset, int offset_location);
```

The `offset_location` determines where the `offset` is from. It is one of three possible values:

```
SEEK_SET /*** Offset is from the beginning of the file. ***/
SEEK_END /*** Offset is from the end of the file.       ***/
SEEK_CUR /*** Offset is from the current position.      ***/
```

Clearly, `offset` must be a zero or positive value if the `offset_location` is `SEEK_SET`. A negative offset from `SEEK_SET` would indicate a seek to a position *before* the beginning of the file—clearly an error. Likewise, any `offset` from `SEEK_END` must be a zero or negative value; you shouldn't seek to a position after `EOF`! An `offset` from `SEEK_CUR` can be positive or negative. `Fseek()` returns zero on success and non-zero on failure.

In the last diagram, you see a seek to a position that is two `int` units from the beginning of the file. This moves `fp` from the 1 to the 3 as shown.

```
fwrite(&k, sizeof(int), 1, fp);
```

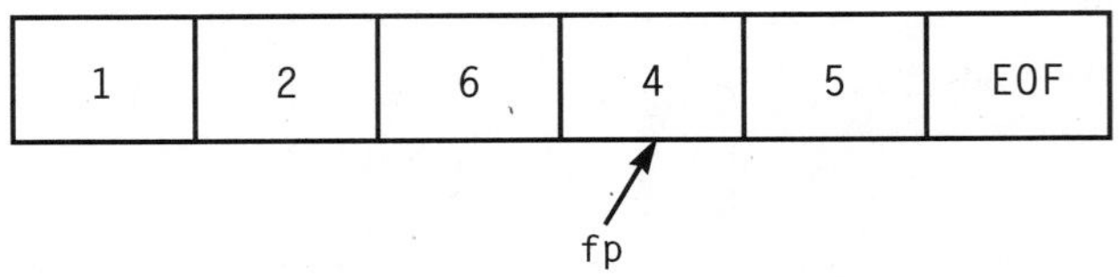

The `fwrite()` writes one integer (the 6) and then advances the file pointer to the next position. You must remember that an `fread()` or `fwrite()` always

advances the file pointer after the read/write. Note that we must pass &k because fwrite() requires that the first argument be a pointer.

```
fseek(fp, -1 * sizeof(int), SEEK_CUR);
```

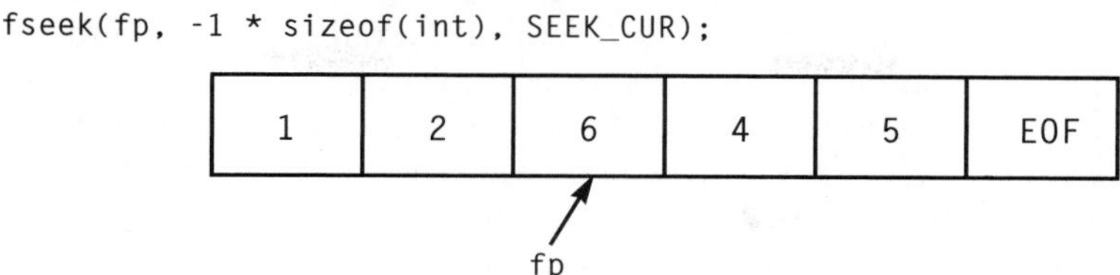

This moves the file pointer (fp) back one int unit. After this statement, the program calls fread() to read the 6 written by the fwrite(). The 6 is then output to the screen to prove that our overwrite operation was successful. Indeed, it was.

```
fseek(fp, -1 * sizeof(int), SEEK_END);
```

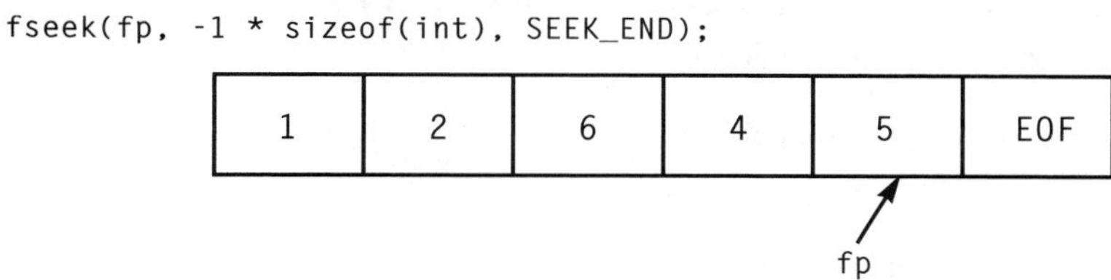

This fseek() moves the file pointer one int unit before the end of file.

```
fwrite(&k, sizeof(int), 1, fp);
```

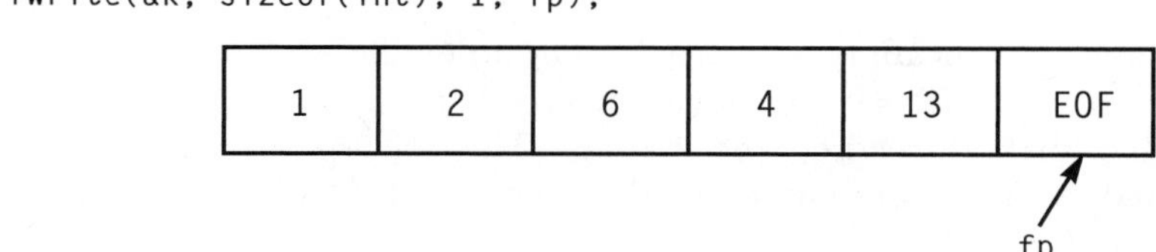

The fwrite() overwrites the 5 with k's value, which is 13. The file pointer is then advanced and is now at the end of file.

As we did after overwriting the 3 with a 6, we back up one int unit and read the area we just overwrote. As the program output proves, we have successfully overwritten the 5 with 13. After the final fread(), fp is now at the end of the file again. Our byte offset from the beginning of the file is 5 * sizeof(int). Because my computer has four-byte ints, the ftell() function should return 20 into variable pos. The output proves the truth of this assertion.

The ANSI C prototype for the ftell() function is

```
long ftell(FILE *fp);
```

Ftell() returns a -1 on error, and a platform-dependent positive value is placed in the built-in variable errno. Does this mean that you need only check `ftell`'s return value to establish an error? Surprisingly, the answer is no. The reason is that it is legal to seek before the beginning of a file or after the end of a file. It's only when you try to *read* or *write* at these positions that problems occur. But the bottom line is that `-1` is a valid offset from the beginning of a file, so you must also check for a positive `errno` value.

The ANSI C functions `fgetpos()` and `fsetpos()` duplicate the functionality of `ftell()` and `fseek()`, respectively. They were added to ANSI C because they allow file offsets that are bigger than a `long`. A `long` on a 32-bit computer has a value of around 2 billion. The vast majority of files are much smaller than this. As 64-bit computers become common (this may occur very soon), the original reasons for adding `fgetpos()` and `fsetpos()` may become irrelevant. Stay tuned!

5.2 `Fopen` Modes and Random Access Files—Advice and Warnings

In the last section, the code example opened the file via

```
fp = fopen(argv[1], "w+b");
```

There are three appropriate modes for writing binary files for random access:

```
w+b
r+b
a+b
```

The `w+b` specification says, "I am going to create a *new* binary file that I may also read." The `r+b` specification says, "I am going to open an *existing* binary file for both reading and writing." The `a+b` specification says, "I am going to open an *existing* binary file that I may read. All of my writes will go to the end of the file."

Thus, if a + is in the `fopen()` mode, it means you're intending to do both reading and writing. Of course, if you are going to do only reading or only writing, you should leave the + out.

The `b` in the mode specifies that a file is to be a binary file. But what if your file contains fixed-length *character* records? Should you use the `b` or not? Because characters are one byte in length on all platforms, the answer would seem to be that it makes no difference. However, many operating systems, such as VAX/VMS, put hidden bytes into the records of nonbinary files. Therefore, when you want "clean" files, don't forget the `b` in the `fopen()` mode.

We've already seen that `FILE *` variables are not like other pointers. We cannot manipulate them except through `stdio.h` functions. Another peculiarity of `FILE *` variables is their behavior when passed to functions. If the file pointer is moved inside a function, that fact will be reflected in the calling environment. However, if a file's open/close status changes inside a function, you should pass the file pointer as a `FILE **`. Otherwise, you will get very bizarre behavior in your program when you return from the function.

Thus, if you want an open file to be manipulated by a function `foo()` that *closes the file when it is done,* your code structure should look like this:

The call: `foo(&fp, /*** Other parameters here. ***/)`
Inside the function:

```
void foo(FILE **fp, /*** Other
parameters here. ***/)
{
    /*** Some code is here. ***/
    fclose(*fp);
}
```

You won't find this in any C manual, so I must reluctantly ask you to memorize this fact!!

5.3 Record-Oriented Binary Files

The types of data most frequently written to binary files are not usually simple numbers. They are generally `struct`s or arrays of `struct`s. However, I must tell you that this makes a file platform-dependent. Why? You must look at the "fine print" in the definition of a `struct` to find out why. Each computer pads a `struct` with "filler" bytes. This is usually done to make `struct`s end neatly on a word boundary. A "word" on most computers is identical to `sizeof(int)`.

The platform-dependence noted above is usually not very pertinent unless you are doing network data transmission between *different* computer architectures. If this is the case, the fixed-length records should *not* be `struct`s. It is then best to write records as long character strings, because, as we saw in Chapter 4, it is very easy to convert all or part of a string into numeric value(s). Given the distributed (i.e., networked) nature of many applications, it may pay to reread the relevant sections of Chapter 4.

The great advantage of `fread()` and `fwrite()` is that enormous amounts of data can be read or written in one read or write operation. This is important because it is much faster to write 10,000 records one time than to write one record 10,000 times. Here is a simple code example of a large-scale `fwrite()` and `fread()`. And just to get a jump on the next topic in this chapter, we'll create a hashed file.

Example 5.2 Writes to and Reads from a Hashed File

```
#include <stdio.h>
#include <stdlib.h>
#include <string.h>
```

```
struct record
{
    char key[50] ;  /*** A very simple record!!  ***/
};

main(int argc, char *argv[])
{

    FILE *fp;
    /*** Next line initializes all record bytes to zero! ***/
    struct record hashtable[100] = {""};
    struct record temprec;
    long hash = 0;
    char line[100], *mover;

    fp = fopen(argv[1],"w+b");

    while(printf("Enter key:"), gets(line),
          strcmp(line,"quit") != 0)
    {
        hash = 0;
        /****  Hash formula is same as used in Chapter 3. ****/
        for (mover = line; *mover != '\0'; mover++)
        {
            hash = hash + (*mover) * (*mover) * (*mover);
        }
        hash = hash % 100;
        strcpy(hashtable[hash].key, line);
        printf("Hash value on output is: %ld \n", hash);
    }

    /*****  Write entire hash table to disk.  *****/
    fwrite(hashtable, sizeof(struct record), 100, fp);
    printf("\nEnd of write.  Beginning of reads.\n\n");

    while(printf("Enter key:"), gets(line),
          strcmp(line,"quit") != 0)
    {
        hash = 0;
        for (mover = line; *mover != '\0'; mover++)
        {
            hash = hash + (*mover) * (*mover) * (*mover);
        }
        hash = hash % 100;
        fseek(fp, hash * sizeof(struct record),
              SEEK_SET);
        fread(&temprec, sizeof(struct record), 1, fp);
        /****  If first byte of requested record is zero ****/
        /****  then the record isn't there!              ****/
```

```
        if (memcmp(&temprec, "", 1) == 0)
        {
            printf("Sorry!  Record not found!\n");
        }
        printf("Hash value on input is: %ld  Key is: %s\n",
                hash, temprec.key);
    }
}

/**************  Sample Program Session Below  ************/

Enter key: foobar
Hash value on output is: 79
Enter key: mouse
Hash value on output is: 49
Enter key: bat
Hash value on output is: 61
Enter key: dog
Hash value on output is: 58
Enter key: wombat
Hash value on output is: 80
Enter key: quit

End of write.  Beginning of reads.

Enter key: foobar
Hash value on input is: 79  Key is: foobar
Enter key: bat
Hash value on input is: 61  Key is: bat
Enter key: wombat
Hash value on input is: 80  Key is: wombat
Enter key: snafu
Sorry!  Record not found!
Hash value on input is: 69  Key is:   /** Nothing there! **/
Enter key: quit
$  /*** Operating System Prompt.  Execution terminated!  ***/
```

As this piece of code illustrates, `fwrite()` and `fread()` don't care whether you are writing or reading one record or a million records. A standard initialization trick was used to zero out all 100 records in the file. The trick was

```
struct record hashtable[100] = {""};
```

Recall, from Chapter 2, the assertion that if a declaration-time initialization contains fewer initializers than there are elements in the array, the remaining elements are zeroed out. The empty string is the value given to the key of `hashtable[0]`—a string with just a `'\0'` in it. One initializer is clearly fewer than 100, so the other 99 elements are given the default initialization value, zero. If zero is the value of the first character of every string in hashtable, this is equivalent to the empty string, because the ASCII value of '\0' happens to be zero. Thus, before we fill up hashtable, it is full of empty strings.

The key field of each struct (the only field in each struct!) was hashed in the same manner as in the hashing example in Chapter 3: by doing a modulo 100 on the sum of the cubes of the ASCII characters in the char key. However, we are not using the computed hash value to access an index in an array of pointers as we did in Chapter 3. We are using the hash value to tell fseek() where to put the file pointer in the statement

```
fseek(fp, hash * sizeof(struct record), SEEK_SET);
```

Because hash is the result of a modulo 100 calculation, its value range is 0 to 99—exactly the correct range in a file that can hold 100 records. A hash value of zero means an offset of zero from SEEK_SET—the first record position in the file. A hash value of 99 means that we skip over 99 records and the file pointer is positioned at the first byte of the 100th (and final) record.

However, now I'm going to surprise you by asserting that the code in Example 5.2 is a good illustration of binary record reading and writing but a terrible illustration of hashing to disk!

Why? Remember that in Chapter 3 we spoke of *collisions*, two or more records with different keys but the same hash value. This was no problem with an array of lists; we simply put all the collidees in the same list. With the algorithm in Example 5.2, if we entered a new record with the same hash value as the "foobar" record, the "foobar" record would simply be overwritten—a disaster.

Furthermore, in a real-world application, you would seldom create the hash table in memory as we did in Example 5.2 and then write it to disk. Such an application might involve hundreds of thousands or even millions of structs—memory that your computer might not be willing to give you! Therefore, the correct method is to create an empty hash file with room for the thousands of records. Then you hash and add the records to the file, one at a time.

Disk is inherently less flexible than memory. A one-struct hash slot can hold one struct, period. Therefore, we must come up with methods to resolve the collision problem for hashing to disk. Hence ... the next section!

5.4 Standard Collision-Handling Methods for Hashing to Disk

There are two standard methods for handling collisions when one hashes to disk: rehashing and hash buckets. *Rehashing* means computing a second hash value for a record in the event of a collision or even a third or a fourth if the rehashes continue to produce collisions. A better practical solution is using *hash buckets* with overflow areas.

The following is a diagram of a file design using hash buckets and overflow areas.

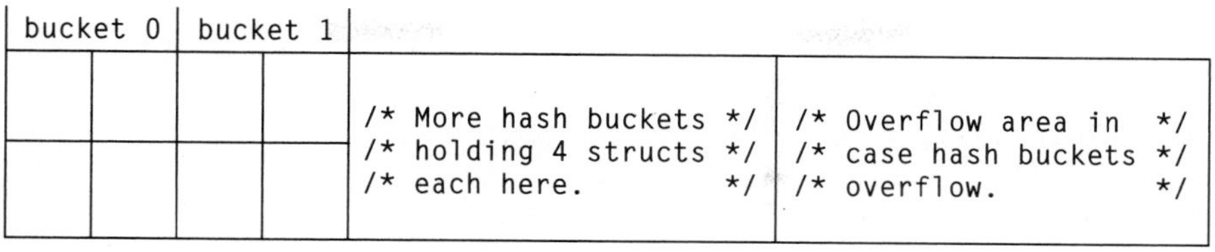

bucket 0		bucket 1			
				/* More hash buckets */ /* holding 4 structs */ /* each here. */	/* Overflow area in */ /* case hash buckets */ /* overflow. */

As you can infer from the diagram, when a record is hashed using this method, it goes into a "bucket" that holds a predetermined number of records (`structs`). Each bucket can hold some maximum number of collidees. If any bucket is filled with collidees, there is an offset value (which can be a fixed constant) that can be used to put new collidees into slots in the overflow area.

This can get ridiculous, with overflow areas having secondary overflow areas and so on. Can we avoid disaster without bogging our code down with complexity? Yes, by making the number of `structs` per bucket high and by making sure the file never gets full. Will this completely eliminate the chance that disaster will occur: the chance of both the buckets *and* the overflow area for a given hash value will overflow? Unfortunately, there is no mathematical certainty that any bucket size will guarantee overflow protection!

Now that I've induced anxiety, let me calm your nerves by telling you that when the bucket size approaches 10 with a file that is, say, 25% to 50% full, the chances of overflow come very close to zero. That is, *you may not even need an overflow area if the bucket size is large enough.* Thus, if you were designing a data retrieval system for a student record file with a projected maximum of 20,000 students, you might consider 10,000 hash buckets with room for 8 `structs` each; that way the file will not be more than 25% full. If you add an overflow area, the chances of overflowing the overflow area, even if it is of modest size, approach nil.

Entire books (especially graduate student dissertations) have been written about the mathematics of hashing and collision resolution. But you are reading this book to see *real code* and to obtain rules of thumb that might enable you to implement real-world systems without a Ph.D. in math. Therefore, we'll "cut to the chase" with a code example that implements a reasonable hashing-to-disk scheme for the minimalist one-field records from Example 5.2.

Example 5.3 Hashing to Disk: Declarations and Main Function

```
#include <stdio.h>
#include <stdlib.h>
#include <string.h>
```

```
#define TABSIZE 100
#define OFLOWSIZE 100
#define BUCKETSIZE 4    /*** Structs per bucket. ***/
#define INSERT 1
#define SEARCH 0

typedef struct record RECORD;

struct record
{
    char key[50] ;
};

main(int argc, char *argv[])
{

    FILE *fp;
    FILE *create_hash_file(char *filename);
    void search_or_insert(FILE *fp, int insertflag);

    fp = create_hash_file(argv[1]);
    search_or_insert(fp, INSERT);
    search_or_insert(fp, SEARCH);
}
```

Although the hashing algorithm is the same as the one used in Chapter 3, we will present it again here for your convenience.

Example 5.4 Hashing to Disk: Hashing Function

```
int hashkey(char *key)
{
     long hash;
     char *mover;

     hash = 0;
     for (mover = key; *mover != '\0'; mover++)
     {
         hash += (*mover) * (*mover) * (*mover);
     }
     hash = hash % TABSIZE;
     return hash;
}
```

Now we present the function that creates the empty hash file by dumping an empty hash table (100 four-`struct` buckets) and an empty overflow area (100 `structs`) into a new file.

Example 5.5 Hashing to Disk: Creation of Empty Hash File

```
FILE *create_hash_file(char *filename)
{
    FILE *fp;

    /******  In a real-world application involving   ******/
    /******  many thousands of records, you might     ******/
    /******  be forced to write ONE zeroed-out        ******/
    /******  record at a time because your computer   ******/
    /******  might not allow you to allocate room     ******/
    /******  for the whole hashtable at once!         ******/

    RECORD hashtable[TABSIZE][BUCKETSIZE] = {{"","","",""}};
    RECORD overflow[OFLOWSIZE] = {""};

    if ((fp = fopen(filename, "w+b")) == NULL)
    {
        printf("Could not open file %s. Aborting!\n");
        exit(1);
    }

    /****** Check for fwrite errors just to be safe.  ******/
    if (fwrite(&hashtable[0][0], sizeof(RECORD),
        TABSIZE * BUCKETSIZE, fp) < TABSIZE)
    {
        printf("Hash table could not be created. Abort!\n");
        exit(2);
    }
    if (fwrite(overflow, sizeof(RECORD), OFLOWSIZE, fp) <
        OFLOWSIZE)
    {
        printf("Could not create overflow area. Abort!\n");
        exit(3);
    }
    rewind(fp);
    return fp;
}
```

Here we give you a little prelude to multidimensional array initializing. The initializing trick

```
{{"","","",""}};
```

says that the first row (left index 0 of `hashtable`) should be four empty strings. This initializes all other rows to zeroes—also empty strings because `'\0'` and integer 0 are the same value.

Note that `fwrite()` writes out the whole empty array to the file in *one* write operation for the hash table and then the overflow area. Of course, we could have just written a one-dimensional array of 500 empty `structs`, but this function tells the reader how we have constructed both the `hashtable` and the `overflow` area. The small loss in efficiency is more than made up for by the information the reader gains about how we wish to divide the file up.

Now let's look at the function that gets user input/search requests.

Example 5.6 Hashing to Disk: User Input Function

```
void search_or_insert(FILE *fp, int insertflag)
{
    char line[100], *token;
    long hash;
    int hashkey(char *key);
    void insert_record(char *key, long hash, FILE *fp);
    void search_record(char *key, long hash, FILE *fp);

    while(printf("Enter key:"), gets(line),
          strcmp(line,"quit") != 0)
    {
        token = strtok(line, "\040\t");
        if (!token) continue;  /*** I love this!  ***/
        hash = hashkey(token);
        if (insertflag)
        {
            insert_record(token, hash, fp);
        }
        else
        {
            search_record(token, hash, fp);
        }
    }
}
```

Note that we use `strtok()` to clean whitespace out of the user's input. Although this is irrelevant to the topic at hand (hashing), we want to use as much of what we have learned as possible!

Finally, we present the "workhorse" functions that insert records into the hash file and search for records in the hash file. Because these two functions have much in common, they are presented together.

Example 5.7 Hashing to Disk: Hash Table Insertion and Searching

```
void insert_record(char *key, long hash, FILE *fp)
{
    RECORD detect, temp;
    int i;

    strcpy(temp.key, key);
    /********  Go to beginning of hash bucket.  ********/
    if (fseek(fp, hash * BUCKETSIZE * sizeof(RECORD),SEEK_SET)
        != 0)
    {
        printf("Fatal seek error! Abort!\n");
        exit(4);
    }
    /********  Find first available slot in bucket.  ********/
    for (i = 0; i < BUCKETSIZE; i++)
    {
        fread(&detect, sizeof(RECORD), 1, fp);
        if (*detect.key == '\0')    /*** Available slot!  ***/
        {
            fseek(fp, -1L * sizeof(RECORD), SEEK_CUR);
            fwrite(&temp, sizeof(RECORD), 1, fp);
            printf("Record: %s : added to bucket %ld.\n",
                   temp.key, hash);
            return;  /*** Nothing left to do!  ***/
        }
    }
    /*******  If I got this far, I must look at  *******/
    /*******  the overflow area.                 *******/
    fseek(fp, TABSIZE * BUCKETSIZE * sizeof(RECORD),SEEK_SET);
    for (i = 0; i < OFLOWSIZE; i++)
    {
        fread(&detect, sizeof(RECORD), 1, fp);
        if (*detect.key == '\0')    /*** Available slot!  ***/
        {
            fseek(fp, -1L * sizeof(RECORD), SEEK_CUR);
            fwrite(&temp, sizeof(RECORD), 1, fp);
            printf("Record:%s: added to overflow slot %d.\n",
                   temp.key, i);
            return;  /*** Nothing left to do!  ***/
        }
    }
    /*******  If I got this far, I am in big trouble.  *******/
    printf("Hash table overflow! Abort!\n");
    exit(5);
}
```

```
void search_record(char *key, long hash, FILE *fp)
{
    RECORD detect;
    int i;

    if (fseek(fp, hash * BUCKETSIZE * sizeof(RECORD),SEEK_SET)
        != 0)
    {
        printf("Fatal seek error! Abort!\n");
        exit(4);
    }
    /********  Find first available slot in bucket.  ********/
    for (i = 0; i < BUCKETSIZE; i++)
    {
        fread(&detect, sizeof(RECORD), 1, fp);
        if (strcmp(detect.key, key) == 0)  /** Found it!! **/
        {
            printf("You found %s at hash bucket %ld.\n",
                   key, hash);
            return;  /*** Nothing left to do!  ***/
        }
    }
    /*******  If I got this far, I must look at  *******/
    /*******  the overflow area.                 *******/
    fseek(fp, TABSIZE * BUCKETSIZE * sizeof(RECORD),SEEK_SET);
    for (i = 0; i < OFLOWSIZE; i++)
    {
        fread(&detect, sizeof(RECORD), 1, fp);
        if (strcmp(detect.key, key) == 0)  /** Found it!! **/
        {
            printf("You found %s in overflow area.\n", key);
            return;  /*** Nothing left to do!  ***/
        }
    }
    /*****  If I got this far, the record isn't there.  *****/
    printf("Record with key: %s : not found.\n", key);
}
```

And now, before we discuss the inner workings of this code, let's view a sample session with this program.

Example 5.8 Hashing to Disk: Sample Execution of Program

```
Enter key: 1234
Record: 1234 : added to bucket 8.

Enter key: 1243
Record: 1243 : added to bucket 8.
```

```
Enter key: 4321
Record: 4321 : added to bucket 8.

Enter key: 4312
Record: 4312 : added to bucket 8.

Enter key: 4123
Record: 4123 : added to overflow slot 0.

Enter key: 4213
Record: 4213 : added to overflow slot 1.

Enter key: 6767
Record: 6767 : added to bucket 78.

Enter key: 8791
Record: 8791 : added to bucket 33.

Enter key: quit  /**** End of additions. Begin searches. ****/

Enter key: 9999
Record with key: 9999 : not found.

Enter key: 4123
You found 4123 in overflow area.

Enter key: 1234
You found 1234 at hash bucket 8.

Enter key: 6767
You found 6767 at hash bucket 78.

Enter key: 5555
Record with key: 5555 : not found.

Enter key: quit
$  /*** Operating system prompt. End of execution.  ***/
```

Notice that one thing this program does *not* do is prohibit duplicate record entry. This is feasible with hashing to *memory*, because the average size of each list in the memory hash table is likely to be quite small. Therefore, you lose very little efficiency by searching the whole list.

With hashing to disk, however, you'd have to search the entire overflow area to establish that you were not entering a duplicate. This would to a large extent negate the speed of hashing. In all likelihood, a separate program would be built to prune duplicates from the file. Database management systems, for example, have many auxiliary systems to ensure that files are not corrupted.

The algorithm for the `insert_record()` function can be stated in English quite simply:

1. Go to the beginning of the hash bucket.
2. Read the first record of the bucket.
3. If byte 1 of this record is a `'\0'` character, the slot is available. An empty string cannot possibly be in the file as real data!
4. If the slot is available, copy the new record to it and return. If the slot is not available, look at the next slot.
5. Continue until the bucket is exhausted.
6. If no slot in the hash bucket is available, move the file pointer to the beginning of the overflow area.
7. Search the overflow area linearly until an empty slot is found. Copy the new record to that slot.
8. If the overflow area is also exhausted, terminate the program with a fatal error.

The `search_record()` function looks through the hash buckets and the overflow area in the same way as `insert_record()`. Therefore, we will leave it to the reader to create this algorithm. Looking through the eight steps listed for the `insert_record()` algorithm, you might wonder why we look at the first character of a `struct` on file to see whether a slot is available. To answer this, look at the user interface function, `search_or_insert()`. It does not accept an empty token (a string with just `'\0'`). If a user enters nothing or nothing plus whitespace, no token is collected and the user is simply reprompted. This is how nearly all commercially available software works. It does not "punish" the user or issue an error message when the user does not enter a valid token in response to a prompt. It just silently reprompts with no message. Thus no actual record in the file will contain the empty string as an actual `key`.

Finally, we don't want the testing session to go unnoticed! Keys were entered such that we eventually overflowed hash bucket 8. The code then reacted correctly by putting new records with hash value 8 into the overflow area. In the search, we deliberately entered record keys that were not represented in the file. The program correctly issued a `"Not found"` error message.

Looking at the `search_record()` code, note how efficient the search is when a record is there and how inefficient it is when a record is not there—it has to search the entire overflow area! Is this a problem? Not when you consider that users generally try to look for records they know are there. *Always make the most likely event the one that is most efficiently handled.*

5.5 Random Access to Variable-Length Record Files

In the last couple of sections, you saw that `fseek()` could be used to go to a certain record number in a file. Because the records were fixed-length, you could be certain which record the file pointer was pointing at. Does that mean random access cannot be done with files whose records are variable-length? Surprisingly, the answer is no.

For example, suppose you were writing a file browser and, because files can be quite large, you didn't want to read the lines of the file into memory. What you could do is read the file a line at a time and, after every line read, put the byte offset of the first character of each line into an *index*. Here is a diagram of an array used as an index:

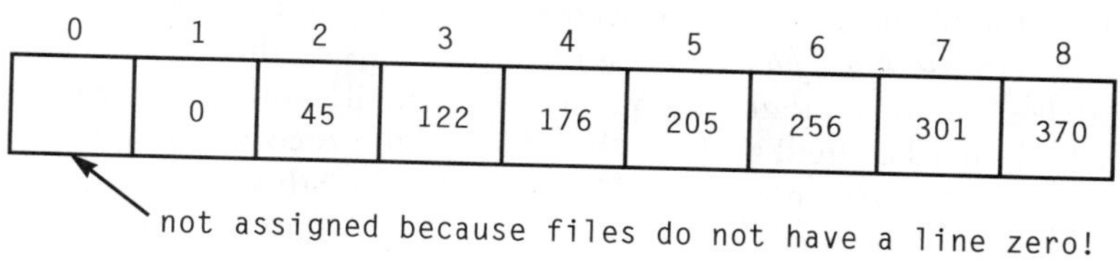

As you can see, the array index corresponds to a line number in the file. Let's assume that the array in the diagram above is called `offsets`. The offset of the first byte of line 4 from the beginning of the file would be held in `offsets[4]`. To go directly to the beginning of this line in the file, you would simply say

```
fseek(fp, offsets[4], SEEK_SET);
```

You might be wondering about the time it takes at the beginning of program execution to sweep through a file and put all the offsets in such an array. However, look at the cost of *not* doing so. If a user wanted to display lines 500 through 530 on the screen, you'd have to read all the irrelevant lines before line 500 just to get to the start of the desired range of lines!

Also, the construction of `offsets` is a one-time cost—the delay occurs before the first prompt only. Thereafter, the program fetches the desired lines at lightning speed. Another good rule of thumb in programming is that *it is much better to delay users a lot on one prompt than to delay them moderately on every prompt.* Even if a file is a million lines, it is better to have users wait 20 seconds for index array construction than to make them wait 5 seconds on every prompt.

When you are using an array of `long` as an index in our file browser application, how do you know how many elements to allocate? You don't! You should start with a modest allocation (say 1000 `long`s) and use `realloc()` (see Section 4.10, "Arrays of Strings") to make the array larger, if needed. This means that the array must start its life as a pointer, because you cannot realloc() true arrays—they are pointer constants. Therefore, you might do this to start the array's life:

```
long  *offsets;
if ((offsets = (long *) malloc(1000 * sizeof(long)))
    == NULL)
{
    printf("Fatal malloc error!\n");
    exit(1);
}
```

Then later use realloc() to expand the array if the file has more than 999 lines.

Another common method of indexing is to keep the index *on disk inside the file.* Thus the file would have two sections: the index and the data. Yet another method is to use *index files* to access data files. This method is commonly used in database management systems. The index file will have two fields per record: (1) the key field and (2) the offset of the record containing that key field in the database file itself. The advantage of this method is that data records can be accessed in ASCII order by key, where any component of a record can be a key.

For example, suppose you have data records with the following field structure:

```
lastname  firstname  SS number  age  salary department
```

You could construct index files for any of these fields if you wanted to do displays of the records in name order, age order, salary order, and so forth. Here's what an index file for lastname might look like:

Appleby	Barnes	Caine	Edwards	Martin	Perry	Quinn
20001	14558	17777	5015	19089	624	7856

Byte offset of Appleby's record in database file.

Readers who are interested in index file construction and other related issues should consult a book on database internals or a treatise on file structures. An excellent choice is *File Structures* by Folk and Zoellick (Reading, MA: Addison-Wesley).

In an exercise at the end of this chapter, you will be asked to construct a file browser using the index array approach outlined at the beginning of this section.

5.6 Advanced and Obscure Uses of the Printf and Scanf Families

We deprived you of code in the previous section (not our style at all!), so we'll proceed immediately to a demonstration of advanced `printf()` and `scanf()` formatting.

Example 5.9 Advanced Printf and Scanf Formatting

```
/*******************************************************/
/*                                                     */
/*  The input file used for this example consists of the */
/*  three lines of data below this comment.            */
/*                                                     */
/*******************************************************/

This is a bunch of junk, followed by a bunch of junk!
8 3
20 150.33333


#include <stdio.h>
main(int argc, char *argv[])
{
    FILE *fp ;
    char stuff[100], junk[100],
         *digits = "0123456789", p1[10], p2[10];
    int i, f1, f2;
    float x;

    fp = fopen(argv[1],"r");
    fscanf(fp,"%s", stuff);
    printf("%10s\n%-10s\n", stuff, stuff);
    rewind(fp);
    fscanf(fp,"%[a-zA-Z ]", stuff);
    printf("%s\n", stuff);
    rewind(fp);     /*** Re-read with [^...] scan set. ***/
    fscanf(fp,"%[^,]", stuff);
    fgets(junk,100,fp);
    printf("%s\n%s\n",stuff,junk);
    fscanf(fp,"%d %d", &f1, &f2);
    fscanf(fp,"%d %f", &i, &x);
    printf("%05d\n%-5d\n%5o\n%5x\n", i, i, i, i);
    printf("%12.3f\n%-12.3f\n%12.5e\n%*.*f\n",
           x, x, x, f1, f2, x);
    printf("%.5s\n", digits);
    printf("%10.5s\n", digits);
```

```
    printf("%*.*s\n", f1, f2, digits);
    rewind(fp);
    fscanf(fp, "%s %*s %*s %s", p1, p2);
    printf("%s %s\n", p1, p2);
}
/****************  Program Output Below  ****************/

      This        /*** Printf %10s format. ***/
This              /*** Printf %-10 format. ***/
This is a bunch of junk  /*** Read with [A-Za-z ] scanset ***/
This is a bunch of junk  /*** Read with [^,] scanset.  ***/
, followed by a bunch of junk!

00020          /*** Printf %05d format. Zero fill!!  ***/
20             /*** Printf %-5d format.  ***/
24             /*** Printf %5o format. Octal output!  ***/
14             /*** Printf %5x format. Hex output!    ***/
    150.333    /***  Printf %12.3f format.  ***/
150.333           /***  Printf %-12.3f format. ***/
    1.50333e+02 /***  Printf %12.5e format.  ***/
    150.333       /***  Printf %*.*f format. (%8.3f) ***/
01234          /***  Printf %.5s format.   ***/
    01234      /***  Printf %10.5s format. ***/
    012        /***  Printf %8.3s format. (%8.3s) ***/
This bunch     /***  Read with assignment suppression.  ***/
```

The first `fscanf()` gets the first word from the first line, "`This`". The subsequent `printf()` outputs it in both `10s` format and `-10s` format. Because `This` contains only four characters, the `10s` format right-justifies the field in a width of 10. The ASCII space character is used to "fill out" the field width of 10. A negative sign in front of the field width in a format, such as `-10s`, specifies that you want left-justification.

After `rewind`'ing the file, the next two `fscanfs` use a *scan set* format descriptor. The two forms of scan sets are `[...]` and `[^...]`. The first form says, "Read characters into the variable so long as they are members of the set enclosed in brackets." The second form says, "Read characters into the variable so long as they are not members of the set enclosed in brackets."

The scan set in the second `fscanf()` says, "Read characters into `stuff` so long as they are letters or the space character." The scan set in the third `fscanf()` says, "Read characters into stuff so long as they are not a comma." As it turns out, both of these `fscanfs` put "This is a bunch of junk" into the string variable `stuff`. Although range notations (like `A-Z`) and the `[^...]` scan set form are not officially recognized in ANSI C, the author has yet to see a compiler that does not acknowledge them.

The `fgets()` should be self-explanatory. `Fgets()` reads from the file pointer's current position to the end of the line. The variable `junk`, therefore, has ", followed by a bunch of junk!" in it, as well as the '\n' character that fgets() keeps and gets() does not keep. When using fgets(), remember to allow room for the terminating '\0' character. Never use a string without a terminating '\0'!

The next batch of printfs show how to output in octal format (%o), hexadecimal format (%x), floating-point format (%f), and exponential floating-point format (%e) with both left- and right-justification. Note the printf() that said

```
printf("%12.3f\n%-12.3f\n%12.5e\n%*.*f\n",
       x, x, x, f1, f2, x);
```

F1 and f2 correspond to the two asterisks in the format *.*f. We have seen this before. It is variable formatting. If f1 is 8 and f2 is 3, the final x will be output in 8.3f format. In fact, that is the case in Example 5.9; the 8 and 3 on the second data line in the input file were assigned to f1 and f2, respectively.

A couple of fprintfs display string processing. This is an area where mistakes are easily made. For example, say a string s consists of "ABCDEF" and you type

```
fprintf("%3s", s);
```

What will appear on the screen? If you said "ABC", you were tricked! When *any* type of data is being output, if a simple integer field width is smaller than the actual value being printed, C ignores the field width and uses whatever space is needed. If you really want ABC to go to the screen, then you need to type

```
fprintf("%.3s", s);
```

Now you know why the fprintf("%10.5s\n", digits) in Example 5.9 outputs 01234 in a right-justified field width of 10. The .5 says to use only 5 of the 10 characters in digits.

Finally, the last fscanf() in Example 5.9 illustrates *assignment suppression.* In any member of the scanf() family, a format that starts with %* means "Do not assign the obtained value to any member of the variable list." Thus %*s says, "Collect a string but don't assign it to anything." This can be very useful if you are given a preformatted file and are interested only in selected pieces of data on each line of the file.

Before we adjourn to the "Facts About Functions" section, I want to talk about the most neglected members of the scanf() and printf() families, sscanf() and sprintf(). People often forget that these functions exist and use inferior methods. For example, suppose you have four strings s1, s2, s3, and s4. You want to concatenate them together in variable bigstring. A lot of people would do this:

```
strcpy(bigstring, "");
strcat(bigstring, s1);
```

```
strcat(bigstring, s2);
strcat(bigstring, s3);
strcat(bigstring, s4);
```

when they could have done it all at once with

```
sprintf(bigstring, "%s%s%s%s", s1, s2, s3, s4);
```

`Sscanf()` is a very good partner when used with `gets()`. You collect a whole line from the screen with the `gets()` and then read the values in the string with `sscanf()`. This approach offers a major advantage over using `scanf()`, because `scanf()` will not collect the `'\n'` at the end of the line. This often causes programmers a lot of grief! Thus the rule for reading from the terminal is simple: *Get the whole line with* `gets()` *and then read the obtained line with* `sscanf()`.

Facts About Functions

<stdio.h> Functions

Function: `int fseek(FILE *fp, long offset, int offset_location);`

Fact: 1) Returns zero if successful and non-zero if an error occurs.

Fact: 2) A seek before the beginning of a file or after the end of a file is *not* an error. It is an error only if you try to access those disk areas! Thus a non-zero return is likely when the seek is to a disk address that does not exist or if `fp` is closed.

Fact: 3) The `offset` is relative to the `offset_location`. The three `offset_location` values are the built-in constants `SEEK_SET` (beginning of file), `SEEK_END` (end of file), and `SEEK_CUR` (current position of file pointer).

Fact: 4) Negative `offsets` from `SEEK_SET` make no sense, and neither do positive `offsets` from `SEEK_END`.

Function: `long ftell(FILE *fp);`

Fact: 1) Returns the offset from the beginning of the file or `-1` on an error.

Fact: 2) Because `-1` is a valid offset (!), you should check to see if `errno` is zero or positive. If `errno` is positive, then the `-1` return from `ftell()` confirms an error. Remember that when using `errno`, you must include `errno.h` and set `errno` to an initial value of zero.

Fact: 3) Be sure to remember to obtain `ftell`'s return value in a `long` (not `int`) variable.

Function: `void rewind(FILE *fp);`

Fact: 1) Equivalent to `fseek(fp, 0, SEEK_SET);`

Fact: 2) Places the file pointer at the first byte of the file.

Function: `size_t fread(void *pointer, size_t size, size_t count, FILE *fp);`

Fact: 1) Returns zero if an error occurred (if the file is closed or the disk sector is out of bounds, for example).

Fact: 2) Returns the number of items read, if successful. If `EOF` occurs, that number could be less than `count`.

Fact: 3) The `size` parameter is the byte size of each item read. Generally, the `sizeof()` function is used to obtain the `size`.

Fact: 4) The first parameter can be a pointer to any type. `Void` pointers, in general, are com patible with any C pointer type.

Function: `size_t fwrite(void *pointer, size_t size, size_t count, FILE *fp);`

Fact: 1) Returns zero if an error occurred (if the file is closed or the disk sector is out of bounds, for example).

Fact: 2) Returns the number of items written, if successful.

Fact: 3) The `size` parameter is the byte size of each item written. Generally, the `sizeof()` function is used to obtain the `size`.

Fact: 4) The first parameter can be a pointer to any type. `Void` pointers, in general, are compatible with any C pointer type.

Fact: 5) As is usual with any C function that features `size_t` return types or parameter types, this type is compatible with members of the `int` family, but on most computers, `size_t` is equivalent to a `long`.

Function: `FILE *fopen(char *filename, char *mode);`

Fact: 1) Returns `NULL` if `filename` cannot be successfully opened.

Fact: 2) Returns file pointer if successful.

Fact: 3) The following modes are pertinent to the material in this chapter and are likely to be new to beginning and intermediate C programmers.

Mode	Meaning
`rb`	Read binary data.
`wb`	Create new binary data file.
`ab`	Append binary data to existing binary file.
`r+b`	Read and write an existing binary file.
`w+b`	Read and write a new binary data file.
`a+b`	Read and append to an existing binary data file.

Exercises

■ **1.** A program has declared a `FILE *` variable `fp`. Given this information, do the following operations. Declare any variables you need (except `fp`).

a. Open existing binary file `foobar.dat` for reading and writing, and attach it to `fp`.

b. Assume that `foobar.dat` is a binary file with an unknown number of `struct foo`. Print to screen the number of `struct foo` in the file.

c. Read the "middle" `struct foo` in the file, where "middle" is the number of `struct foo` divided by 2—for example, it is the 30th `struct foo` if the file has 60 or 61. Use the result of part b.

d. Transpose each pair of `struct` in the file (the 1st and 2nd, 3rd and 4th, and so on).

e. Turn the file's contents backwards so that the last record is the first, the next-to-last is the second, and so on.

■ **2.** Write a function that

   a. Has one `char *` parameter containing the name of a file.

   b. Opens the file, assuming that it exists, is binary, and will be read.

   c. Reads the whole file into an array of `struct foo` in one read operation. *Hint:* Your answer will have one call to `fread()`.

   d. Returns the array read in part c to the calling environment. This array will have all the data in the file and one sentinel `struct foo` that is zeroed out.

3. Write a program that

   a. Allows the user to pass the name of an input file on the command line.

   b. Expects the file to be text and, therefore, opens it as a binary file for reading.

   c. Sweeps through the file putting the byte offsets of line beginnings into an index array.

   d. Repeatedly prompts the user for a line number or line number range (two numbers separated by whitespace).

   e. Checks the user's numbers for validity. You must decide what *validity* means!

   f. Prints the line(s) requested by the user on the screen.

   g. Uses `strtok()` and `strtol()` to get the numbers from the user's input line and convert them to `long`.

   h. Uses `fseek`s to get to the correct place in the file to fetch the user's lines. *Do not read the input file into a data structure in memory.*

   i. Do full error checking! Make no assumptions about the size of the input file.

4. Write a function that deletes a record from the on-disk hash table constructed by the code in Examples 5.3 through 5.7.

■ **5.** In each of the following parts, indicate what is printed to the screen.

   a.
```
int  i = 64;
printf("%05o", i);
```

   b.
```
int  i = 64;
printf("%5x", i);
```

   c.
```
float  x = 23.123456;
int i = 6, j = 2;
printf("%*.*f", i, j, x);
```

   d.
```
char *s = "abcdefghij";
printf("%-10.4s", s);
```

   e.
```
char *s = "abcdefghij";
printf("%4s", s);
```

f.
```
char *s1 = "This is a sentence.  So is this!", s2[25];
sscanf(s1, "%s", s2);
printf("%s", s2);
```
g.
```
char *s1 = "This is a sentence. So is this!", s2[25];
sscanf(s1, "%[^S]", s2);
printf("%s", s2);
```
h.
```
char *s1 = "What's up, Doc?", *s2 = "Elmer Fudd?",
s3[25], s4[25];
sscanf(s1, "%[^D]", s3);
sprintf(s4, "%s%s", s3, s2);
printf("%s", s4);
```
i.
```
char *s1 = "AFGH1236", s2[10];
sscanf(s1, "%[A-Z]", s2);
printf("%s", s2);
```
j.
```
char *s1 = "What's up, Doc?";
printf("%s", strchr(s1, ',') + 1);
```

6. Your boss at the Financial Aid Department of Whatsamatta University wants you to write a program that allows additions to, deletions from, or displays of database records in a financial aid database. The records in this database will consist of the following fields:

Field	Format
`lastname`	Variable length up to 20 characters.
`firstname`	Variable length up to 20 characters.
`amount`	2 digits after the decimal point and at least 2 before the decimal point. Min = 10.00, Max = 99999.99
`student_id`	*Exactly* 4 digit characters. No more, no less!

Your program must

a. Do complete error checking for added records. You may assume that names consist only of letters, that the student id can be any 4-digit combination, and that the amount of financial aid is between 10.00 and 99999.99 and must be entered *rigidly* with 2 digits after the decimal point.

b. Report and reject record additions that would overflow the 4-record bucket for each hash location.

c. Put names in the file in one case or the other, but *not* mixed!

d. Abort if the file is empty *or* is the wrong size!

e. Report *every* error on a user's input line when he or she tries to *add*.

Do not use overflow areas. This challenging project involves more than 400 lines of code and uses everything from this chapter. It uses `strtok()`

and `strtod()` and possibly other `string.h` functions. Indeed, it will be a good way for you to test whether you have understood all the material up to this point.

■ **7.** Write a program that accepts text lines from the user at the terminal and enters them into a binary file. In case you are wondering, this will create an output text file that is free of platform-independent junk! You will use this file in Exercise 8.

■ **8.** Write a program that accepts an input file argument. The program will rewrite this same file so that it is backwards. The output file must be *the same file* given as an argument. Do not use a separate file for output!

9. Do the same as in Exercise 8, but this time make the output file *a different file.* You'll notice that this is approach is much easier (and saner, too). Of course, this means that the command line invoking your program will have two arguments instead of one.

10. Assume that you have done Exercise 6. Write a program that enables a user to swap the positions of any two records in the file. Users will be allowed to swap pairs until they enter some indication that they wish to quit.

Chapter 6

Bit Manipulation

Some people have jokingly referred to ANSI C as "the greatest assembly language ever invented." One of the reasons they say such things is that C allows the user to operate at the bit and byte level normally associated with assembly languages. We have seen some of that in the `string.h` functions `memcpy()`, `memset()`, and `memcmp()`, which do bitwise copies, value assignments, and comparisons, respectively.

Bit manipulation is featured in an amazing variety of different areas, such as graphics, robotics and industrial automation, cryptography, and game theory. We will start with the basic operations and then move to large-scale operations that combine them.

6.1 Bitwise AND, OR, Exclusive OR, and NOT

The simplest way to show how the AND (the C & operator), OR (the C | operator), and XOR (the C ^ operator) operators work is to show what happens when two bits (binary digits) are AND'ed, OR'ed, or XOR'ed via *truth tables*. They are virtually self-explanatory.

Bitwise AND: Operator is &

	1	0
1	1	0
0	0	0

As you can see, only two ones results in a one. All other combinations result in a zero. Now that we've seen how bitwise AND works on two bits, let's see how it works on variables with many more bits.

Example 6.1 Demonstration of Bitwise AND

```
#include <stdio.h>
main()
{
    unsigned short a = 12, b = 4, c;

    c = a & b;
    printf("a & b = %hu\n", c);
}
/****************  Program Output Below *******************/

a & b = 4
```

Let's see why we got this result in a diagram that incorporates the knowledge we have of bitwise AND from the truth table above. We show a and b in their binary forms along with the result.

```
a  =  0 0 0 0 0 0 0 0 0 0 0 0 1 1 0 0
b  =  0 0 0 0 0 0 0 0 0 0 0 0 0 1 0 0
--------------------------------------
c  =  0 0 0 0 0 0 0 0 0 0 0 0 0 1 0 0

  /**** Binary 100 is decimal 4. ****/
```

We have assumed that on our computer, an unsigned short is 16 bits (2 bytes). The result is 4, because it is only in the "4" position that both a and b have ones—the only way to get a one with a bitwise AND.

Now let's look at the truth table for bitwise OR.

Bitwise OR: Operator is |

	1	0
1	1	1
0	1	0

As you can see, the only way to get a zero from a bitwise OR is if *both* bits are zeroes. Given this knowledge, let's demonstrate bitwise OR with 16-bit numbers.

Example 6.2 Demonstration of Bitwise OR

```
#include <stdio.h>
main()
{
    unsigned short a = 12, b = 16, c;

    c = a | b;
    printf("a | b = %hu\n", c);
}
/******************  Program Output Below  *****************/

a | b = 28
```

Let's see why we got this result in a diagram that incorporates the knowledge we have of bitwise OR from the truth table above. We show a and b in their binary forms along with the result.

```
a  =  0 0 0 0 0 0 0 0 0 0 0 0 1 1 0 0
b  =  0 0 0 0 0 0 0 0 0 0 0 1 0 0 0 0
---------------------------------------
c  =  0 0 0 0 0 0 0 0 0 0 0 1 1 1 0 0

/**** Binary 11100 is decimal 28. ****/
```

Let's look at the truth table for bitwise exclusive OR (better known as XOR).

Bitwise XOR: Operator is ^

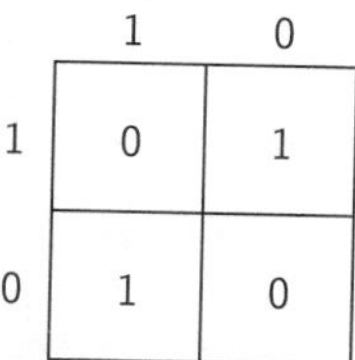

	1	0
1	0	1
0	1	0

As you can see, XOR results in a one if one of the two bits is a one. If both are one or both are zero, the result is a zero. Given this knowledge, let's test XOR with two 16-bit numbers.

Example 6.3 Demonstration of Exclusive OR (XOR)

```
#include <stdio.h>
main()
{
    unsigned short a = 28, b = 20, c;

    c = a ^ b;
```

```
    printf("a ^ b = %hu\n", c);
}
/*****************  Program Output Below  ******************/

a ^ b = 8
```

Let's see, via a diagram, why the result above was achieved.

```
a  =  0 0 0 0 0 0 0 0 0 0 0 1 1 1 0 0
b  =  0 0 0 0 0 0 0 0 0 0 0 1 0 1 0 0
--------------------------------------
c  =  0 0 0 0 0 0 0 0 0 0 0 0 1 0 0 0

/**** Binary 1000 is decimal 8. ****/
```

By the way, you may have noticed that we used the `printf()` format descriptor `%hu` to output our `unsigned short` numbers. As you may have guessed, the `u` means "unsigned" and the `h` means "half of an `int`" or, in other words, a `short`.

The bitwise `AND` (&), `OR` (|), and `XOR` (^) operators are known as *binary operators*. That does not mean that they operate on binary numbers. It means that they take two operands. The bitwise `NOT` (~) operator is a *unary operator*. It takes only one operand. The bitwise `NOT` simply inverts the value of every bit. That is, each one becomes a zero and each zero becomes a one.

The largest `unsigned short`, if they are 16-bit types on your computer, is 65,535. Thus, if we take the bitwise `NOT` of 65,534, the result should be one. The following diagram shows why.

```
binary 65,534   1 1 1 1 1 1 1 1 1 1 1 1 1 1 1 0
~65,534         0 0 0 0 0 0 0 0 0 0 0 0 0 0 0 1    ====>>>  1
```

Let's see if a little code backs up our guess.

Example 6.4 Demonstration of Bitwise NOT

```
#include <stdio.h>
main()
{
    unsigned short a = 65534, b;

    b = ~a;
    printf("b = %hu\n", b);
}
/*******************  Program Output Below  ****************/

b = 1
```

Before we go on to the next section, a special mention should be made of the XOR (^) operator. It has very special applicability to cryptography, the science of encrypting and decrypting data. The reason is illustrated in the following example.

Example 6.5 Demonstration of Exclusive OR for Data Encryption and Decryption

```
#include <stdio.h>
main()
{
     unsigned short a = 17, b = 11;

     a = a ^ b;
     a = a ^ b;    /**** Value of "a" should be 17 again. ****/
     printf("a = %hu\n", a);
}
/****************  Program Output Below  ******************/

a = 17
```

We can look at b in Example 6.5 as an *encryption/decryption key*. We used b to encrypt a to some other value. Then we used b again with the encrypted a. Lo and behold, we got the original value of a back again—17! If you read any books on the subject of cryptography, you will notice that XOR plays a huge role in these algorithms.

6.2 Bit Shifting

There are two other bit manipulation operators in C. They are the left shift (<<) and right shift (>>) operators. Generally, you should always do bit shifting with unsigned data types, especially the right shift. This is because the ANSI C standard says that it is up to the implementor of the compiler whether the right shift operator shifts zeroes in from the left or sign bits. Don't play brinksmanship; if you use unsigned data types, zeroes are always shifted in, whether you have done a left shift or a right shift.

It's time to display the basic operation of these two operators through a code example.

Example 6.6 Demonstration of the Bitwise Left Shift and Right Shift Operators

```
#include <stdio.h>
main()
```

```
{
    unsigned short a = 3, b = 7, c = 32768, d;

    d = a << 3;
    printf("a << 3  = %hu\n", d);
    d = b >> 2;
    printf("b >> 2  = %hu\n", d);
    d = c >> 14;
    printf("c >> 14 = %hu\n", d);
}
/******************  Program Output Below  ****************/

a << 3  = 24
b >> 2  = 1
c >> 14 = 2
```

Let's see, through diagrams, why these results were obtained.

```
a =  0 0 0 0 0 0 0 0 0 0 0 0 0 0 1 1          /** Binary 11 is decimal 3. **/
a   << 3  =  0 0 0 0 0 0 0 0 0 0 0 1 1 0 0 0  /** Binary 11000 is decimal 24. **/

b = 0 0 0 0 0 0 0 0 0 0 0 0 0 1 1 1           /** Binary 111 is decimal 7. **/
b   >> 2  =  0 0 0 0 0 0 0 0 0 0 0 0 0 0 0 1  /** Binary 1 is decimal 1. **/

c = 1 0 0 0 0 0 0 0 0 0 0 0 0 0 0 0           /** This is 32768 in decimal. **/
c    >> 14 = 0 0 0 0 0 0 0 0 0 0 0 0 0 0 1 0  /** Binary 10 is decimal 2. **/
```

Notice that a left shift of a number by *n* is the same as multiplying it by 2 to the *n*th power. Thus `a << 3` is like a multiplication by 8 (2 to the third power). But be careful! If any ones are shifted out, this is *not* true.

A right shift of a number by *n* is the same as dividing it by 2 to the *n*th power. But this holds only when zeroes are shifted out. Thus `b >> 2` is not 7 divided by 4, because the two ones at the right edge of `b` are shifted out. Thus `b >> 2` is one.

Finally, we did a right shift of a really large number, `c`. The value 32768 in a two-byte `unsigned short` has the leftmost bit "set" (value 1) and all the other bits "unset" (value 0). When we right-shift `c` by 14, it is shifted all the way down to the second bit position, creating a value of 2.

Obviously, in all shifting operations, you must make sure that the number of bits you are shifting (the number to the right of the `>>` or `<<`) makes sense. For example, if `unsigned shorts` are 16 bits on your computer, don't try to shift by 20!

6.3 Bit Masking Formulas

In this section, you will see how to set, unset, or toggle a range of bits. *Toggling* is a common word that means "changing to the opposite value." If a light is on, toggling it turns it off. If a light is off, toggling it turns it on. First, let's see how you can set a range of bits. *Setting* bits means giving them a value of one.

Example 6.7 Demonstration of Formula to Turn On a Range of Bits

```
#include <stdio.h>
main()
{
    unsigned short a = 32, b = 13, c;
    int numbits = 3, startbit = 2;

    c = a | (~((unsigned short) ~0 << numbits) << startbit);
    printf("c = %hu\n", c);    /*** Result should be 60! ***/

    numbits = 3; startbit = 1;
    c = b | (~((unsigned short) ~0 << numbits) << startbit);
    printf("c = %hu\n", c);    /*** Result should be 15! ***/
}
/*****************  Program Output Below  *****************/

c = 60
c = 15
```

I often call these formulas the "line noise" formulas because they look like the characters that appear on your screen when your modem malfunctions! The formula shown turns on `numbits` bits, starting at bit position `startbit`. Let's break this formula apart in a series of diagrams.

```
                         bit position 15                     0
a)(unsigned short) ~0          = 1 1 1 1 1 1 1 1 1 1 1 1 1 1 1 1
b)result of a) << numbits (3)  = 1 1 1 1 1 1 1 1 1 1 1 1 1 0 0 0
c)~ of result of b)            = 0 0 0 0 0 0 0 0 0 0 0 0 0 1 1 1
d)result of c) << startbit (2) = 0 0 0 0 0 0 0 0 0 0 0 1 1 1 0 0
e)value of variable a (32)     = 0 0 0 0 0 0 0 0 0 0 1 0 0 0 0 0
----------------------------------------------------------------
f)OR'ing result of d) and e)   = 0 0 0 0 0 0 0 0 0 0 1 1 1 1 0 0 == 60
```

The code in Example 6.7 also turns on three bits of the number 13 starting at bit position 1 to illustrate a point about this formula. That point is that *bits that are already set, stay set.* Here's the proof.

```
                         bit position 15                     0
a)(unsigned short) ~0          = 1 1 1 1 1 1 1 1 1 1 1 1 1 1 1 1
b)result of a) << numbits (3)  = 1 1 1 1 1 1 1 1 1 1 1 1 1 0 0 0
c)~ of result of b)            = 0 0 0 0 0 0 0 0 0 0 0 0 0 1 1 1
d)result of c) << startbit (1) = 0 0 0 0 0 0 0 0 0 0 0 0 1 1 1 0
e)value of variable a (13)     = 0 0 0 0 0 0 0 0 0 0 0 0 1 1 0 1
----------------------------------------------------------------
f)OR'ing result of d) and e)   = 0 0 0 0 0 0 0 0 0 0 0 0 1 1 1 1 == 15
```

Notice that the bits in b that were already set in positions 2 and 3 stayed set, as did the bit in position zero that was unaffected by the OR.

You will be quite surprised to find that the formula for turning *off* a range of bits is only slightly different from the formula for turning a range of bits *on*. Here is some code demonstrating this formula.

Example 6.8 Demonstration of Formula to Turn Off a Range of Bits

```
#include <stdio.h>
main()
{
    unsigned short a = 31, b = 19, c;
    int numbits, startbit;

    numbits = 3;  startbit = 1;
    c =  a & ~(~((unsigned short) ~0 << numbits) << startbit);
    printf("c = %hu\n", c);
    c =  b & ~(~((unsigned short) ~0 << numbits) << startbit);
    printf("c = %hu\n", c);
}
/*****************  Program Output Below  *****************/

c = 17
c = 17
```

As you can see, unsetting bits involves one more level of bitwise negation (~) plus the use of bitwise AND (&) instead of bitwise OR (|). Just as the bit setter formula left bits set that were already set, the bit unsetter formula leaves bits unset that were already unset. For example, in Example 6.8 we unset three bits (numbits) starting at bit position 1 (startbit). The value being operated upon was 19 (b), which in binary is

```
0 0 0 0 0 0 0 0 0 0 0 1 0 0 1 1
```

The mask constructed by the awesome formula in the code will be

```
1 1 1 1 1 1 1 1 1 1 1 1 0 0 0 1
```

Now let's line up these two bit strings and bitwise AND (&) them as we did in Example 6.8.

```
0 0 0 0 0 0 0 0 0 0 0 1 0 0 1 1
1 1 1 1 1 1 1 1 1 1 1 1 0 0 0 1
-------------------------------
0 0 0 0 0 0 0 0 0 0 0 1 0 0 0 1
```

As you can see, we did zero out three bits starting at bit position 1, and the two bits in positions 2 and 3 which were already off, stayed off. Try following each operation in the unsetting formula as we did in the diagram for the bit-setting formula.

Of course, there is also a formula to "toggle" `numbits` bits starting at bit position `startbit`. Guess what? You will be given this as an exercise in the end of the chapter. Don't worry, the answer is in the Appendix. A giant hint: Use `XOR` to develop this formula.

The next trick you will be shown is how to overlay a bit pattern onto a range of bits. You may want more flexibility than the "all-or-nothing" approach of turning a range of bits all on or all off. You may want, for example, to overlay the bit pattern 11001 onto an `unsigned short` starting at bit number 2, or something like that. The next piece of code will show you how to accomplish this feat.

Example 6.9 Overlaying a Bit Pattern on a Range of Bits

```
#include <stdio.h>
main()
{
    unsigned short word = 127;    /*** 1111111 in binary.  ***/
    unsigned short pattern = 9;   /*** 1001 in binary.     ***/
    unsigned short overlay(unsigned short word, int startbit,
                int numbits, unsigned short pattern);

    word = overlay(word, 2, 4, 9);
    printf("word = %hu\n", word);
}

unsigned short overlay(unsigned short word, int startbit,
            int numbits, unsigned short pattern)
{
    word &= ~(~((unsigned short) ~0 << numbits) << startbit);
    word |=  pattern << startbit;
    return word;
}
/********************  Program Output Below  ***************/

word = 103
```

Notice that the bit overlay method first uses the bit unsetter formula to zero out the bits that will be overlaid. Thus, the bit pattern in `word` goes from 1111111 to 1000011 because the bit unsetter turns off four bits (`numbits`) starting at bit position 2 (`startbit`). Note that the bitwise operators can be used in assignments like +, *, and so on. Therefore,

```
word &= whatever;
```

is the same as

```
word = word & whatever;
```

In the code of Example 6.9, we have unset four bits of `word` starting at bit position 2. Then we `OR` the result (which is in `word`) with `pattern << startbit`, resulting in the following operation:

```
                    a  = 0 0 0 0 0 0 0 0 0 1 0 0 0 0 1 1
pattern << startbit  = 0 0 0 0 0 0 0 0 0 0 1 0 0 1 0 0
------------------------------------------------------------------
           bitwise OR  = 0 0 0 0 0 0 0 0 0 1 1 0 0 1 1 1  = 103 decimal
```

6.4 Bit Rotation Methods

In assembly languages, there are often commands for *rotating* bits. First, we have to answer the question "What does that mean?" Let's say we have a string of bits like this:

```
1 0 0 0 0 0 0 0 0 0 0 0 0 0 0 1
```

A right rotation of this bit pattern by two bits would result in

```
0 1 1 0 0 0 0 0 0 0 0 0 0 0 0 0
```

Now, if we rotated *this* pattern to the *left* by three bits, the result would be

```
0 0 0 0 0 0 0 0 0 0 0 0 0 0 1 1
```

Notice, however, that we do not need a formula to do both left and right rotation. A left rotation by `n` bits results in the same value as a right rotation by `16 - n` bits. Here is some code that accomplishes a right rotation.

Example 6.10 Demonstration of Right Rotation of Bits

```
#include <stdio.h>
main()
{
    unsigned short word = 3;
    unsigned short rightrot(unsigned short word,
                            int numbits);

    word = rightrot(word, 1);
    /***  Word is Binary:  0000000000000011 ***/
    /***  which becomes:   1000000000000001 ***/
    /***  which is decimal 32769.  ***/
    printf("Word = %hu\n", word);
}
```

```
unsigned short rightrot(unsigned short word, int numbits)
{
    unsigned short nleft;

    nleft = word <<  (sizeof(short) * 8 - numbits);
    word = word >>  numbits;
    word = word | nleft;
    return word;
}
/******************  Program Output Below  ****************/

Word = 32769
```

6.5 Testing Individual Bits and Printing Bit Strings

Sometimes you also need to know whether an individual bit is set or unset. Here is a piece of code that gives the on/off value for an individual bit and outputs an `unsigned short` as a bit string.

Example 6.11 Testing and Printing Bit Set/Unset Values

```
#include <stdio.h>
main()
{
    unsigned short word = 127;
    int testbit(unsigned short word, int bit_to_test), i;
    void printbits(unsigned short word);

    for (i = 0; i < 10; i++)
    {
        printf("Bit %d of word is %s\n\n",
               i, testbit(word, i) ? "ON" : "OFF");
    }
    printbits(word);
}

/***************************************************/
/******                                     *******/
/******  Return 1 if bit_to_test is set and 0  *******/
/******  if it is unset.                    *******/
/******                                     *******/
/***************************************************/
int testbit(unsigned short word, int bit_to_test)
{
    word >>=  bit_to_test;
```

```
    word &= 1;
    return word;
}

/**********************************************/
/******                                  ******/
/******  This uses a trick to print an un- ******/
/******  signed short as a string of 16   ******/
/******  bits.                            ******/
/******                                  ******/
/**********************************************/
void printbits(unsigned short word)
{
    int i, testbit(unsigned short word, int bit_to_test);

    for (i = 15; i >= 0; i--) printf("%1d", testbit(word,i));
}
/******************** Program Output Below ****************/

Bit 0 of word is ON
Bit 1 of word is ON
Bit 2 of word is ON
Bit 3 of word is ON
Bit 4 of word is ON
Bit 5 of word is ON
Bit 6 of word is ON
Bit 7 of word is OFF
Bit 8 of word is OFF
Bit 9 of word is OFF

0000000001111111   /* This is what 127 looks like as bits! */
```

The `testbit()` function uses a very simple principle: when you perform the operation

```
something & 1;
```

it can have only two possible outcomes—one or zero. It's easy to see this in binary.

```
    1 1 0 0 1 1 1 1 1 1 0 0 1 1 0 1
    0 0 0 0 0 0 0 0 0 0 0 0 0 0 0 1
    -------------------------------
&   0 0 0 0 0 0 0 0 0 0 0 0 0 0 0 1
```

Thus the trick used by `testbit()` is to shift the bit you wish to test into the rightmost position. If that bit is set, the result is one. If that bit is not set, the result is zero. The `printbits()` function actually uses `testbit()` to do its job!

6.6 Applications for Bit Manipulation Formulas and Concepts

Bit manipulation algorithms and formulas are used in a wide variety of applications. For example, when your modem sends data out or receives data, it is often in a compressed form. This compression can be done in many ways, but one way is to use bit patterns such that the most frequently used characters have the smallest bit pattern and the least frequently used characters have the largest bit pattern.

Another application for bit manipulation is in cryptography. Earlier in the chapter, we saw how the exclusive OR operator is used to encrypt and decrypt data. If you buy any book on data encryption and security, you will see bit manipulation performed in virtually every algorithm.

Probably the most promising area for bit manipulation is in industrial automation. That's because a bit represents the most fundamental state of a machine (1 for "on" and 0 for "off"). Imagine a set of 16 lights on a theater stage. Suppose that you are operating a software-controlled console to control the on/off status of these lights. You could place the on/off status of the whole bank of lights in one `unsigned short`. A variation of this very problem is given in the exercises in the end of this chapter.

Graphics is another area where bit "twiddling" (as it is popularly called) is common. Often the state of each screen pixel (an industry nickname for "picture element") is held in a *bit map*. The most elementary kind of bit map represents an unlit screen pixel as a zero and a lit pixel as a one. If you ever work with graphics at the device level, you are bound to become involved in programming at the bit level.

Finally, many problems in common games are solved with bit manipulation. You are going to be given an exercise at the end of this chapter where you will write the code for such a game. But first we must tell you how the game works. The game is a variation of an old set of games known as Nim games. Here is how the one you're going to program works.

```
Pile 1:    |   |   |   |   |   |   |
Pile 2:        |   |   |   |   |
Pile 3:            |   |   |
Pile 4:                |
```

There are four piles of sticks containing 7, 5, 3, and 1 sticks, respectively. Two players play. On each turn, the player may take anywhere from a single stick to the whole pile but may choose from one pile only. Whoever takes the last stick wins.

What's the secret? Exclusive OR. Let's look at the exclusive OR of the four piles at the start of the game.

```
Pile 1:    1 1 1        /****  Binary 7.   ****/
Pile 2:    1 0 1        /****  Binary 5.   ****/
```

```
Pile 3:    0 1 1          /****  Binary 3.  ****/
Pile 4:    0 0 1          /****  Binary 1.  ****/
```

Notice that the exclusive OR of the four piles is zero. As it turns out, no matter what the first player does, if the second player knows what he or she is doing, he or she can always choose from one of the piles in such a way as to return the XOR of all four piles to zero.

Therefore, when you solve this problem in the exercises, make the computer go first so that the human opponent has a chance to figure out the game and win! The computer can start the game by taking one stick from pile 1 and wait for the human's response. Thereafter, the computer will do one of the following: (1) choose one stick from the pile with the most sticks if the human continues to play correctly, or (2) if the human makes a mistake (XOR of four piles is *not* zero after his or her turn), choose such that the XOR of the four piles is zero.

Notice that the XOR of the four piles is zero only when there are an even number of "set" bits in each column of the binary representations. For example, at the start of play, the ones column has all four bits set, the twos column has two bits set, and the fours column has two bits set. Remember, when you play, that zero is also an even number. This game can be programmed in about four pages of code and is fun to play! With that we will close this chapter on one of the author's favorite subjects!

Facts About Functions

No new functions were introduced in this chapter, nor were any old functions used in a new way.

Exercises

■ **1.** Given these declarations:

```
unsigned short a = 7,  b = 8,  c = 5, d = 15, e = 6;
```

find the value of the following expressions.

a. `a >> 3`

b. `a ^ a`

c. `d ^ a`

d. `d & a`

e. `d && a`

f. `c << 1`

g. `b | ~((unsigned short) ~0 << 2) << 1`

h. `(d << 2) & 3`

i. `(d << 2) | 3`

j. `a & b`

2. Write a program to implement the Nim game as described in Section 6.6.

3. A theater stage has a set of computer-controlled lights. There are 16 lights. A theater employee is working the lights, and you can assume that the on/off situation of the lights is entirely dependent on an `unsigned short` variable in your program. Make sure your program makes no assumptions about the size of an `unsigned short`. Your program will supply the following menu:

```
 1)   turn on all lights
 2)   turn on center stage lights (lights 5-10)
 3)   turn on left stage lights (lights 11-15)
 4)   turn on right stage lights (lights 0-4)
 5)   turn off all lights
 6)   turn off center stage lights
 7)   turn off left stage lights
 8)   turn off right stage lights
 9)   overlay on/off pattern onto light configuration
10)   quit the menu
```

Your program must

a. Use the bit set/unset formulas as given in this chapter.

b. Seek to reduce redundant code.

c. Use `strtok` to get user tokens. Assume whitespace (tabs or spaces) might surround any user response (i.e., to the menu or a prompt that you supply).

d. Use `strtol` to convert strings (user responses to menu choices) to integers.

e. Perform complete error checking of user input.

f. Simply reprompt a user if the user gives no token in response to the menu.

g. Allow a user to use an empty response to any prompt to get back to the main menu. A user should never be *forced* to respond to any prompt!

h. After each menu choice (except the "quit" choice), output the on/off status of the 16 lights.

i. If a user chooses option 9 (the bit overlay option), prompt the user for a bit string and the starting light number where the overlay should start. This is tricky. You must make sure that the given pattern is a valid bit string (*Hint:* Use `strtol()` with base 2) and fits into the bit string given the starting location.

4. Do a variation of Exercise 3 where each light can have a `RED` or `WHITE` color. A user who turns lights `ON` will also get a color prompt. You can put the colors for the 16 lights either in the other half of a 32-bit `long` (the first 16 bits will be the on/off statuses) or use a separate `unsigned short` for the color bits. On some old personal computers, even a `long` is 16 bits, so be sure to find out what kind of architecture your machine has.

■ **5.** Write a function that takes two parameters: (a) a character string containing a bit pattern, and (b) an `unsigned short`. This function will search for the bit pattern within the `unsigned short` and return the starting location. If the bit pattern is too long, return `-1`. If the bit pattern is invalid (assume all characters in this argument are supposed to be ones or zeroes) return `-2`. If the bit pattern is O.K. but cannot be found in the `unsigned short`, return `-3`.

6. Do a variation of Exercise 5 in which the user passes the pattern as a decimal `unsigned short` and your program turns it into a bit string.

7. Write a function that takes an `unsigned short` parameter and returns an `unsigned short` with the bits in the parameter turned backwards. Thus, if the parameter has a binary value of 1111111100000000, your function will return a value whose binary representation is 0000000011111111.

8. Write a function that encrypts a data file by exclusive `OR`'ing all of the characters in the original file with the letter `X`. Write another function that decrypts the encrypted file back to its original form. Yes, it's a rather primitive encryption/decryption scheme, but if you want, you can use a more complicated encryptor/decryptor than `X`!

9. Write a function that does a left bit rotation. Look at Section 6.4 if you have forgotten how we did a right rotation.

■ **10.** Write a function that toggles `numbits` bits starting at bit position `startbit`. Assume that the user gives sensible values for `numbits` and `startbit`.

■ **11.** Write a function that returns the bit pattern of an `unsigned short` from bit `endbit` down to bit `startbit` *as a string*. Do full error detection inside the function, and make no assumptions about the size of an `unsigned short` on the target computer. Return a `NULL` pointer if the user's `startbit` or `endbit` values are illegal.

Chapter 7

Recursion and Binary Trees

Recursion is simple to explain and hard to follow. It is simply the ability of a C function to call itself. The problem with recursion is that the algorithms that employ it are often slow, consume many system resources, and may be difficult to understand. However, some data structures, especially binary trees, are manipulated rather well with recursive algorithms.

We will look at some very simple recursive algorithms (computation of factorials and the Fibonacci sequence) and then see how to convert them to iterative algorithms (algorithms that do not use recursion). After we've explored the fundamental ideas about recursion, we will move to a data structure that is very useful and is usually manipulated with recursion (that is, binary trees).

7.1 Recursive Computation of a Factorial

The *factorial* of an integer `n` is `n * (n - 1) * (n - 2) ... * 1`. For example, the factorial of 5 is

```
5 * 4 * 3 * 2 * 1 = 120
```

As you can see, the factorial of 5 can be said to be `5 * factorial(4)`. In general, the factorial of any number `n` can be said to be `n * factorial(n - 1)`. The fact that we can create a definition of the factorial function that refers to *itself* makes the recursive computation of the factorial of any integer `n` rather easy to follow. Here's the code and the output created by the code.

Example 7.1 The Recursive Computation of the Factorial of a Number

```
#include <stdio.h>
main()
{
    long fact(int number);
    int number;
    char line[80];

    while(printf("Enter an integer: "), gets(line),
          sscanf(line, "%d", &number), number != 0)
    {
        printf("The factorial of %d is %ld\n", number,
               fact(number));
    }
}

long fact(int number)
{
     if (number == 1) return 1;
     else return number * fact(number - 1);
}
/*****************  Sample Output Below  ****************/
Enter an integer: 1
The factorial of 1 is 1
Enter an integer: 2
The factorial of 2 is 2
Enter an integer: 3
The factorial of 3 is 6
Enter an integer: 5
The factorial of 5 is 120
Enter an integer: 7
The factorial of 7 is 5040
Enter an integer: 8
The factorial of 8 is 40320
Enter an integer: 0  /***  End of input indicator.  ***/
$  /*** Operating system prompt.  We're done!  ***/
```

Of course, we intentionally simplified this code by not dealing with negative numbers. We should just reject them. The `fact()` function, though remarkably simple and short, displays the two cases that every recursive algorithm must have: (1) the *stopping* case, which causes the recursive calls to stop, and (2) the *recursive* case, which causes the current level of recursion to call the function yet another time.

You must have the stopping case. Otherwise, your function will recurse until the end of time or your machine runs out of stack space, whichever comes first. The stopping case in the `fact()` function says, if the parameter `number` passed to it is one, `return 1`. The recursive case says, if `number` is anything other than one, `return number * fact(number - 1)`.

Let's diagram how this function works until it hits the stopping case and then winds back through all the recursive calls and returns to `main()`.

```
Call 1: return 5 * fact(4);
Call 2: return 4 * fact(3);
Call 3: return 3 * fact(2);
Call 4: return 2 * fact(1);
Call 5: return 1; /****  The stopping case!!!  ****/
Return to Call 4: return 2 * 1;
Return to Call 3: return 3 * 2;  /*** The 2 is returned by
                                  Call 4.  ***/
Return to Call 2: return 4 * 6;  /*** The 6 is returned by
                                  Call 3.  ***/
Return to Call 1: return 5 * 24; /*** The 24 is returned by
                                  Call 2. ***/
                                 /***  120 Returned to
                                  main(). ***/
```

This was an easy recursion to follow, but I want to make it perfectly clear that we are using the `fact()` function merely to illustrate recursion. Here's how you would actually write `fact()`.

Example 7.2 Iterative (Nonrecursive) Version of the Factorial Function

```
long fact(int number)
{
     int total = 1;

     while (number) total *= number--;
     return total;
}
```

7.2 Recursive Computation of the Fibonacci Number Sequence

The Fibonacci number sequence looks like this:

```
1  1  2  3  5  8  13  21  34  55  89  ... and so on
```

Notice that once you get past the second number in the sequence, each number in the sequence is the sum of the two previous numbers; for example,

5 + 8 = 13. This makes the generation of the Fibonacci sequence easy to express recursively:

```
Fibonacci(n)  =  Fibonacci(n - 1)  +
                 Fibonacci(n - 2)       /*** For n > 2 ***/
```

Let's look at the C code that implements this.

Example 7.3 Recursive Generation of the Fibonacci Number Sequence

```
#include <stdio.h>
main()
{
   int fibonacci(int number), number, result;
   char line[80];

   while ( printf("Enter an integer: "), gets(line),
           sscanf(line,"%d", &number), number != 0)
   {
      result = fibonacci(number);
      printf("Fibonacci number %d is: %d\n", number, result);
   }
}  /*** End of main()  ***/


int fibonacci(int number)
{
   if (number == 1 || number == 2) return 1;
   else return fibonacci(number - 1) + fibonacci(number - 2);
}
/*************  Sample Program Session Below  *************/

Enter an integer: 1
Fibonacci number 1 is: 1
Enter an integer: 2
Fibonacci number 2 is: 1
Enter an integer: 3
Fibonacci number 3 is: 2
Enter an integer: 4
Fibonacci number 4 is: 3
Enter an integer: 5
Fibonacci number 5 is: 5
Enter an integer: 6
Fibonacci number 6 is: 8
Enter an integer: 7
Fibonacci number 7 is: 13
Enter an integer: 8
Fibonacci number 8 is: 21
```

```
Enter an integer: 9
Fibonacci number 9 is: 34
Enter an integer: 10
Fibonacci number 10 is: 55
Enter an integer: 0
$  /*** Operating system prompt.  Session is done.  ***/
/******  Sequence is correct: 1 1 2 3 5 8 13 21 34 55  ******/
```

Unlike the factorial algorithm, this algorithm is tough to follow! That's because the recursive case has two recursive calls in the `return`. The best way to deal with this is to follow a *recursion tree* diagram. What is that? Look below!

We will draw a diagram to compute the seventh Fibonacci number. In order to have enough room in the diagram, we will abbreviate the name of the function to `fib()`.

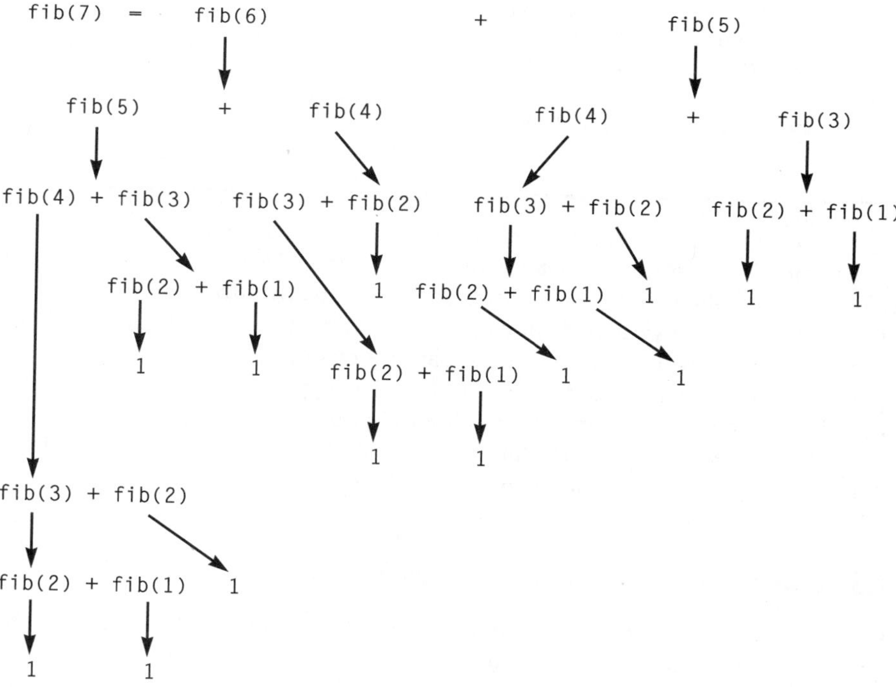

Pretty scary. Now I'm going to ask you to count all of the 1's in the diagram. There are 13 of them, aren't there? Look at the code output for the seventh Fibonacci number. That's right—it's 13, just the number we arrived at by following all the recursive calls out to their stopping cases in the diagram. The diagram does not represent an elegant proof, but it is certainly conclusive!

As usual, the Fibonacci sequence can, and should, be generated with an iterative algorithm. One look at the foregoing diagram should convince you that the function-call overhead for the recursive algorithm is way too expensive. Think how many calls there would be for, say, the 50th Fibonacci number! Thus, we now present the iterative version of the Fibonacci number generator.

Example 7.4 Iterative (Nonrecursive) Version of the Fibonacci Function

```
int fibonacci(int number)
{
    int curnum = 1, prevnum = 1, sum;

    if (number == 1 || number == 2) return 1;
    else number -= 2;
    while (number--)
    {
        sum = curnum + prevnum;
        prevnum = curnum;
        curnum  = sum;
    }
    return sum;
}
```

This is certainly a lot longer than the recursive version of `fibonacci()`, but believe me, it will run a lot faster. Count the calls to `fibonacci()` in the tree diagram that followed all the recursive calls out to the stopping case. That's right—there are 24 calls to `fibonacci()`. That's a lot of overhead. And this overhead increases depending on the parameter value.

The algorithm presented in Example 7.4 will perform *exponentially better* than the recursive algorithm as the value of `number` increases.

Now we're ready to look at a data structure that is usually inserted, searched, and traversed via recursive algorithms: the binary tree data structure.

7.3 The Binary Tree Data Structure

Thus far, we have looked at two types of storage structures: lists and list-like structures, and hash tables. List-like structures are excellent if you have a relatively small data volume and you need sequential record-processing capabilities. After all, because lists are ordered, once you find a record with a certain key, you can process the keys that immediately follow it.

However, access times for lists are slow. If you have 10,000 records, a search for an average record will take 5000 record accesses. Hash tables, as we have seen, provide lightning-fast record access. However, the keys in hash table records are in no particular order. Therefore, we cannot use hash tables if we are going to do sequential record processing.

The binary tree data structure makes possible rapid data access (not quite as good as hash tables but close enough!) and allows for sequential record processing. We will look at recursive and iterative algorithms for inserting into, deleting from, traversing, and searching binary trees. First, let's see how insertion into a binary tree works graphically. We'll assume that our records are minimal and have only one field, a string. Let's also assume that the record keys are entered in this order:

```
middle
zoo
cat
poodle
barge
riddle
mailer
apple
person
giraffe
```

Here's a view of how the tree will change after every two insertions (after the "middle" node).

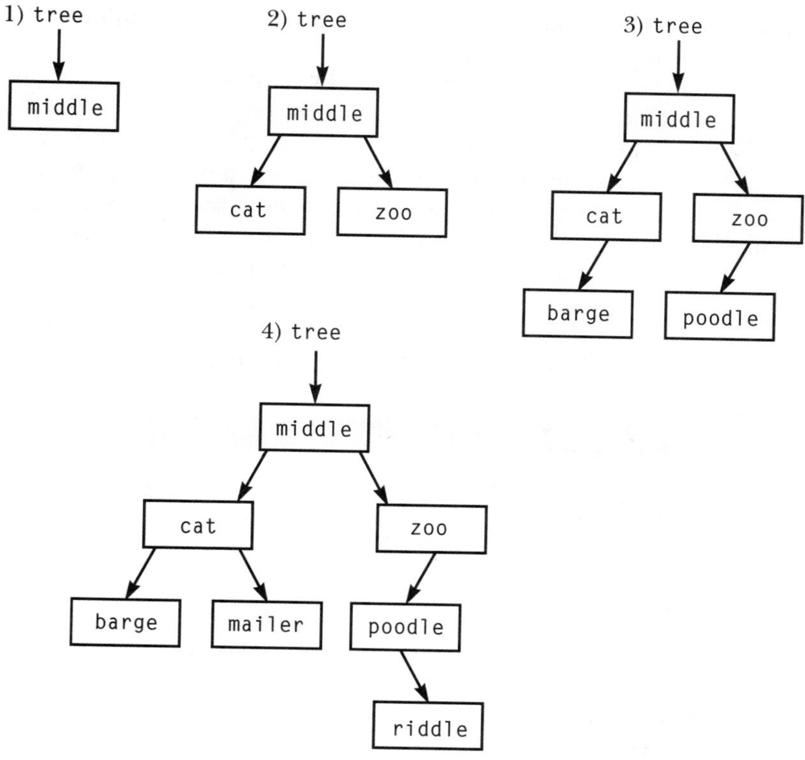

And now the final picture of the tree after all 10 insertions have been made:

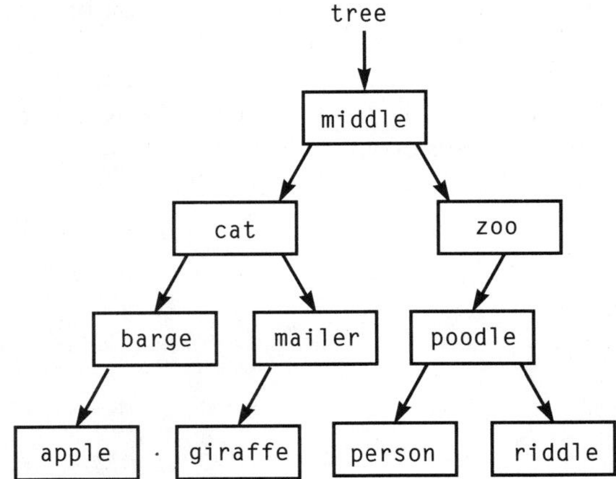

Unlike the trees in your yard, computer trees have their roots in the air and their leaves on the ground. All new nodes are *leaf* nodes. It is called a *binary* tree is because each node has two pointers (a "left" pointer to a node whose key value is less than the given node and a "right" pointer to a node whose key value is greater than the given node).

In the two diagrams above, all unused left or right pointers coming out of a node have the value `NULL`, so this is really an easy concept. When a new node is to be placed in the tree, you start at the *root* node (the one pointed at by the `tree` pointer) and ask the question "Is the key to my new node greater or less than the key to the node being pointed at?" If the answer is "less than," you follow the left pointer. If the answer is "greater than," you follow the right pointer. This process continues until a left or right pointer is found that is `NULL`.

Without further ado, we will look at two different versions of the tree insertion routine. The first is recursive and the second is iterative.

Example 7.5 Recursive Tree Insertion Code

```
void insert(char *word, NODE **tree)
{
   int compare;

   if (!(*tree))
   {
       if ((*tree = (NODE *) malloc(sizeof(NODE))) == NULL)
       {
           printf("Fatal malloc error!\n");
           exit(1);
```

```
        }
        if (((*tree)->word = (char *)
            malloc(strlen(word) + 1)) == NULL)
        {
            printf("Fatal malloc error!\n");
            exit(2);
        }
        (*tree)->left = (*tree)->right = NULL;
        strcpy((*tree)->word,word);
        return ;
    }
    compare = strcmp(word, (*tree)->word);
    if (compare < 0) insert(word,&(*tree)->left);
    else if (compare > 0) insert(word,&(*tree)->right);
    else printf("Word is already in tree.\n");
}
```

Well, you already know that this algorithm is bound to be slower than the iterative one, so let's proceed immediately to the correct version of `insert()`.

Example 7.6 Iterative Tree Insertion Code

```
/**************  NONRECURSIVE TREE INSERTION  ************/
NODE *insert(char *word, NODE *tree)
{
    NODE **tree_ptr_ref = &tree;
    int compare;

    while (*tree_ptr_ref)
    {
        compare = strcmp(word, (*tree_ptr_ref)->word);
        if (compare > 0)
        {
            tree_ptr_ref = &(*tree_ptr_ref)->right;
        }
        else if (compare < 0)
        {
            tree_ptr_ref = &(*tree_ptr_ref)->left;
        }
        else
        {
            printf("Node already in tree!\n");
            return tree;
        }
    }
    if ((*tree_ptr_ref = (NODE *) malloc(sizeof(NODE))) ==
        NULL)
```

```
    {
        printf("Fatal malloc error!\n");
        exit(1);
    }
    if ((((*tree_ptr_ref)->word =
        (char *) malloc(strlen(word) + 1)) == NULL)
    {
        printf("Fatal malloc error!\n");
        exit(2);
    }
    strcpy((*tree_ptr_ref)->word, word);
    (*tree_ptr_ref)->left  = (*tree_ptr_ref)->right = NULL;
    return tree;
}
```

Let me admit straightaway that many purists will howl with indignation at the iterative `insert()`, because it uses double indirection (the variable `tree_ptr_ref`) and they would substitute a version that is something like the tree version of the "chasing pointers" method we used with linked lists.

The beauty of the iterative `insert()` is that when it gets down to an insertion point (a `NULL` pointer), it has a *reference* to that `NULL` pointer called `tree_ref_ptr`. The following diagram shows exactly what is going on just after the `while` and before the `malloc()`.

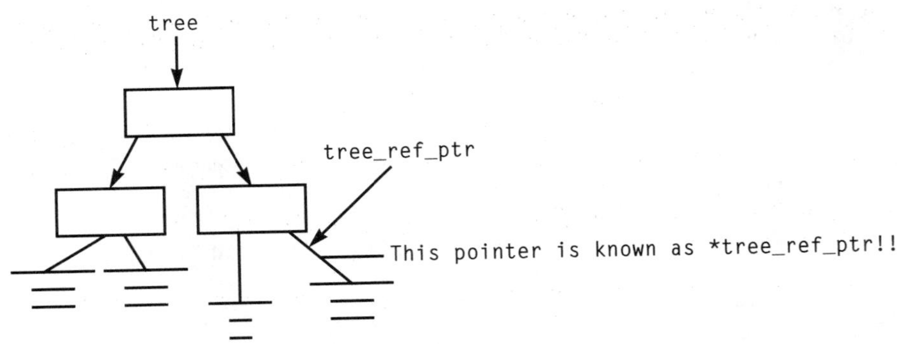

Assuming that the new insertion is to go off the right pointer of the right second-level node, the `tree_ref_ptr` has the address of this `NULL` pointer, and `*tree_ref_ptr` is its name! We leave it to the reader to understand the not-very-difficult recursive version of `insert()`. It, too, uses the dreaded double indirection, because if the tree is empty, then the value of `tree` will change, and therefore we must pass its address so that it comes back to the calling environment *with a changed value.* Otherwise, the tree would (mistakenly!) stay empty forever.

Searching for a node in a tree is not very much different from inserting a node into a tree. You do the same kind of key comparison seen in `insert()`. Again we show a recursive version followed by an iterative version.

Example 7.7 Recursive Tree Searching Code

```
NODE *find(char *word, NODE *tree)
{
    int  compare;

    if (!tree) return NULL;  /***  Got to the end      ***/
                             /***  of the tree. No     ***/
                             /***  success!!          ***/
    compare = strcmp(word,tree->word);
    if (compare < 0)       return find(word,tree->left);
    else if (compare > 0) return find(word,tree->right);
    else return(tree);    /****  We found it!!  ****/
}
```

Example 7.8 Iterative Tree Searching Code

```
NODE *find(char *word, NODE *tree)
{
    int  compare;
    NODE *mover;

    for (mover = tree; mover != NULL; )
    {
        compare = strcmp(word,mover->word);
        if (compare < 0)         mover = mover->left;
        else if (compare > 0)    mover = mover->right;
        else return mover;       /**** Found it!! ****/
    }
    return NULL;    /****  Got to the end of the tree  ****/
                    /****  without finding the node!!  ****/
}
```

In this case, the iterative `find()` isn't even more notationally formidable than the recursive `find()`.

7.4 Search Times in Binary Trees

Before we look at binary tree traversal and deletion, let's take a small look at the search times to find a target node in a binary tree. It's quite surprising. If you have a *randomly inserted* binary tree, the time it takes to find a target node is roughly

```
1.4 * log2 Number-of-Nodes
```

Thus if you had 1024 nodes (2 to the tenth power), you would find the target node, on average, in 1.4 × 10 searches—that is, 14 searches. In a linked list, it would take 512 searches! And the larger the number of nodes, the more the comparison favors trees. If you had about 16,000 nodes, your binary tree search would access about 1.4 × 14 (about 20) nodes. The linked list would need to access 8000 nodes—that's a lot!

But how can you ensure that your insertions are random? If you insert nodes that are already sorted, your binary tree is just a linked list that wastes all of its left pointers! If each node that comes in has a key greater than the preceding node, only right pointers will be followed.

If you read a data structures book, you will see many algorithms for creating *balanced binary trees.* These are trees whose height differs by no more than one level from any node's point of view. Here's a picture showing a balanced tree and one that is not balanced.

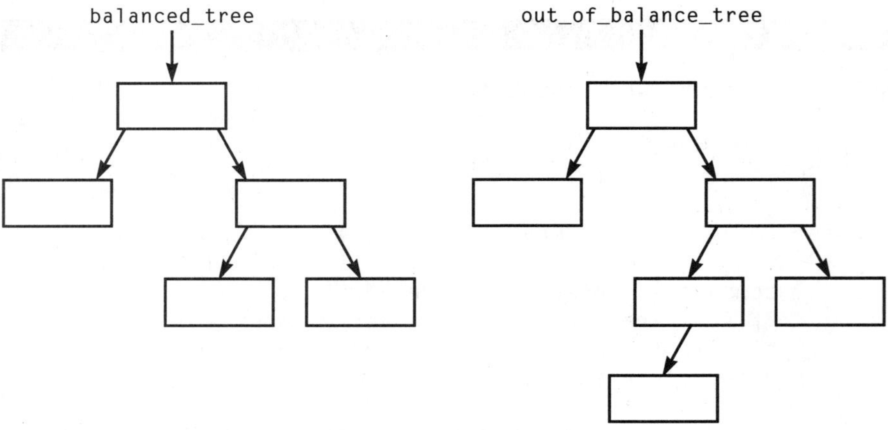

In the balanced tree, from the root node's point of view, there is a difference of only one level between its left and right subtrees. In the out-of-balance tree, there is a difference of two levels between its left and right subtrees. Does this mean that we must use a balancing algorithm?

It turns out that the balancing algorithms may consume more time than they are worth. Another ugly fact is that the code is quite complex. Therefore, it may pay big dividends to *randomize input before it is inserted into a tree structure.* How can you do this? By using random numbers.

Let's say you had a minimal data file with only one field per line. You would read the file and create a temporary output file with *one extra field per line*—a random number generated by the ANSI C `rand()` function. Then you would use your operating systems's sort utility and sort the records by this random number. The next piece of code will show this for a file that is in sorted order (an order that creates a horrid tree unless randomized).

Example 7.9 Randomizing a Sorted File

```
#include <stdio.h>
#include <stdlib.h>  /*** Has srand() and rand()  ***/
#include <string.h>  /*** Has strchr().            ***/
main(int argc, char *argv[])
{
    FILE *fpin, *fpout;
    char outfile[80], line[512];

    fpin  = fopen(argv[1],"r");
    sprintf(outfile, "new%s", argv[1]);
    fpout = fopen(outfile, "w");
    srand(5);  /***  Create seed for random number gen. ***/
    while (fgets(line, 512, fpin))
    {
        *(strchr(line,'\n')) = '\0';  /** Overwrite '\n' with
                                          '\0' **/
        fprintf(fpout, "%s %d\n", line, rand());
    }
}

/********************  Original File Below  ****************/

foo
bar
apple
papa
crab
banana
moo

/***********  Randomized File with Random Numbers  **********/

foo 18655
bar 8457
apple 10616
papa 31877
crab 10193
banana 25964
moo 18104

/***********  File Sorted by the Random Numbers  ***********/

bar 8457
crab 10193
apple 10616
```

```
moo 18104
foo 18655
banana 25964
papa 31877
```

This is just one technique to get rid of the overhead of using a balancing algorithm during program execution. The next section discusses another headache in tree manipulation.

7.5 Deleting Nodes from a Binary Tree

If you look at any data structures book that bothers to include the code (most don't!) for deletion from a binary tree, you will see another real mess that is not worth it. The problem is that the deletion has three possible cases:

1. The deleted node is a leaf node.
2. The deleted node has one child.
3. The deleted node has two children.

The result is a very messy algorithm whether you are talking about the iterative or the recursive version. Is it worth it? Generally, not at all. In most sessions where you are inserting and deleting from a binary tree, you are not going to delete, say, half the tree. But, even if you were, and if you had a 16,000-node tree, your searches will take 10 node accesses instead of 20.

No user will notice any change in program execution speed when such small numbers of node accesses are involved. They'll notice the difference between, say, 10 and 1000 (like the difference in access times between trees and lists), but not between 10 and 20. Thus the best deletion method is known as *lazy deletion.* In this method, you simply put in the key a character that is not part of any legitimate key. In the exercises, you will show how doing so changes insertion, deletion, and traversal of binary keys.

7.6 Traversing a Binary Tree

Traversal is the only binary tree operation that can't be done in a reasonable way without recursion. The following is the code for traversal, given our minimum nodes with only a string key and the left/right pointers.

Example 7.10 Traversing a Binary Tree

```
void printtree(NODE *tree)
{
    if (!tree) return;
    printtree(tree->left);
```

```
        printf("%s\n",tree->word);
        printtree(tree->right);
    }
```

This algorithm is exceedingly hard to explain. Fortunately, it is used as a kind of "canned" algorithm that doesn't require deep comprehension of its inner workings. You need to realize that this algorithm will visit every node on a binary tree. Thus, it is a good model for any algorithm that must perform some operation on every tree node.

A primitive but effective way to understand the algorithm is to think of it as no node's contents being printed until a left subtree is exhausted. Only after a left subtree is exhausted is a node printed, and then when `printtree (tree->right)` is called, once again, the call to `printtree(tree->left)` creates further recursions until a left subtree is, again, exhausted!

Now that we have seen all of the relevant functions, let's drive them with a `main()` function.

Example 7.11 Demonstration of Execution of Binary Tree Functions

```
#include <stdlib.h>
#include <string.h>
#include <stdio.h>

typedef struct node NODE;

struct node
{
    char word[20];
    NODE *left, *right;
};

main()
{
    char word[20];
    NODE *tree = NULL;
    NODE *find(char *word, NODE *tree);
    NODE *insert(char *word, NODE *tree);
    void printtree(NODE *tree);

    while (printf("Enter a string: "), gets(word),
            strcmp(word, "quit") != 0)
    {
        tree = insert(word, tree);
    }

    printf("\nEnd of insertions. Start searches.\n\n");
```

```
    while (printf("Enter a string: "), gets(word),
           strcmp(word, "quit") != 0)
    {
        if (find(word, tree)) printf("Found \"%s\"\n", word);
        else printf("Did not find \"%s\"\n", word);
    }

    printtree(tree);
}

/***************  Sample Program Session Below  ************/

Enter a string: mouse
Enter a string: dog
Enter a string: quiet
Enter a string: pan
Enter a string: house
Enter a string: raven
Enter a string: zoo
Enter a string: tree
Enter a string: quit

End of insertions. Start searches.

Enter a string: foo
Did not find "foo"
Enter a string: mouse
Found "mouse"
Enter a string: raven
Found “raven"

Enter a string: slap
Did not find "slap"
Enter a string: quit

dog        /*****  Execution of printtree()  *****/
house
mouse
pan
quiet
raven
tree
zoo
```

Notice that we called the `find()` function inside an `if` conditional. In this case, it works out well because the `if` reads like English—if I find the word in the tree, print it! Of course, if `find()` does not find `word` in the tree, it returns `NULL`, which conveniently equals "false" in an `if` conditional.

7.7 Forests and Other Tree Variants

Just as lists had variants such as arrays of lists, lists of lists, lists of queues, and so on, there are limitless variations on the basic binary tree data structure. A *forest,* as its name implies, is a group of two or more trees. For example, if last name was a key of a node and you wanted a tree for each letter starting a last name, you would create a forest of 26 trees.

Tree nodes, like any other kind of dynamic node, may point to a queue, a list, a stack, or even another tree. In the exercises, you will be given an assignment to build a concordance of identifiers in a file containing a C program. This will require that each tree node have a queue of line numbers. Your data structures will look like this:

```
struct linenumber
{
    long linenum;
    struct linenumber  *next;
};


struct treenode
{
    char *key; /**** Yes, we want totally dynamic
                 nodes! ****/
    struct treenode  *left, *right;
    struct linenumber  *front, *rear;
};
```

Conceptually, a tree of queues will be no harder to deal with than the Operating System Queues example of Chapter 3 (examples 3.20–3.23) or Exercise 5 of Chapter 3. This data structure, a hybrid of a linear data structure (a queue) and a tree, represents the final level of pointer-handling complexity addressed in this book. Have fun with Exercise 9!

Remember, above all, that when you are constructing a binary tree, the performance of the tree in insertions and searches depends, to a large degree, on how random the insertions were. If you cannot guarantee randomness, then you must rely on tree-balancing algorithms. These algorithms are inherently difficult to understand and create a considerable runtime cost.

The message here is simple: Randomize the data *before insertion.* This may involve creating a couple of utility programs to do so, but once created, these programs will enhance tree performance meaningfully at runtime. Your users will be happier.

Facts About Functions

`<stdlib.h>` Functions

Function: `void srand(unsigned int seed);`

Fact: 1) Initializes the C random number generator.

Fact: 2) If you want a different random number sequence than the one `rand()` is giving you, you must give `srand()` a different seed value. Otherwise, you are likely to get the same sequence.

Function: `int rand(void);`

Fact: 1) Generates a random number between 0 and the largest integer representable on your computer.

Fact: 2) The largest integer representable on your computer is the `INT_MAX` constant in the `limits.h` header file. This file generally contains limits for members of the `int` family, whereas `float.h` has limits for members of the `float` family.

Exercises

■ **1.** Write a function that reads an indefinitely long string and prints it backwards. This string will be terminated when the user hits the Return key. *Hint:* Recursion is involved.

■ **2.** Write a function that will count the nodes in a binary tree of `struct foo`s.

3. A binary tree has nodes with `int` keys. Nodes are inserted into the tree with keys in the following order: 22, 14, 35, 2, 23, 19, 29, 17, 6, 9, and 12. Draw a diagram showing what this tree will look like.

4. A tree has been created that looks like this:

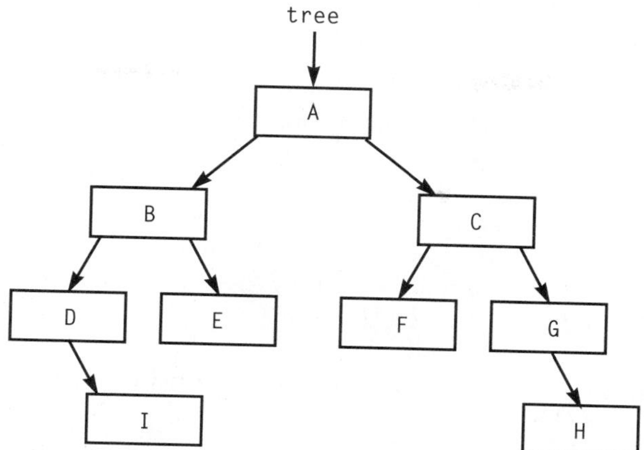

Show the order in which these nodes would be printed if this tree were printed out using the `printtree()` algorithm shown in this chapter.

■ **5.** Assume that lazy deletion was used on nodes in a tree whose nodes look like the ones in this chapter. Also assume that no node will have an asterisk (`*`) as part of the key. Show how the `find()` and `printtree()` algorithms will change.

6. Write a function `double power (int exponent, double number)` that computes and returns `number` to the `exponent` power. Write two versions: a recursive one and an iterative one. `Exponent` can be positive, negative, or zero.

■ **7.** Write a function that prints the part of a tree whose keys are equal to or greater than a key given as an argument. *Hint:* Do it recursively.

8. Write a program that will generate a concordance of an English text file. A concordance will list tokens in lowercase ASCII order in the following manner:

```
apple:      6.22  10.44  /* Page 6, line 22 and page 10,
                            line 44. */
astronaut: 7.55   22.56  /* Your output should be NEATLY
                            FORMATTED, too!! */
```

... etc...

When you read your text file, tokens will consist of any combination of the following:

a. Letters.

b. Digits.

c. Single quotes such as in the words *can't* and *won't.* A single quote must have a letter on both sides.

d. Hyphens, provided that they have a letter or digit on both sides.

Thus, `"a25"` will be a token. `"123"` will be a token. "`Bill-bob`" will be a token. "`Haven't`" will be a token. You may assume that all other ASCII characters will *not* be part of a token. Convert all letters in tokens to lowercase.

You will store all tokens in a binary tree whose nodes each contain the word and also pointers to the front and rear of a page number or line number queue. Make any assumption you wish about the number of lines per page.

9. Write a program that will read a user's C source file as specified on the command line and allow users to

a. Request a display of lines where a user-supplied identifier can be found. Users can do this repeatedly until they say "quit."

b. Request a cross-reference file after they say "quit" in task a. A cross-reference file will list identifiers and their line numbers like this:

```
apple       3  10  20
banana      5   8  15  25  30
cat         4   7
```

Your program will accomplish this task with the following rules applying:

a. A C identifier starts with a letter or underscore followed by any combination of letters, underscores, and digits.

b. No identifier occurs in comments or quoted strings (single or double!).

c. Identifiers will be put in tree nodes. Each tree node has a line number queue hanging off it.

d. Create an array of offsets of beginnings of line numbers so that user requests for lines that contain some identifier can be complied with *quickly.*

This exercise uses everything this book has taught you. Good luck!

■**10.** Write a function that gets integers from the user at the terminal and writes them into a binary file of `int`s *in the reverse order of their entry.* Do not enter invalid `int`s into the file. Tell the user when an entry has been rejected. The function must be recursive and accept one argument, the `FILE *` of the file to be created. You may assume that the file will be opened and closed outside of this function. The answer in the Appendix (and yours, too!) will also include a `main()` function to drive this recursive function.

Chapter 8

Multidimensional Arrays and Arrays of (Non-Char) Pointers

Multidimensional arrays introduce many problems that never arise when we are using arrays of only one dimension. They are more difficult to traverse and initialize. They introduce notational difficulties and hidden syntactic pitfalls. This chapter will show you a collection of tricks to help you get around the most formidable problems.

8.1 What Is an Element of a Multidimensional Array?

If you have used only one-dimensional arrays in C, you have been introduced to the idea that the name of an array is a pointer constant. It contains the address of the first element. Unfortunately, this is true only for one-dimensional arrays. For example, look at the following piece of code.

```
int  a[3][3];
memset(a, 0, 9 * sizeof(int));
```

Given what you have been told about arrays, this looks correct. But it is wrong! A good compiler should give you a type mismatch error on the argument `a` of `memset()`. It turns out that an *element* of a two-dimensional array is a one-dimensional array. Therefore, I'm going to give you a simple rule to memorize: *For arrays of dimension two or higher, you must pass the address of the first element to a function through notation using the & operator.*

Thus the foregoing memset() call should have been

```
memset(&a[0][0], 0, 9 * sizeof(int));
```

If you want to declare an int * variable p to point at the first element of array a, your declaration should be

```
int  *p = &a[0][0];   /***  Correct!  ***/
```

not

```
int  *p = a;   /***  Wrong!  Type of a is not int  *.  ***/
```

Because the rule we have stated is true for arrays of dimension two or higher, you should have no trouble with the above operations on arrays of three, four, or more dimensions. To set all elements of a 3-by-3-by-3 array a to be zeroes, you should say

```
memset(&a[0][0][0], 0, 27 * sizeof(int));
```

8.2 Declaration-Time Initialization of Multidimensional Arrays

We will start this section by demonstrating the initialization of two- and three-dimensional arrays.

Example 8.1 Initializing Two- and Three-Dimensional Arrays

```
#include <stdio.h>
main()
{
    int array2d[3][4] = { {0},              /* Init row 0 */
                          {1,2},            /* Init row 1 */
                          {3, 5, 4, 1}};    /* Init row 2 */

    int array3d[3][3][3] =
        { {{1, 2, 3}, {4}, {5, 6}},        /* Left index 0 */
          {{7} , {8}, {0}},                /* Left index 1 */
          {{0},  {9}, {10, 11, 12}}};      /* Left index 2 */

    int array2dnew[3][4] = {5, 7};
    int i, j, k;  /* Loop indices. */

    for (i = 0; i < 3; i++)
        for (j = 0; j < 4; j++)
        {
            printf("Array2d[%d][%d] = %d\n",
                   i, j, array2d[i][j]);
```

```
        }

    for (i = 0; i < 3; i++)
        for (j = 0; j < 4; j++)
        {
            printf("Array2dnew[%d][%d] = %d\n", i, j,
                    array2dnew[i][j]);
        }

    for (i = 0; i < 3; i++)
        for (j = 0; j < 3; j++)
            for (k = 0; k < 3; k++)
        {
            printf("Array3d[%d][%d][%d] = %d\n", i, j, k,
                    array3d[i][j][k]);
        }
}
/*****************  Program Output Below  *****************/

Array2d[0][0] = 0
Array2d[0][1] = 0
Array2d[0][2] = 0
Array2d[0][3] = 0
Array2d[1][0] = 1
Array2d[1][1] = 2
Array2d[1][2] = 0
Array2d[1][3] = 0
Array2d[2][0] = 3
Array2d[2][1] = 5
Array2d[2][2] = 4
Array2d[2][3] = 1

Array2dnew[0][0] = 5
Array2dnew[0][1] = 7
Array2dnew[0][2] = 0
Array2dnew[0][3] = 0
Array2dnew[1][0] = 0
Array2dnew[1][1] = 0
Array2dnew[1][2] = 0
Array2dnew[1][3] = 0
Array2dnew[2][0] = 0
Array2dnew[2][1] = 0
Array2dnew[2][2] = 0
Array2dnew[2][3] = 0

Array3d[0][0][0] = 1
Array3d[0][0][1] = 2
Array3d[0][0][2] = 3
Array3d[0][1][0] = 4
```

```
Array3d[0][1][1] = 0
Array3d[0][1][2] = 0
Array3d[0][2][0] = 5
Array3d[0][2][1] = 6
Array3d[0][2][2] = 0
Array3d[1][0][0] = 7
Array3d[1][0][1] = 0
Array3d[1][0][2] = 0
Array3d[1][1][0] = 8
Array3d[1][1][1] = 0
Array3d[1][1][2] = 0
Array3d[1][2][0] = 0
Array3d[1][2][1] = 0
Array3d[1][2][2] = 0
Array3d[2][0][0] = 0
Array3d[2][0][1] = 0
Array3d[2][0][2] = 0
Array3d[2][1][0] = 9
Array3d[2][1][1] = 0
Array3d[2][1][2] = 0
Array3d[2][2][0] = 10
Array3d[2][2][1] = 11
Array3d[2][2][2] = 12
```

The initialization of the two-dimensional array illustrates two principles: (1) You can do initialization on a row-by-row basis, and (2) the "insufficient initializers" rule that applied to one-dimensional arrays applies here as well. This rule states that if a declaration-time initialization has fewer initialization values than there are array elements, then the remaining unspecified values will be zero.

`Array2d` in Example 8.1 has three rows with four values in each row. Because the first row is given only one initializing value (`0`), the remaining three elements on that row are all zeroes. The second row is given two initializing values (`1` and `2`). The remaining two elements on that row are therefore given a value of zero. The third row is fully initialized with `3, 5, 4,` and `1`.

Multidimensional arrays in C are arranged in memory in *row major order.* For two-dimensional arrays, this means that `array2d` has its elements in memory in the following order:

[0][0]	[0][1]	[0][2]	[0][3]	[1][0]	[1][1]	[1][2]	[1][3]	[2][0]	[2][1]	[2][2]	[2][3]
0	0	0	0	1	2	0	0	3	5	4	1

An easy way to remember what row major order means is to remember that the row number is the leftmost index and that this index changes only after all values of the rightmost indices change. We will see shortly how this applies to three-dimensional arrays.

The array `array2dnew` in Example 8.1 was put there to illustrate that you are not required to initialize two-dimensional arrays on a row-by-row basis. In the initialization for `array2dnew`, the initializer is simply

```
{ 5, 7 };
```

This means that `array2dnew[0][0]` is assigned the value 5, `array2dnew[0][1]` is assigned the value 7, and all of the other elements of `array2dnew` are assigned zero.

Whereas it is easy to see what row major order means for a two-dimensional array, it is somewhat more difficult to see what it means for a three-dimensional array. However, all you have to do is understand the rule we just noted: The indices' "speed" of change goes from leftmost = slowest to rightmost = fastest. Keeping this in mind, you should find that the following memory layout of `array3d` from Example 8.1 makes sense.

[0][0][0]	[0][0][1]	[0][0][2]	[0][1][0]	[0][1][1]	[0][1][2]	[0][2][0]	[0][2][1]	[0][2][2]
0	2	3	4	0	0	5	6	0

[1][0][0]	[1][0][1]	[1][0][2]	[1][1][0]	[1][1][1]	[1][1][2]	[1][2][0]	[1][2][1]	[1][2][2]
7	0	0	8	0	0	0	0	0

[2][0][0]	[2][0][1]	[2][0][2]	[2][1][0]	[2][1][1]	[2][1][2]	[2][2][0]	[2][2][1]	[2][2][2]
0	0	0	9	0	0	10	11	12

This diagram, showing the change in indices in `array3d`, supports our theory that the general meaning of row major order layout of arrays in memory is that the leftmost index changes slowest and the rightmost the most rapidly. Can we give a more formal definition? Yes.

> *For any array of dimension* `[i][j][k]`, *the leftmost index will change its value i times, the middle index will change its value* $i \times j$ *times, and the rightmost will change its value* $i \times j \times k$ *times.*

If you simply count the changes in the foregoing diagram, you can see the truth of the rule just stated. The leftmost index changes its value 3 times, the middle index changes its value 3×3 times, and the rightmost index changes its value $3 \times 3 \times 3$ times.

In the initialization of the three-dimensional array, we create initializers for each row, where *row* is defined as each possible combination of the left and middle indices (nine combinations). As with two-dimensional arrays, you are not forced to do this kind of row-oriented initialization. For example, if we had initialized array3d like this:

```
int array3d[3][3][3] = { 1, 2, 3, 6};
```

then we would have gotten the following assignments:

```
array3d[0][0][0]:  1
array3d[0][0][1]:  2
array3d[0][0][2]:  3
array3d[0][1][0]:  6
All other elements of array3d: 0
```

Another common way to give array elements an initial value is at runtime with the memset() function from the string.h header file. However, this function is only really useful for giving all elements a starting value of zero. Let's look at memset's prototype again to see why.

```
void *memset(void *pointer, int value, size_t
                number_of_bytes);
```

Memset() puts value in each of the bytes starting at pointer and continuing for number_of_bytes. Thus if you wanted to give array3d elements a starting value of zero, you would say

```
memset(&array3d[0][0][0], 0, 27 * sizeof(int));
```

And this would work, because if each byte of a four-byte int is zero, the whole int is a zero. However, if you wanted to give all elements of array3d a starting value of 3, the following would be disastrous:

```
memset(&array3d[0][0][0], 3, 27 * sizeof(int));
```

This would put a 3 in *every byte* for 27 * sizeof(int) bytes starting at address &array3d[0][0][0]. Clearly, if a four-byte int has a 3 in each of its four bytes, the value of that int will not be 3! If you want to do such runtime initializations, I'm afraid you will have to resort to the "blunt instrument" of a thrice-nested for loop, such as

```
for (i = 0; i < 3; i++)
    for (j = 0; j < 3; j++)
        for (k = 0; k < 3; k++)
            array3d[i][j][k] = 3;
```

8.3 Row- and Column-Oriented Operations on Matrices

Two-dimensional arrays are usually referred to as tables or matrices. We will use the term *matrix* (plural, *matrices*) to refer to a two-dimensional array.

It is very common to perform operations on matrices where only a row or a column is operated upon. For example, if we had a file full of student test scores where each line in the file had N scores per student, we might read the scores into a matrix. If we averaged the scores over a row, we would produce the average score for one student. If we averaged the scores over a column, we would produce the class average on test K, where K is the column (test) number.

Let's look at some code that does row and column averaging.

Example 8.2 Averaging Across a Row or Column of a Matrix

```
/*   50 60 65 70       Contents of input file
     70 72 74 72
     80 85 90 85
     75 90 82 83
     67 73 67 73   */

#include <stdio.h>
#define NUMTESTS 4
main(int argc, char *argv[])
{
    FILE *fp;
    double colavg(int matrix[][NUMTESTS], int numstudents,
                  int testnum),
           rowavg(int matrix[][NUMTESTS], int numtests,
                  int studentnum);
    double result1, result2;
    int i,j;
    int matrix[5][4];  /****  Holds all the scores. ****/

    fp = fopen(argv[1],"r");
    for (i = 0; i < 5; i++)
        for (j = 0; j < 4; j++)
        fscanf(fp,"%d",&matrix[i][j]);

  /****  When users use this program, they will number  ****/
  /****  students and tests starting at one, not zero.  ****/
  /****  The averaging functions called below take this ****/
  /****  into account.                                   ****/

    result1 = colavg(matrix, 5, 2);
    result2 = rowavg(matrix, 4, 4);

    printf("Average score on test 2 for 5 students  = %f\n",
           result1);
    printf("Average score for student 4 for 4 tests = %f\n",
           result2);
}
```

```
double colavg(int matrix[][NUMTESTS], int numstudents,
              int testnum)
{
    long sum = 0;
    int i, *rowptr = &matrix[0][testnum - 1];

    for (i = 0; i < numstudents; i++)
    {
        sum +=  *rowptr;
        rowptr += NUMTESTS;
    }
    return (double) sum/numstudents;
}


double rowavg(int matrix[][NUMTESTS], int numtests,
              int studentnum)
{
    long sum = 0;
    int i, *colptr = &matrix[studentnum - 1][0];

    for (i = 0; i < numtests; i++)
    {
        sum += *colptr++;
    }
    return (double) sum/numtests;
}
/*****************  Program Output Below  *****************/

Average score on test 2 for 5 students  = 76.000000
Average score for student 4 for 4 tests = 82.500000
```

The key to understanding the `colavg()` function lies in understanding the declaration

```
int *rowptr = &matrix[0][testnum - 1];
```

This initializes `rowptr` to point at the `testnum - 1` column in row 0. The other tricky statement is

```
rowptr += NUMTESTS;
```

After we have added the score for the current student to the accumulator `sum`, we must skip over four test scores in `matrix` to get to the identical test for the next student. Each student took `NUMTESTS` tests, so this means adding `NUMTESTS int` storage units to whatever is in `rowptr` to get to the desired score.

Averaging scores for one student is easier than averaging a particular test for all students. This is because, once we arrive at the proper row, the four tests taken by that student lie contiguously in memory. Thus the declaration

```
int *colptr = &matrix[studentnum - 1][0];
```

gets us to the first test score of the proper student (`studentnum - 1`). Then, to get to the next test score for that student, we need only perform

```
colptr++;
```

8.4 Useful Tricks with Matrices

In the last section, we averaged over a row or column of a matrix. Obviously, one row of a matrix is a one-dimensional array. A column of a matrix is also a one-dimensional array. Moreover, because all of the scores added together in `rowavg()` lie next to one another in memory, could we write `rowavg()` differently so that we give it *only the address of the desired row?*

The problem, syntactically, is how we pass one row of a matrix to a function. The following code will show you how.

Example 8.3 How to Pass a Row of a Matrix into a Function

```
/*    50 60 65 70        Contents of array in input file
      70 72 74 72
      80 85 90 85
      75 90 82 83
      67 73 67 73    */

#include <stdio.h>
#define NUMTESTS 4
main(int argc, char *argv[])
{
    FILE *fp;
    double rowavg(int *rowptr, int numtests);
    double result;
    int i,j;
    int matrix[5][4];  /****  Holds all the scores. ****/

    fp = fopen(argv[1],"r");
    for (i = 0; i < 5; i++)
        for (j = 0; j < 4; j++)
            fscanf(fp,"%d",&matrix[i][j]);

    result = rowavg(matrix[2], 4);  /*** Student 3's row ***/
```

```
    printf("Average score for student 3 for 4 tests = %f\n",
        result);
}


double rowavg(int *colptr, int numtests)
{
    long sum = 0;
    int i;

    for (i = 0; i < numtests; i++)
    {
        sum += *colptr++;
    }
    return (double) sum/numtests;
}
/*****************  Program Output Below  ****************/

Average score for student 3 for 4 tests = 85.000000
```

It worked! But why? Remember that an element of a two-dimensional array of `int` is not one `int`. It's a row! Why? Let's look at two expressions:

```
matrix[2][3]
*(*(matrix + 2) + 3)
```

You may have guessed from your experience with the array and pointer versions of elements of one-dimensional arrays that these two expressions represent identical values. Hence the name `matrix`, just as I claimed earlier, is not an `int *`; it's an `int **`. Thus `matrix[2]` in Example 8.3 is really `*(matrix + 2)`, and the data type of that is `int *`—the `int *` that points to the first element of the third row (the one with index `2`).

Confused? Remember how pointer arithmetic works in C: When you add a value to a pointer, it jumps a certain number of *storage units* dictated by the type of the pointer. I have told you that `matrix` actually points at a *row*, so adding 2 to it jumps two rows of `int`s. Thus `*(matrix + 2)` (which is the same as `matrix[2]`) jumps two rows from where `matrix` points, and the dereference gives us the first `int` in that row.

This trick cannot work for column averaging for one simple reason—the numbers in a column do not lie next to one another in memory. Therefore, we must stick with the version of `colavg()` that we have, where we passed the entire matrix to the function.

Another useful trick with matrices is to treat a matrix as a one-dimensional array. Where would this be useful? Suppose we wanted a function to compute the average of all test scores in the class. We could do this with the following function.

Example 8.4 Averaging Over a Whole Matrix (Bad Version!)

```
double class_average(int matrix[][NUMTESTS], int numstudents)
{
    int *mover = &matrix[0][0];
    long sum = 0;
    int i;

    for (i = 0; i < NUMTESTS * numstudents; i++)
    {
        sum += *mover++;
    }
    return (double) sum/(NUMTESTS * numstudents);
}
```

This is a very undesirable solution for two reasons: (1) we need to have a constant like `NUMTESTS` so that we can pass the second dimension of `matrix` to the function, and (2) the function, therefore, works only on matrices with `NUMTESTS` columns. If a matrix is of dimension `N`, the function header must be given the rightmost `N - 1` dimensions. It's the law!

Thus the function in Example 8.4 is highly deficient. The function that follows is the correct way to average over a whole matrix.

Example 8.5 Averaging Over a Whole Matrix (Good Version!)

```
double class_average(int *matrix_ptr, int numscores)
{
    long sum = 0;
    int i;

    for (i = 0; i <  numscores; i++)
    {
        sum += *matrix_ptr++;
    }
    return (double) sum/numscores;
}
```

The calling statement for `class_average` would look like this:

```
average = class_average(&matrix[0][0], numscores);
```

The beauty of this function is that, in fact, it can be used on arrays *of any dimension.* You simply pass the address of the first element of the array and the total number of scores. C doesn't care how few or how many dimensions the original array had.

8.5 The C Memory Mapping Formula for Arrays

Before we move to our next topic, let's clear up a mystery that has existed since the day you discovered C arrays. Why, when passing an array to a function, do you *not* need to pass the size of the leftmost dimension? And, of course, if the array is a one-dimensional array, you don't have to pass the dimension at all!

The answer lies in the algorithm C uses to find a particular element when you ask for it. For example, suppose you have an array declared as

```
int array[2][3][4];
```

If you ask for a particular `array[i][j][k]`, C finds it by using a formula that it constructs for this array. It is

```
*(&array[0][0][0] + (3 * 4 * i) + (4 * j) + k)
```

Thus, if we wanted `array[1][2][2]`, we would expect it to be

```
(3 * 4 * 1) + (4 * 2) + 2 = 22
```

22 `int` units past `array[0][0][0]`. That is exactly correct. But notice what is missing in the memory map formula for `array`: the size of the leftmost dimension—that is, 2! It isn't needed, and that is the reason why, when passing an array to a function, you need not specify the size of the leftmost dimension. It makes no difference how many dimensions an array is; the memory map formula will not include a coefficient for the leftmost dimension.

8.6 Array Tricks to Be Avoided: A Little Knowledge Is Dangerous!

When some programmers find out that `array[2][2]` is the same as `*(*(array + 2) + 2)`, many actually try this out in a real program. Don't! It is dreadfully unreadable, and this negates any speed advantage you might obtain by avoiding the memory map formula that is applied when indexing is used.

Another legal but horrible practice involves indexing tricks such as this:

```
int array[3][4], j;
/***** Some code assigns the elements of array here! *****/
j = array[0][6];
```

Wait a minute! If the number of columns in `array` is 4, how can I use 6 as the value of the second index? Remember that, in C, indices merely hide pointer arithmetic. `Array[0][6]` just breaks down to `*(*array + 6)`, which gets the sixth integer past the one that `*array` points at. This turns out to be the same `int` as `array[1][2]`.

Believe it or not, the compiler and the runtime system will let you get away with `array[0][6]`! The lack of extra runtime checking is one of the reasons why C code executes so swiftly. This blessing is also a curse if programmers are more interested in being clever than in producing crystal-clear code. Unfortunately, many untamed egos have ruined software. Just make sure that, for the good of all concerned, you leave your ego outside of your code!

8.7 "Ragged" Arrays and Arrays of Non-Char Pointers

It is also possible to create multidimensional arrays whose row sizes vary from row to row. Here is an example.

Example 8.6 Creation of a Ragged Two-Dimensional Array of Int

```
#include <stdio.h>
main()
{
    int *p[3], i;
    int a[3] = {1, 2, 3};
    int b[5] = {6, 7, 8, 9, 10};
    int c[4] = {9, 10, 11, 12};

    p[0] = a;
    p[1] = b;
    p[2] = c;

    /***** Now p is a "ragged" 2-D array because the  *****/
    /***** row sizes are all different!               *****/

    for (i = 0; i < 3; i++)
        printf("p[0][%d] = %d\n", i, p[0][i]);
    for (i = 0; i < 5; i++)
        printf("p[1][%d] = %d\n", i, p[1][i]);
    for (i = 0; i < 4; i++)
        printf("p[2][%d] = %d\n", i, p[2][i]);
}
/*******************  Program Output Below  ***************/

p[0][0] = 1
p[0][1] = 2
p[0][2] = 3
p[1][0] = 6
p[1][1] = 7
p[1][2] = 8
p[1][3] = 9
```

```
p[1][4] = 10
p[2][0] = 9
p[2][1] = 10
p[2][2] = 11
p[2][3] = 12
```

As you can see, the program in Example 8.6 creates a "pseudomatrix" with rows of 3, 5, and 4 ints, respectively. I call it a pseudomatrix because it is not a real matrix. Remember that in a real matrix, all elements from the first to the last lie next to one another in memory. That is not the case with variable p in Example 8.6 for the obvious reason that we have no guarantee that arrays a, b, and c lie next to one another in memory.

Therefore, you cannot process p in the same way that we processed a matrix in Example 8.5. The same caution applies when you create a matrix from scratch, as shown in Example 8.7.

Example 8.7 Creation of a Ragged Array via Dynamic Allocation

```
#include <stdio.h>
#include <stdlib.h>    /***  Contains malloc() and exit.   ***/
main()
{
    int **p, **mover, i;

    /******  Make p point at 5 (unassigned) pointers.  ******/
    if ((p = (int **) malloc(5 * sizeof(int *))) == NULL)
    {
         printf("Fatal malloc error!\n");
         exit(1);
    }
    /****** Allocate space for all pointers in p to     ******/
    /****** point at something. Each pointer in p will ******/
    /****** point to a row of integers.  Each row       ******/
    /****** will be a different size!                    ******/
    for (mover = p, i = 0; i < 5; i++, mover++)
    {
         if ((*mover = (int *) malloc((i + 2) * sizeof(int)))
              == NULL)
         {
              printf("Fatal malloc error!\n");
              exit(2);
         }
    }
/****  Row sizes of p: 2, 3, 4, 5, and 6, respectively. ****/
}
```

Here, too, we must call `p` a pseudomatrix because there is no guarantee that the memory we request from `malloc()` will lie next to the memory given to us by a previous call to `malloc()`. Some mathematical applications use ragged arrays. They are rather rare in nonmathematical applications.

Finally, recall from Chapter 4 that arrays of pointer to `char` are ragged arrays. Reread the section on using `realloc()` (Section 4.11) before turning to the exercises in this chapter.

Facts About Functions

No new functions were introduced in this chapter, nor were any old functions used in a new way.

Exercises

■ **1.** An identity matrix is a matrix with ones on its main diagonal (same row and column index) and zeroes everywhere else. Declare and initialize a 4-by-4 identity matrix `m`. You should give yourself full credit for the shortest answer only!

■ **2.** A program has the following declarations:

```
int  a[3][4] = { {1, 3, 5},
                 {2, 4},
                 {6} };
int  *p = &a[1][1];
```

You know that the computer running this program has four-byte `int`s and pointers and that `&a[0][0]` is 1000. Give the value of the following expressions, or give `error` if the expression is not correct.

a. `**p` **b.** `*(*(a + 1) + 1)`

c. `*(*a + 1) + 1` **d.** `a[1][1]`

e. `**a` **f.** `sizeof(p)`

g. `sizeof(a)`
h. `*(p + 3)`
i. `p[2]`
j. `a[0][5]`
k. `p`
l. `p - a[1]`
m. `p - (*a)`
n. `*p * (**a)`
o. `p[-1]`
p. `*a[2]`
q. `*a[-1]`
r. `p - a`
s. `*a + 1`
t. `&p[2]`

3. Write a function that gets one `int *` parameter representing an array and one `int` parameter containing the number of elements in the array. The function will return an array containing the addresses of all array elements whose value is zero. *Hint:* Use `realloc()`. *Another hint:* The returned array should waste no space except for the `NULL` sentinel value in the last element. You have to figure out what the return type of the function is all by yourself.

■ **4.** Write a function that processes the array returned by the function in Exercise 3. This function will return the number of elements from the array parameter in Exercise 3 that had a value of zero.

■ **5.** A program has the following declaration:

```
int a[5][4][3][2];
```

Give the memory map formula that C will construct to access `a[q][r][s][t]`.

6. Write a function that takes three parameters:

a. An array of pointer to `int`.
b. An array of `int` where each element has the row size of each row of `int`s in the first parameter.
c. The number of elements in the first parameter (and the second, by implication).

Your function will report the row numbers of any two rows in the first parameter that *are contiguous in memory.*

7. An `int` array `a` has `num` elements. Write a code fragment that will put the address of every odd-indexed element of `a` in `p`. You must declare `p` as well.

■ **8.** A program has the following declaration:

```
int **p;
```

Assume that `p` is built into a ragged array of `int` with the last pointer in the array given `NULL` as a sentinel value. Each row of `int`s ends with a `-1` sentinel value. Write a function to compute and return the sum of all nonsentinel values in `p`.

9. Write a declaration and initialization of the matrix `m` if it is to have five columns and four rows and all array elements are zeroes except `m[0][2] = 4`, `m[1][1] = 5`, `m[1][3] = 2`, and `m[2][2] = 6`.

■**10.** You do not know how many bits are in an `unsigned long` on your computer. You have an array of `unsigned long` called `array`. Show how to turn every bit of every element of `array` on. You must do it in *one statement.* You are given the condition that `array` has `N` elements.

■**11.** Write a function that will create and return a ragged two-dimensional array. The function will be given an `int` array argument whose first element contains the number of rows in the ragged array and the remaining elements contain the row sizes. The function should return `NULL` if it is unable to create the ragged array. *Note:* You are merely creating the space for the ragged array—you are *not* assigning values to the elements. The answers to Exercises 11 and 12 are given together in the Appendix, along with a `main()` driver function to show that they work.

■**12.** Assume that the array created in Exercise 11 has been populated with values. Write a function that will take the same argument as Exercise 11 along with the ragged array itself and will print out all the values in the ragged array. See the note at the end of Exercise 11.

Chapter 9

Potpourri: Part One

The last two chapters of this book present topics that, though important, do not contain enough material to fill an entire chapter. Don't be misled by the brevity of coverage of these topics. They're important—they just don't take many pages to cover!

In this chapter, we will discus the ANSI C time functions, pointers to functions, functions with variable-length argument lists, and understanding difficult data type declarations. The time functions are particularly important. You would be hard pressed to think of any aspect of computing where time calculations are not involved. Business reports are usually dated. Database systems keep track of the time when database changes and searches are made. Operating systems keep track of who made what request and *when* they made it. Performance benchmarking of programs is accomplished using the time functions to compute the wall-clock time it takes for a code fragment to execute. The list is endless.

Pointers to functions is a topic in C that deserves more attention than it gets. System function libraries for many operating systems include routines that require that one of the arguments be a pointer to a function. The most confusing aspect of using pointers to functions is the syntax, because the ANSI and pre-ANSI methods are quite different. Read Section 9.2 and you will learn both.

Have you ever wondered how `printf()`, `scanf()`, and other functions in the C library work? Unlike the functions you've written, they allow argument lists of any size. In Section 9.3, you'll find out how you can write such functions yourself.

Finally, Section 9.4 will help programmers understand such difficult declarations as arrays of function pointers, functions returning a pointer to a function, and so forth by using the right-left rule. You won't want to miss this!

9.1 The ANSI C Time Functions

Example 9.1 Using the ANSI C Time Functions

```
#include <stdio.h>
#include <time.h>  /****  Location of time functions.  ****/
main()
{
    struct tm *timeptr;  /*** Notice lack of allocation!  ***/
    time_t timeval;
    char *chtime;   /****  No space allocation again!!  ****/
    char buffer[80];

    time(&timeval);  /*** Timeval = seconds since 1/1/70. ***/

    timeptr = localtime(&timeval);
    printf("Local time: %d hours, %d minutes\n\n",
           timeptr->tm_hour, timeptr->tm_min);

    timeptr = gmtime(&timeval);
    printf("Greenwich time:  %d hours, %d minutes\n\n",
           timeptr->tm_hour, timeptr->tm_min);

    chtime = asctime(timeptr);
    printf("Greenwich ASCII time from asctime: %s\n\n",
           chtime);

    timeptr = localtime(&timeval);
    chtime = asctime(timeptr);
    printf("Local ASCII time from asctime:  %s\n\n", chtime);

    /******  Difference between ctime() and asctime()  ******/
    /******  is that asctime() takes a struct tm        ******/
    /******  pointer, ctime() takes a time_t pointer.  ******/
    chtime = ctime(&timeval);
    printf("Local ASCII time from ctime: %s\n\n", chtime);
}
/****************  Program Output Below  ****************/

Local time: 19 hours, 47 minutes
```

```
Greenwich time:  3 hours, 47 minutes

Greenwich ASCII time from asctime: Fri Nov 22 03:47:18 1996

Local ASCII time from asctime:  Thu Nov 21 19:47:18 1996

Local ASCII time from ctime: Thu Nov 21 19:47:18 1996
```

Notice that the `time()` function is the core time function. Although its return value is seldom used directly, the return value is used by virtually *all the other time functions*. The return value from `time()`, though it is not forced by the ANSI C standard, is generally the number of seconds since January 1, 1970. The prototype for the `time()` function is

```
time_t time(time_t *timeval);
```

As was the case with the `size_t` data type, the `time_t` type was invented to ensure portability between systems but is almost always defined as a `long` in actual practice. The return value is the same as the value placed into the parameter, so it need not be used. The functions `localtime()`, `gmtime()`, and `asctime()` all use the `time_t *` variable acquired by the `time()` function to produce the current time in different forms. The prototypes for these three functions are

```
struct tm *localtime(time_t *tptr);
struct tm *gmtime(time_t *tptr);
char *asctime(time_t *tptr);
```

Notice that both `localtime()` and `gmtime()` return a `struct tm` pointer. Notice also, in Example 9.1, that the program allocates space for a `struct tm` *pointer* and not for a `struct tm`. This tells you that `localtime()` and `gmtime()` have a local `static struct tm` whose space allocation persists even after you return from these functions. Likewise, `asctime()` must have a local `static char *`, because you will notice in Example 9.1 that we have not allocated space for the `char *` variable `chtime`.

The components of the `struct tm` data type are as follows:

Component	Meaning	Values
`tm_sec`	Seconds after current minute	0 to 59
`tm_min`	Minutes after current hour	0 to 59
`tm_hour`	Current hour (military time)	0 to 23
`tm_mday`	Day of the current month	0 to 31
`tm_wday`	Days since the most recent Sunday	0 to 6
`tm_yday`	Days since January 1	0 to 365
`tm_mon`	Months since January	0 to 11
`tm_year`	Years since 1900	`Current_year -1900`

Component	Meaning	Values
tm_isdst	Daylight savings time?	Positive if it is. Zero if it isn't. Negative if unknown.

In Example 9.1, we used only a couple of the components in the struct tm returned by localtime() and gmtime(). However, another time function that we will look at later uses all of the components—the strftime() function.

Generally, if a programmer wants a complete local time specification with day, month, year, hour, minute, and second, localtime() and gmtime() are overkill because your printf() has to specify all the components of the struct tm used. Ctime() is the function to use when you want the most time information with the least effort! The prototype for ctime() is

```
char *ctime(time_t *tptr);
```

Notice that this is easier to use than asctime(), because asctime() requires a struct tm * argument. Thus asctime() must be called after either localtime() and gmtime(), and these two functions must be called after time() is called. Ctime(), on the other hand, can immediately follow a call to time(), because it requires only the time_t * value obtained by time().

One remaining mystery from Example 9.1 is the necessity for the gmtime() function. Gmtime() gives the time in Greenwich, England. The military, airports, and government research stations often issue reports with the time given in Greenwich Mean Time.

However, as mysterious as the use of gmtime() may seem to most civilians, it actually has one very practical use. Because it is the zero time for the world (you'll see what I mean by that), it can be used to compute things like the number of hours and minutes a user has been logged in and the amount of wall-clock time a certain code segment takes to execute. If you are interested in breaking wall-clock time into hours, minutes, and so on, use gmtime() as shown in Example 9.2. If you're interested in seconds only, use difftime() as shown in Example 9.2.

Example 9.2 Program Benchmarking Using Gmtime and Difftime

```
#include <stdio.h>
#include <time.h>
main()
{
    long i;
    float ftime;
    time_t time1, time2, diff;
    struct tm *tptr;
```

```
    time(&time1);
    for (i = 0; i < 1000000000; i++) ;
    time(&time2);
    diff = time2 - time1;
    tptr = gmtime(&diff);
    printf("1 billion for loops took %d seconds!\n",
          tptr->tm_sec);
    ftime = difftime(time2, time1);
    printf("1 billion for loops took %f seconds!\n", ftime);
}
/*****************  Program Output Below  ***************/

1 billion for loops took 16 seconds!
1 billion for loops took 16.000000 seconds!
```

Notice that `difftime()` is less useful if we are benchmarking something that takes a huge amount of wall-clock time to execute, because it gives a floating-point seconds value only. `Gmtime()` can be used to break time into hours, minutes, seconds, and so forth.

Why does the `gmtime()` trick work? Because you want the number of seconds to be *relative to the zero time zone.* Of course, if we looked at the other `struct tm` components returned by `gmtime()`, it would say January 1, 1970 and so forth. But for getting hours, minutes, and seconds, nothing can beat it!

Why does `difftime()` return a `float`? Because it makes no assumption about the units of a `time_t` variable. They might be seconds, milliseconds, microseconds, nanoseconds—who knows? The units might *not* be an integer multiple of seconds, so they played it safe by specifying a `float` return value.

Now let's look at some code that demonstrates the most flexible time function of them all, `strftime()`.

Example 9.3 Demonstration of the `Strftime` Function

```
#include <stdio.h>
#include <time.h>  /****  Location of time functions.  ****/
main()
{
   struct tm *timeptr;  /*** Notice lack of allocation!  ***/
   time_t timeval;
   char buffer[80];

   time(&timeval);

   timeptr = localtime(&timeval);

   strftime(buffer, 80, "%c\n", timeptr);
   printf("Strftime %%c format\n");
```

```
    printf("-------------------\n %s\n", buffer);

    strftime(buffer, 80, "%A, %B %d, %H:%M\n", timeptr);
    printf("Strftime %%A, %%B, %%d, %%H:%%M format\n");
    printf("--------------------------------------\n %s\n",
           buffer);

    strftime(buffer, 80, "%a, %b %d, %H:%M\n", timeptr);
    printf("Strftime %%a, %%b, %%d, %%H:%%M format\n");
    printf("--------------------------------------\n %s\n",
           buffer);

    strftime(buffer, 80, "%a, %b %d, %I:%M %p\n", timeptr);
    printf("Strftime %%a, %%b, %%d, %%I:%%M %%p format\n");
    printf("------------------------------------------\n %s\n",
           buffer);

    strftime(buffer, 80, "%a, %b %d, %I:%M %p, %Y\n",
             timeptr);
  printf("Strftime %%a, %%b, %%d, %%I:%%M %%p, %%Y format\n");
  printf("----------------------------------------------\n %s\n",
         buffer);

    strftime(buffer, 80, "%a, %b %d, %I:%M %p, %y\n",
             timeptr);
  printf("Strftime %%a, %%b, %%d, %%I:%%M %%p, %%y format\n");
  printf("----------------------------------------------\n %s\n",
         buffer);
}
/******************  Program Output Below  ***************/

Strftime %c format
-------------------
 Fri Nov 22 17:02:28 1996

Strftime %A, %B, %d, %H:%M format
--------------------------------------
 Friday, November 22, 17:02

Strftime %a, %b, %d, %H:%M format
--------------------------------------
 Fri, Nov 22, 17:02

Strftime %a, %b, %d, %I:%M %p format
------------------------------------------
 Fri, Nov 22, 05:02 PM
```

```
Strftime %a, %b, %d, %I:%M %p, %Y format
-----------------------------------------------------
 Fri, Nov 22, 05:02 PM, 1996

Strftime %a, %b, %d, %I:%M %p, %y format
-----------------------------------------------------
 Fri, Nov 22, 05:02 PM, 96
```

The annotated output in Example 9.3 should give you a good idea of the differences among the various time format indicators in `strftime()`. `Strftime()` (which stands for `String` `Formatted` `Time`) is like a time-related cousin of `sprintf()`. It allows us to format a time string in lots of different ways: with a 24- or 12-hour clock (`%H` versus `%I`), with a fully spelled-out day versus a three-character day abbreviation (`%A` versus `%a`), with a fully spelled-out month versus a three-character month abbreviation (`%B` versus `%b`), with a four-digit year versus a two-digit year (`%Y` versus `%y`), and with an AM/PM spec (`%p`).

As you can see in the first line of output, the `%c` format gives you a full-time spec similar to that given by the `asctime()` and `ctime()` functions. Therefore, it is seldom used. The list of format variations given here is not a complete list of all available formats, but it shows all of the really useful variants.

9.2 Pointers to Functions

Function pointers are really useful, but they are not given much coverage in most C texts. Many low-level system calls in most operating systems have functions with pointer-to-function parameters. Many mathematical functions also require pointer-to-function parameters—for example, `sin(x)` on one call versus `cos(x)` on another call to the same function. Two code examples follow. The first illustrates pointers to functions using the pre-ANSI C syntax. The second illustrates the easier ANSI C syntax.

Example 9.4 Demonstration of Old (Pre-ANSI) Style Pointers to Functions

```
#include <stdio.h>
main()
{
    float reciprocal(int), square(int),
          funsum(int, float (*f)(int));

    printf("Sum of 5 reciprocals: %f\n",
           funsum(5,reciprocal));
    printf("Sum of 3 squares: %f\n", funsum(3,square));
}
```

```
float funsum(int n, float (*f)(int))
{
    float sum = 0.0;
    int i;

    for (i=1; i <= n; i++) sum += f(i);
    return sum;
}
float reciprocal(int k)
{
    return 1.0/k ;
}

float square(int k)
{
    return (float) k * k;
}

/*****************  Program Output Below  ****************/

Sum of 5 reciprocals: 2.283334
Sum of 3 squares: 14.000000
```

Example 9.5 Demonstration of New (ANSI) Style Pointers to Functions

```
#include <stdio.h>
main()
{
    float reciprocal(int), square(int),
          funsum(int, float f(int));

    printf("Sum of 5 reciprocals: %f\n",
           funsum(5,reciprocal));
    printf("Sum of 3 squares: %f\n", funsum(3,square));
}


float funsum(int n, float f(int))
{
    float sum = 0.0;
    int i;

    for (i=1; i <= n; i++) sum += f(i);
    return sum;
}
```

```
float reciprocal(int k)
{
    return 1.0/k ;
}


float square(int k)
{
    return (float) k * k;
}

/******************  Program Output Below  ****************/

Sum of 5 reciprocals: 2.283334
Sum of 3 squares: 14.000000
```

The difference between the old style and the new style can be seen in the two declarations:

```
float (*f) (int)
float f (int)
```

The new, ANSI style was invented because it's easier to use, but is it clearer? I don't think so. The old, pre-ANSI style makes it much clearer that `f` really is a pointer. This is one of the very few areas where I disagree with the ANSI committee. I hate the "dumbing down" of a language when the feature really isn't hard to use.

With either style, note that you pass the function pointer to `funsum()` by just giving the name of the function to be passed. Inside of `funsum()`, the call to function `f()` is really a sneaky call to whichever function was passed (`reciprocal()` in one call to `funsum()` and `square()` in the other call).

The final point to be made about pointers to functions is that the syntax is the same whether you are passing a pointer to a function that *you* wrote or to a function that is in the C library. Thus, if you want a function to use the `sin()` of a variable `x` in one call to the function, and the `cos()` of `x` in another, and the function is called `trig()`, its prototype may look like this:

```
double trig (double x, double (*trigfunc) (double x));
```

A call to `trig()` that passes the `math.h` `sin()` function may look like this:

```
varname = trig(x, sin);
```

All of the functions whose names you pass as parameters *must have the same return type and the same number and type of parameters.* Thus you couldn't call `trig()` with a pointer to a function with, say, two `int` parameters or a `struct` pointer return type. Don't forget this important point! You'll get a compile-time error if you do.

9.3 Functions with Variable-Length Argument Lists

Writing functions with variable-length argument lists is actually quite easy, because it is a very static technology. All such functions feature the same three functions (`va_start()`, `va_arg()`, and `va_end()`) and a new data type (`va_list`). As usual, the easiest way to show how to write such a function is to offer an example.

Example 9.6 Functions with Variable-Length Argument Lists

```
#include <stdarg.h> /** Contains va_start, va_arg, va_end,  **/
                    /** and the va_list data type.          **/
#include <stdio.h>
#include <string.h>
main()
{
    double sumargs(int n,...);
    void   char_find(char *,...);

    /*********  Sumargs' first argument says how    *********/
    /*********  many unnamed arguments follow.      *********/

    printf("Sum of three arguments is %f\n",
           sumargs(3,10.0,20.0,30.0));
    printf("Sum of two arguments is %f\n",
           sumargs(2,10.0,20.0));
    printf("Sum of zero arguments is %f\n\n",  sumargs(0));

    /**********  Char_find uses '#' as a sentinel  **********/
    /**********  to warn that it is the final un-  **********/
    /**********  named argument.                   **********/

    char_find("Hello",'e','l','i','k','o','#');
}


/**********  Sum all of the unnamed arguments.  *************/
/**********  First argument tells function how  *************/
/**********  many unnamed arguments follow.     *************/
double sumargs(int n, ...)
{
    va_list argp;
    float sum = 0.0;

    /*********  Va_start initializes argp to point  *********/
    /*********  at the first unnamed argument after *********/
    /*********  the last named argument (n).        **********/
    va_start(argp,n);
```

```
    while (n--)
    {
        sum += va_arg(argp,double);  /*** Get unnamed arg. ***/
    }                                /*** Move argp to     ***/
                                     /*** next unnamed arg.***/

    va_end(argp);  /* REQUIRED!! */
    return sum;
}



/**********  Report whether unnamed char constant  **********/
/**********  arguments are in string or not.       **********/
void char_find(char *string, ...)
{
    va_list argp;
    char c;

    va_start(argp,string);
    while ((c = va_arg(argp,int)) != '#') /* # is sentinel! */
    {
       printf("The character %c is%s in %s\n",
              c, strchr(string,c) ? "" : " not", string);
    }
    va_end(argp);
}
/****************  Program Output Below  ****************/

Sum of three arguments is 60.000000
Sum of two arguments is 30.000000
Sum of zero arguments is 0.000000

The character e is in Hello
The character l is in Hello
The character i is not in Hello
The character k is not in Hello
The character o is in Hello
```

The code really says it all here! All functions that use variable-length argument lists specify this list using an ellipsis (`...`). The unnamed arguments denoted by `...` must follow the last named argument. There *must* be at least one named argument. The `va_start()`, `va_arg()`, and `va_end()` functions that appear in all such functions are in the header file `stdarg.h`. The unnamed argument list pointer is of type `va_list`, whose definition is also in `stdarg.h`.

The function `va_start()` will appear in every function that uses variable-length argument lists. It initializes a pointer of type `va_list` so that it points at the first unnamed argument. The prototype for `va_start()` is

```
void va_start (va_list argp, type-of-last-named-argument
               name-of-last-named-arg);
```

Thus, in `sumargs()`, the following diagram is the state of affairs after the call to `va_start()`.

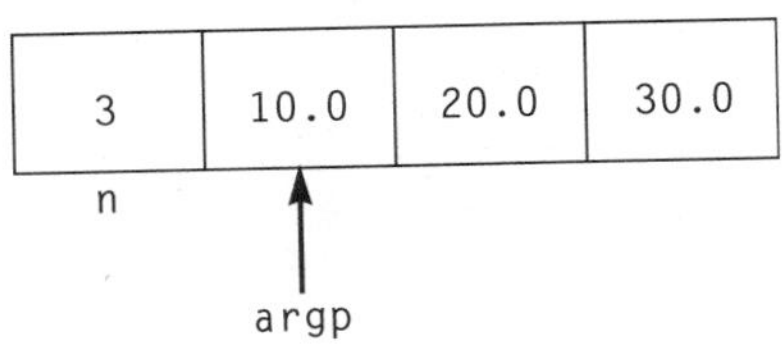

As you can see, `argp` is pointing at the first byte of the first unnamed argument. After the first call to `va_arg()`, the following is the state of affairs inside of `sumargs()`.

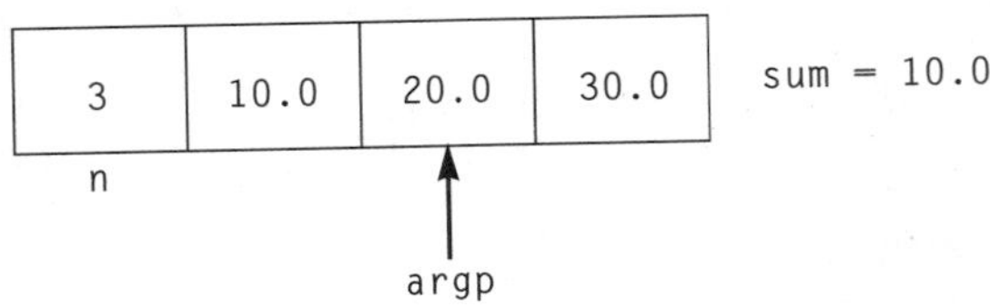

`Va_arg()` has fetched the first unnamed argument value (10.0) and added it to `sum`. This process of collecting unnamed arguments and adding them to `sum` continues until the `while` loop header reaches zero. The named argument (`n`) tells the `while` how many times to loop. Notice that `va_arg()` fetches unnamed arguments and also moves `argp` to the next unnamed argument.

The prototype for the `va_arg()` function is

```
type-of-unnamed-arg va_arg(va_list argp, type-of-unnamed-arg)
```

You must be very careful to put the proper type name in the second parameter of `va_arg()`. Otherwise, the `argp` pointer will not move the proper number of bytes after each call to `va_arg()`. It is useful to know that floating-point constants (such as `10.0`) are of type `double` and that character constants (such as `'x'`) are of type `int`. The unnamed arguments can be of all different types. The critical point is to give `va_arg()` the proper type *on each call.*

The `va_end()` call cleans up the unnamed argument stack so that your program behaves normally after the variable-length argument list function terminates. Although it appears to do nothing, you risk dire consequences when you exclude it! The prototype for `va_end()` is

```
void va_end(va_list va_argp);
```

Finally, notice that `sumargs()` and `char_find()` use two different methods to detect the end of the unnamed argument list. `Sumargs()` does it by using the named parameter `n` to tell its code how many unnamed arguments follow `n`. `Char_find()` does it by requiring that the user enter a pound sign (`'#'`) as the last item in the unnamed argument list. When `va_arg()` collects the `'#'` in the unnamed argument list, the `while` loop is terminated.

Before we go to the section on difficult C declarations, I want to refer back to the section on pointers to functions. Remember that a function that has a pointer to function parameter requires that each function actually called through the pointer must have the *same type and number of parameters.* After reading this section, you now realize that you can use variable-length argument list functions to get around this restriction if you ever need to. Try thinking this through!

9.4 How to Write and Read Difficult C Declarations

There is an amazingly simple rule for figuring out how to read or write difficult C declarations. It is the *right-left* rule. It is easiest to show how this rule works by illustrating it in action with successively more difficult problems. Let's start with

```
int  *p[5];
```

Start at the variable name, and work right and then left.

```
p[5]        /**** P is an array of 5 "somethings".  ****/
*p[5]       /**** P is an array of 5 pointers to "somethings". ****/
*p[5]       /**** Nothing to the right of [5] so go left! ****/
int *p[5]   /**** P is an array of 5 pointers to ints! ****/
```

Do you see it? We went right, then left, then right, then left—until we were done.

Let's try it on something harder.

```
int (*f) (int i);
```

This is harder, because there is one extra rule I didn't tell you about: You must finish off parentheses around the variable name first. So...

```
(f)                /**** Nothing to right of f—go left!  ****/
(*f)               /**** F is a pointer to "something". ****/
(*f)(int i)        /**** F is a pointer to a function with an int
                         parameter. ****/
int (*f) (int i)   /**** F is a pointer to a function with an int
                         parameter that returns an int. ****/
```

Again we went right-left-right-left. Now let's go to even more difficult declarations.

```
int (*p)[20];
```

Remember, you've got to finish off the parentheses around p first! So...

```
(p)             /**** Nothing to right of p—go left! ****/
(*p)            /**** P is a pointer to "something". ****/
(*p)[20]        /**** P is a pointer to an array of 20
                      "somethings". ****/
int (*p)[20]    /**** P is a pointer to an array of 20 ints. ****/
```

Notice the difference between `int *p[20]` and `int (*p)[20]`. The first is an array of 20 pointers to `int`s. The second is *one* pointer to an array of 20 `int`s. Using `p` in the example just shown, how many storage units would `p` move if you said `p++`? The answer: `20 * sizeof(int)`. Why? Because ++ always adds to a pointer according to the size of the thing it points at. In this case, the thing `p` points at is 20 `int`s long!

Let's figure this one out:

```
int  (*f[5]) (float f);
(f[5])                  /**** F is an array of 5 "somethings". ****/
(*f[5])                 /**** F is an array of 5 pointers to
                              "somethings".  ****/
(*f[5])(float f)        /**** F is an array of 5 pointers to
                              functions with one float
                              parameter. ****/
int (*f[5])(float f)    /**** F is an array of 5 pointers to
                              functions with one float parameter and
                              an int return type.   ****/
```

Now we'll show you the toughest one of all—a function header that appears virtually unreadable but can be understood using our trusty friend the right-left rule.

```
int (*func(int num)) (int);
```

Let's begin the "dissection" of this mind-boggler:

```
(func(int num))            /**** Func is a function with an int
                                 parameter.    ****/
(*func(int num))           /**** Func is a function with an int
                                 parameter that returns a pointer
                                 to "something".      ****/
(*func(int num))(int)      /**** Func is a function with an int
                                 parameter that returns a pointer
                                 to a function with an int
                                 parameter.        ****/
int (*func(int num))(int)  /**** Func is a function with an int
                                 parameter that returns a pointer
                                 to a function with an int
                                 parameter and an int  return
                                 type.    ****/
```

There is a function in the C header file, `signal.h`, that has a pointer to a function in its parameter list and returns a pointer to a function. That function, `signal()`, will be discussed in the final chapter. Thus you can see that this was not a purely academic exercise. You're going to use this stuff in its toughest form very soon.

Notice that the right-left rule has a certain "vocabulary" attached to it. When you encounter an asterisk (*), you must substitute the language "*pointer to.*" When you encounter `(parameters)`, you must substitute the language "*function with parameters of type ....*" And when you encounter `[n]`, you must substitute the language "*array of* `n` *'somethings'.*"

The right-left rule can help you decipher the most convoluted data types and function headers. Although you may choose to avoid such difficult declarations in your program, it is a bad mistake to avoid learning about them. This is because (1) you may have to use such declarations in your job, and (2) you may have to read code with such declarations. You have no control over code that already exists, so the latter is going to be unavoidable.

Facts About Functions

`<time.h>` Functions

Function: `time_t time(time_t *timeptr);`

Fact: **1)** You must pass `&` of a `time_t` variable as the parameter.

Fact: **2)** Returns the same `time_t` value that the parameter receives.

Fact: **3)** The time returned is seconds expired since January 1, 1970.

Fact: **4)** There is no absolute guarantee that the units of `time_t` variables are seconds, but the chances are very high that they are.

Fact: **5)** Returns `-1` if it can't get the time.

Fact: **6)** If `timeptr` is passed in with a `NULL` value, `time()` assumes you want to collect the result in a variable that receives the return value.

Fact: **7)** You can't use any of the `time.h` functions described below without calling this first!

Function: `struct tm *localtime(time_t *timeptr);`

Fact: **1)** Uses value returned by `time()` as its parameter.

Fact: 2) Returns a pointer to a `struct tm` that is statically allocated inside of `localtime()` itself! This means that the variable receiving the return value should be just an unallocated `struct tm *`.

Fact: 3) The composition of `struct tm`s is shown in Section 9.1 but will be repeated here for the convenience of the reader.

Component	Meaning	Values
`tm_sec`	Seconds after current minute	0 to 59
`tm_min`	Minutes after current hour	0 to 59
`tm_hour`	Current hour (military time)	0 to 23
`tm_mday`	Day of the current month	0 to 31
`tm_wday`	Days since the most recent Sunday	0 to 6
`tm_yday`	Days since January 1	0 to 365
`tm_mon`	Months since January	0 to 11
`tm_year`	Years since 1900	`Current_year -1900`
`tm_isdst`	Daylight savings time?	Positive if it is. Zero if it isn't. Negative if unknown.

Fact: 4) The time loaded into the `struct tm` is in the local time of your region.

Fact: 5) `NULL` is returned if the time could not be retrieved.

Function: `struct tm *gmtime(time_t *timeptr);`

Fact: 1) Identical in every respect to `localtime()` except that the time loaded into the `struct tm` is in Greenwich Mean Time.

Function: `char *asctime(struct tm *time_struct_ptr);`

Fact: 1) Turns the contents of a `struct tm` into a string that can be easily output by such functions as `printf()` in a form like this:

```
Fri Nov 22 03:47:18 1996
```

Fact: 2) Returns `NULL` if it cannot make the `struct tm`-to-`char *` conversion.

Fact: 3) The string that contains the time is statically allocated inside of `asctime()`. Thus a variable that accepts the return value of asctime() should be an unallocated char * variable.

Function: `char *ctime(time_t *timeptr);`

Fact: 1) Identical to asctime() but easier to use because it requires only a time_t value. Thus it can be called immediately after the time() function, whereas asctime() must be called after time() and either localtime() or gmtime().

Function: `double difftime(time_t time1, time_t time2);`

Fact: 1) Produces the number of seconds resulting from time2 - time1. Because there is some possibility that the time_t units are not an integral number of seconds, the return value is a double-precision floating-point number.

Fact: 2) No error return value.

Fact: 3) Is often used to benchmark code when time() is called before and after a section of code that produces the time1 and time2 values. Gmtime() can also be used for such purposes. See the code in Example 9.2.

Function: `size_t strftime(char *string, size_t string_size, char *format, struct tm *time_struct_ptr);`

Fact: 1) Returns the number of characters stored in string.

Fact: 2) Returns zero if an error occurred converting the struct tm into string using the specs in format.

Fact: 3) Read Example 9.3 (Section 9.1) to get the most important format specifiers usable in format.

Fact: 4) Gives the programmer tremendous flexibility in time output formats.

<stdarg.h> Functions

Function: `void va_start(va_list argp, type-of-last-named-arg name_of_last_named_arg);`

Fact: 1) Initializes argp. Argp points at the first unnamed argument in a function with a variable-length argument list.

All variable-length argument list functions have a header that looks like this:

```
type_name funcname(named_args_list, ...)
```

The unnamed argument list is denoted by an ellipsis (`...`). The ellipsis must come after the last named argument.

Fact: 2) It is imperative that the second argument to `va_start()` be the name of the last named parameter, because the C standard specifies no mechanism to report an error in the execution of `va_start()`. This is because `va_start()` is actually implemented as a *macro* rather than as a *function.*

Fact: 3) Must be called before `va_arg()` is called upon to fetch unnamed arguments.

Function: `return_type va_arg(va_list argp, type_to_fetch);`

Fact: 1) Fetches an unnamed argument of type `type_to_fetch`. The `return_type` will be the same as `type_to_fetch`.

Fact: 2) `Va_arg()` is actually implemented as a *macro,* not as a *function.* Therefore, it is imperative that the `type_to_fetch` conform with the data type of the actual unnamed parameters given in the call to the variable-length argument list function. In practice, this function usually returns an unexpected zero or `NULL` value (depending on the `return_type`) if you've made an error on `type_to_fetch`.

Fact: 3) After `va_arg()` fetches an unnamed argument, the unnamed argument pointer (`argp`) is advanced so that it points at the next unnamed argument.

Function: `void va_end(va_list argp);`

Fact: 1) Is called after the last call to `va_arg()` in a variable-length argument list function.

Fact: 2) `Va_end()` frees the nodes on the unnamed argument list stack.

Fact: 3) Every function with a variable-length argument list must call this function or bizarre memory addressing errors may pop up in other parts of the program. *Don't even think about omitting this call!*

Addendum: 1) Even though we have referred to the variable `argp` of type `va_list` as an "unnamed argument pointer," it is not a pointer in the usual C sense. You should never dereference this pointer!

Addendum: 2) The name of the `va_list` pointer can be anything—we just chose `argp`.

Exercises

1. Write a function that takes an unknown number of string arguments with the empty string acting as a sentinel last argument. This function will attempt to convert the strings to `long ints` and return the sum of them. If any string is not a completely proper `long int`, the function will return `LONG_MIN`, which necessitates the inclusion of `limits.h`. *Hint:* You will need a dummy named *parameter* to solve this.

■ 2. Write a code fragment, with variable declarations, that will print the current local time in a form that looks like this:

```
Friday, Nov. 22, 7:30 PM
```

■ 3. Write a function that will return the number of hours difference between your current local time and Greenwich Mean Time. Subtract one from this difference if your region is currently in daylight savings time.

4. You have written a group of utility functions that perform an operation on `struct st` variables and that return a `long`. Write a function that passes a `NULL`-terminated array of pointers to these functions as an argument. Your function will return a `-1`-terminated array of `time_t`. Each element of the returned array will contain the wall-clock execution time of each function represented in the array-of-function-pointer parameter.

■ 5. Write declarations for the following. Use the variable name `X` in your declarations.

   a. A pointer to an array of 20 unallocated strings.
   b. An array of 20 pointers to unallocated strings.
   c. An array of 20 strings, each of which can hold 10 characters (including the `'\0'`).

d. An array of 20 pointers to `int`.

e. A pointer to an array of 20 `int`s.

f. A 20-by-10 array of `int`s.

g. A pointer to a function returning an `int` and taking two parameters: an `int` and a pointer to a function taking an `int` argument and returning a `double`.

h. A function taking an `int` argument and returning a pointer to a function with a `void *` argument that returns `void`.

i. An array of 5 pointers to functions. Each function takes an `int` argument and returns a string.

j. A pointer to a 20-by-10 array of `int`s.

■ **6.** Write some code to prove that your answers to parts a and j of Exercise 5 are correct. You need not use the array dimensions in the problem to prove understanding. Strings need not be unallocated; indeed, it is hard to prove correctness without allocated strings. This is *very* difficult.

■ **7.** A binary file (`users.dat`) has an unknown number of `struct logins`. The definition of a `struct login` is as follows:

```
struct login
{
    char  username[16];
    time_t  login_time;
};
```

Each currently-logged-in user's login time was obtained from a call to `time()`. Given this, write a function that takes no parameters and returns `void`. This function will construct a text output file (`login.dat`) in which each line has a username followed by the number of days, hours, minutes, and seconds logged in.

8. A function is called as follows:

```
char   **match_positions, *string;
/*****  Lots of code here. String is allocated space and
        filled up.   *****/
match_positions = find_positions(string, "abc", "def",
                                 "jkl", "#");
```

You are told that the purpose of `find_positions` is to put all the starting positions in `string` of all arguments that follow it (except for the "#" sentinel argument) into an array of pointer to `char` that is returned. If any given nonsentinel string argument cannot be found in `string`, then the appropriate element of the returned array is `NULL`. Assume a maximum of 100 nonsentinel constant string arguments.

Write `find_positions()`, and fill the last element of the returned array with address `-1` so that a user traversing the returned array knows when to stop traversal.

9. Write a function called `printstr` that implements a very crude form of `printf()` but accepts only `%s` formats (with signed field widths allowed, such as `%-5s`) for a variable number of strings.

■10. A program uses `struct executes`, which are defined as follows:

```
struct execute
{
    int i;
    int (*function)(int);
};
```

A function is called as follows:

```
run_funcs(dummy_arg, &se1, &se2, NULL); /*** Dummy_arg
                                         is an int.  ***/
```

where a dummy argument is followed by an unknown number of `struct execute*` arguments. A `NULL` is a sentinel value signaling the end of `struct execute` arguments. Write `run_funcs` if its sole purpose is to report the return value of running the function whose pointer is embedded within each `struct execute`. Use the `int` in each `struct execute` as the argument to this function. This is tough, but the answer is in the Appendix.

Chapter 10

Potpourri: Part Two

In this final chapter of the book, we will investigate searching and sorting via the `bsearch()` and `qsort()` functions in `stdlib.h`, signals and interrupts, and some advanced file- and directory-oriented functions.

The `qsort()` and `bsearch()` functions are like cousins. These two array-oriented functions sort arrays and apply a key-driven binary search to arrays. The array given to `bsearch()` is assumed to be sorted, so you can see that these two functions are often used together.

Although we have emphasized self-sorting data structures like linked lists and binary trees in earlier chapters, one should *not* be led into thinking that operations on arrays are not needed. There are many applications where a file's contents are brought into memory, sorted, and then written back out to disk. This makes possible sequential displays of data and the detection of duplicate data entries (because after sorting, the duplicates will be next to one another).

Indeed, when we have an unchanging collection of data where we need to do searching, it is actually far more efficient to use arrays than dynamic data structures. For one thing, when we are using `fread()` to read a file into memory, it can be done in one read operation if we are reading directly into an array. Then the `bsearch()` function offers us search times on the array that are equal to those of a completely balanced binary tree.

The second section in this chapter looks at the `signal.h` library and related libraries used to detect keyboard interrupts, memory leaks, arithmetic overflows/underflows, and other exceptional program events.

Finally, the book concludes with a discussion of a few file- and directory-related functions that do not fit neatly with those discussed in Chapter 5.

10.1 Sorting and Searching with Qsort and Bsearch

The qsort() function uses "quick sort" to sort arrays. This is a sort with a very good best-case performance (with random data) and a very poor worst-case performance (if the array is already sorted). Its best-case performance is needed if the sort needs to be done fast in real time. The very fact that it sorts, regardless of its poor worst-case performance, is useful if we need some kind of sort even when we don't care about its real-time performance. After all, it is the only sort function offered in the ANSI C libraries!

Bsearch() does a binary array search, which is a search done with a "divide-and-conquer" algorithm. Bsearch() looks at the middle element of the sorted array and asks, "Is the element I am looking for less than or greater than this middle element?" If the element is in the first half of the array, it then looks at the middle element of this first half and asks the same question. This process is continued until the desired element is found or is proved to be missing from the array.

The following example gives a demonstration of qsort() and then bsearch(). The example is far less minimalist than most examples in the book, because we also wanted to incorporate such important functions as strtok(), memset(), realloc(), and others. This will be your last exposure to these very important functions, so *read the code!*

Example 10.1 Using Qsort and Bsearch

```
MOLLY BOLT: 57      /****  Start of Input Data File. ****/
WIDGET:28           /****  Two fields per line are   ****/
WING NUT: 89        /****  partname and quantity.    ****/
SLEDGE HAMMER: 27
HAMMER: 45
CEMENT BAGS:  113
VISE: 44
THERMOSTAT:78
RIVET: 89
NAIL: 2345
BRACE:234
CLAMP:  523
SANDER: 99
SAW: 211
SAW BLADE: 675
LEVEL:  122
WRENCH: 452
SOCKET SET: 147
ACETYLENE TORCH: 10
```

```
SCREW DRIVER: 789
PLANE: 67
WALL MOUNT: 90
BOLT (REGULAR): 1311
FLASH LIGHT: 343
WELDING TORCH:89    /**** End of Input Data File ****/

#include <stdio.h>
#include <stdlib.h>  /****  Has qsort() and bsearch().  ****/
#include <string.h>

#define BLOCK 10
#define SENTINEL '~'

typedef struct hardware HARDWARE;

struct hardware
{
    char partname[20];
    int  quantity;
};

main(int argc, char **argv)
{
    FILE *parts;
    HARDWARE *inventory;
    long numparts;
    FILE *open_file(char *filename);
    HARDWARE *read_file(FILE *parts, long *numparts);
    void print_sorted_output(HARDWARE *inventory);
    int compare(const void *part1, const void *part2);
    void find_keys(HARDWARE *inventory, long numparts);

    parts = open_file(argv[1]);
    inventory = read_file(parts, &numparts);
    fclose(parts);
    qsort(inventory, numparts, sizeof(HARDWARE), compare);
    print_sorted_output(inventory);
    printf("\n\n");
    find_keys(inventory, numparts);  /** Calls bsearch()!! **/
}


/****************  Open input file.  Bail    *****************/
/****************  out if unsuccessful.      *****************/
FILE *open_file(char *filename)
{
    FILE *parts;
```

```
    if ((parts = fopen(filename, "r")) == NULL)
    {
        printf("Cannot open file: %s.\n", filename);
        exit(1);
    }
    return parts;
}


/**************** Read input file into array. **************/
/***************** Dynamically increase size of *************/
/**************** array with realloc.          **************/
HARDWARE *read_file(FILE *parts, long *numparts)
{
    HARDWARE *inventory, *mover;
    char line[80], *partname, *pqty;
    long numlines = 0;

    if ((inventory = (HARDWARE *)
         malloc(BLOCK * sizeof(HARDWARE))) == NULL)
    {
         printf("Fatal malloc error!\n");
         exit(2);
    }
    memset(inventory, 0, BLOCK * sizeof(HARDWARE));

    mover = inventory;
    while (fgets(line, 80, parts))
    {
         numlines++;
         partname = strtok(line,":");
         pqty     = strtok(NULL, "\040");
         mover->quantity  =  (int) strtol(pqty, NULL, 10);
         strcpy(mover->partname, partname);
         if (numlines % 5 == 0)
         {
              if ((inventory = (HARDWARE *)realloc(inventory,
              (numlines + BLOCK) * sizeof(HARDWARE))) == NULL)
              {
                  printf("Fatal realloc error!\n");
                  exit(3);
              }
              mover   = inventory + numlines; /** Vital!!! **/
              /******** Zero out new BLOCK of storage ******/
              memset(mover, 0, BLOCK * sizeof(HARDWARE));
         }
         mover++;
     }
```

```
        *mover->partname = SENTINEL;
        *numparts = numlines;
        return inventory;
}


/**************** Print sorted array.  Do not   **************/
/***************  print empty elements or the   **************/
/***************  sentinel record.               **************/
void print_sorted_output(HARDWARE *inventory)
{
    HARDWARE *mover;

    for (mover = inventory; *mover->partname != SENTINEL;
         mover++)
    {
        if (*mover->partname != '\0')
            printf("%-20s%-5d\n",
                   mover->partname, mover->quantity);
    }
}


/****************  Used by qsort AND bsearch to *************/
/****************  compare two keys, i.e., the  *************/
/****************  partname component.  Use     *************/
/****************  memcpy to put parameters in- *************/
/****************  to HARDWARE structs.         *************/

int compare(const void *part1, const void *part2)
{
    HARDWARE p1, p2;

    memcpy(&p1, part1, sizeof(HARDWARE));
    memcpy(&p2, part2, sizeof(HARDWARE));
    /*********  Now we can refer to components of  **********/
    /*********  structs due to the memcpy's.       **********/
    if (strcmp(p1.partname, p2.partname) > 0)
    {
        return 1;
    }
    else if (strcmp(p1.partname, p2.partname) < 0)
    {
        return -1;
    }
    else return 0;
}
```

```
/*************  Get user tokens from terminal. *************/
/*************  Find in array with bsearch.    *************/
void find_keys(HARDWARE *inventory, long numparts)
{
    HARDWARE *mover, *found, temp;
    char line[80];
    void format(char *key);

    while (printf("Enter key:"), gets(line),
           format(line), strcmp(line, "QUIT") != 0)
    {
        if (*line == '\0') continue; /*** Empty response ***/
        memset(&temp, 0, sizeof(HARDWARE));
        strcpy(temp.partname, line);
        found = (HARDWARE *) bsearch(&temp, inventory,
                numparts, sizeof(HARDWARE), compare);
        if (!found) printf("Could not find key: %s\n", line);
        else printf("Found record: %s %d\n",
                   found->partname, found->quantity);

    }
}


/****************  Uppercases all characters  **************/
/****************  in key. Trims leading and ***************/
/****************  trailing space. Puts one   ***************/
/****************  space between tokens in    ***************/
/***************** "key".                     ***************/
void format(char *key)
{
     char line[80], *token, *keyptr = key;

     strcpy(line, "");
     for ( ; token = strtok(keyptr, "\040"); keyptr = NULL)
     {
         strcat(line, token);
         strcat(line, "\040");
     }
     line[strlen(line) - 1] = '\0'; /*** Overwrite space ****/
     strcpy(key, line);
     while (*key != '\0')
     {
         *key = toupper(*key);
         key++;
     }
}  /****  End of program. ****/
/****************** Program Output and   *****************/
/****************** Sample Session Below *****************/
```

```
ACETYLENE TORCH     10     /**** Print After Qsort. ****/
BOLT (REGULAR)      1311
BRACE               234
CEMENT BAGS         113
CLAMP               523
FLASH LIGHT         343
HAMMER              45
LEVEL               122
MOLLY BOLT          57
PLANE               67
RIVET               89
SANDER              99
SAW                 211
SLEDGE HAMMER       27
SOCKET SET          147
THERMOSTAT          78
VISE                44
WALL MOUNT          90
WIDGET              28
WING NUT            89
WRENCH              452

Enter key:  fOobAR
Could not find key: FOOBAR

Enter key: wRenCH
Found record: WRENCH 452

Enter key:  MollY   BoLT
Found record: MOLLY BOLT 57

Enter key:  arg
Could not find key: ARG

Enter key: wing  NUT
Found record: WING NUT 89

Enter key: quit
$  /*** Operating System Prompt. End of Execution. ***/
```

Because it is late in the book and we are assuming a certain level of achievement at this point, we are not going to give a detailed analysis of this program except for a few important points. First, notice that `qsort()` and `bsearch()` both require a pointer to a function as an argument. The function is one that *you* must write! This function, which is called `compare()` in Example 10.1, must have `const void *` argument types. You must convert these arguments to different data types (as we were forced to in compare()) if you need to refer to a struct component.

In the case of qsort(), the comparison function is supposed to return -1, 0, or 1, depending on whether the first argument is less than, equal to, or greater than the second, where *you* define *less than, equal to,* and *greater than.* Bsearch() requires a negative, zero, or positive return from the same function. Thus our -1, 0, and 1 return values in compare() conveniently satisfy the return requirements for both functions.

Notice that the mover pointer in the read_file() function is reassigned whenever a realloc() occurs. Recall that realloc() may pick up the original array and put it somewhere else in memory. Thus any pointers that were pointing somewhere within the original array must be moved as well. Forgetting this can lead to a very stubborn and hard-to-find bug!

Finally, notice how format() alters the user's input string. It uses strtok() to get words in a multi-word part name (like MOLLY BOLT) and puts exactly one space between the words in the output string (line). It also uppercases each letter because the input file's data is all uppercase. Thus the user of the program is not "punished" for entering strings in the wrong case or putting extra spaces in multi-word partnames. I guarantee that you'll use this trick some day!

For formal completeness, we will now discuss the ANSI C prototypes of qsort() and bsearch().

```
void *bsearch(void *key, const void *start_address, size_t
              num_elements,size_t  element_size, int
              (*compare)(const void  *key, const void
              *current_element);

void  qsort(void *key, const void *start_address, size_t
            num_elements, size_t  element_size, int
            (*compare)(const void  *key, const void
            *current_element);
```

So far in this book, we have not shown whether function parameters in library functions should have const in their declaration. That's because, most of the time, it isn't even an issue. However, the compare() function parameters *must* be declared, in the function header, as const void *. Otherwise, C gives you a compile-time type mismatch. That's because qsort() and bsearch() (not you) call compare(). And these functions have the compare() function prototyped internally with the const designation. Hence we have included this necessary key word in the foregoing prototypes.

10.2 Signals, Interrupts, and Error Handling

Thus far, we have dealt only with *synchronous events* in programs. What do I mean by this? Suppose we have a hypothetical set of statements in a program:

```
s1;      /***  Statement one.    ***/
s2;      /***  Statement two.    ***/
s3;      /***  Statement three.  ***/
```

In a normal program, statement s2 is not executed until statement s1 is finished. Accordingly, we say that s1 and s2 are synchronized. However, suppose we want to trap the event of a user hitting a CTRL-C at the keyboard. We have no idea which statement in the program is executing when the user does this. Therefore, we must put code in our program that is *not* synchronized with any statement that detects the CTRL-C no matter when it occurred.

We do this, in ANSI C, through the use of the signal() function in the signal.h header file. The prototype for signal() is

```
void (*signal(int signal_type, void (*handler)(int
      signal_type)))(int);
```

Aren't you glad that we exposed you to difficult declarations in Section 9.4? Fortunately, in practice, the return value of signal() is seldom used, so we'll look just at the two parameters signal_type and handler for now. The signal_type is the asynchronous event you are trying to trap. Most hardware platforms have dozens of signal_types that apply to their hardware only. ANSI C gives the following small set as a standard for all platforms:

Signal Type	Meaning
SIGABRT	Caused by the abort() function.
SIGINT	On most machines, a CTRL-C terminal interrupt.
SIGSEGV	A memory error (dereferencing an invalid address).
SIGFPE	Floating-point overflow or underflow.
SIGTERM	A termination signal, often from another program.

This isn't much, but even this limited set is very helpful. For example, if malloc() or realloc() fails in your program, you may not care much where it failed because it's often an operating system glitch. Instead of testing the return value of malloc() or realloc() for NULL, you could put this one statement at the top of your program:

```
signal(SIGSEGV, handler);
```

Remember, this is useful only when (1) you don't care where memory failures occur, and (2) you've gotten all the memory leaks out of your program so that malloc()/realloc() failures are the only remaining problem source. Both of these conditions must apply! On some architectures, SIGBUS is synonymous with, or is a replacement for, SIGSEGV. Check your reference guide.

SIGFPE almost always occurs when you attempt a divide-by-zero at runtime. SIGTERM is usually sent by another program—often one invoked by a system administrator to terminate your program if it misbehaves. We will discuss SIGABRT later.

What about the second parameter to signal()? It can have three possible values:

```
SIG_DFL    /*** Handle the signal in the "default" fashion.
                Usually, this will terminate a program. ***/

SIG_IGN    /*** Ignore the signal (do nothing). ***/

func_name /*** Go to function func_name() when the signal
               occurs. You may give the function any
               name you wish. ***/
```

If you give the name of a function to be invoked when a certain signal_type occurs, this function is usually referred to as the *signal-handling function.* You may choose to give this function one parameter, int signal_type. How can this be useful if the operating system calls this function when the signal occurs? Because you may choose to go to the same signal-handling function on many different types of signals.

Well, enough theory. Time for some code!

Example 10.2 The Signal Function

```
#include <stdio.h>
#include <signal.h>
main()
{
    void handler(int signum);
    float i, j;
    char line[80], *ptr = NULL;

    signal(SIGINT,  handler);  /* Handler can have any name.*/
    signal(SIGFPE,  handler);
    signal(SIGSEGV, handler);
    for (i = 0; i < 8; i++)
    {
        sleep(1);   /**** Stop program for one second.  ****/
        printf("Ouch!\n");
    }
    printf("Enter two numbers: ");
    gets(line);
    sscanf(line,"%f %f", &i, &j);
    i /= j;
    printf("i = %f\n", i);  /*** Did NOT generate SIGFPE! ***/
    printf("*ptr = %c\n", *ptr);
}
```

```
void handler(int signum)
{
    switch (signum)
    {
        case SIGINT:  printf("SIGINT caught!\n");
                      signal(SIGINT, handler);
                      break;
        case SIGSEGV: printf("SIGSEGV caught!\n");
                      exit(1);
                      break;
        case SIGFPE:  printf("SIGFPE caught!\n");
                      signal(SIGFPE, handler);
    }
}
/***************  Sample Session Below  ****************/

Ouch!
SIGINT caught!
Ouch!
Ouch!
SIGINT caught!
Ouch!
Ouch!
Ouch!
Ouch!
Ouch!
Enter two numbers: i = inf
SIGSEGV caught!
```

Example 10.2 illustrates the blessings and the perils of `signal()`. `SIGFPE` was not trapped on a divide-by-zero on two different platforms. As you can see, it plugged a *string* (`inf`) into `i`, denoting "infinity" (I guess).

The `SIGSEGV` signal was raised when I attempted to dereference a `NULL` pointer. `SIGINT` was raised when I hit CTRL-C but I want you to notice that I reinstalled the handling of the `SIGINT` signal inside of `handler()`. This is imperative, because on some platforms, once a signal is raised, the way of handling it reverts to `SIG_DFL` unless you "refresh" the signal by issuing another call to `signal()` as we did inside `handler()`. The default on most systems on an "unhandled" (default method of handling) CTRL-C is *to abort the program.* Thus reinstallation of signal handling is a must!

Example 10.2 provides a decent model of how `signal()` works but does not fully expose its shortcomings. For example, if you do not `exit()` from the handler function, your program will return control to whichever statement was executing at the time the signal was raised. This is dangerous because some functions are *non-reentrant.* This means you may return control to a function that hangs forever. Is there a way out of this problem? Fortunately, there is.

Example 10.3 Controlled Re-Entry to Code Via Setjmp and Longjmp

```
#include <stdio.h>
#include <signal.h>
#include <setjmp.h>  /*** Contains setjmp/longjmp. ***/
#include <stdlib.h>

jmp_buf env;

main()
{
    void handler(int signum);
    int k;

    signal(SIGINT,  handler); /* Handler can have any name. */
    if (setjmp(env) != 0)
    {
        printf("Got here via longjmp!\n");
        printf("Value of k is: %d\n", k);
    }
    for (k = 0; k < 8; k++)
    {
        sleep(1);
        printf("Ouch!\n");
    }
}

void handler(int signum)
{
        printf("SIGINT caught!\n");
        signal(SIGINT, handler);
        longjmp(env, 1);
}
/***********  Sample Session Output Below  ************/

Ouch!
Ouch!
Ouch!
SIGINT caught!
Got here via longjmp!
Value of k is: 3
Ouch!
Ouch!
Ouch!
Ouch!
Ouch!
Ouch!
Ouch!
Ouch!
```

The functions `setjmp()` and `longjmp()` are located in `setjmp.h`. The first time the `setjmp()` function is called, it automatically returns zero. When we hit CTRL-C in the sample session above, instead of allowing an uncontrolled return to `main()`, the call to `longjmp()` returned us to the `setjmp()` again with a return value of one (the second parameter of `longjmp()`). You cannot throw a 0 back to `setjmp()`. If you try, by saying `longjmp(env, 0)`, it will throw a 1 back instead.

The thing it is most important for you to know about `setjmp()` and `longjmp()` is that *they do not roll back the values of variables.* Notice that k's value upon returning to the `setjmp()` is still 3—the value `k` had when `SIGINT` was raised.

Signal handling can be used for many purposes, and one of the most important is guarding critical code sections. For example, suppose your program is in the process of writing out a critical system file. You do not want the program aborted by a CTRL-C. You can prevent disaster with code such as

```
signal(SIGINT, SIG_IGN);
/******** Critical code in here! ********/
signal(SIGINT, SIG_DFL);
```

Thus CTRL-C interrupts are disabled (ignored) while the critical code is executing and are re-enabled after the critical code has completed execution.

We saw earlier that some systems don't acknowledge some signals they are supposed to acknowledge; remember how `SIGFPE` was ignored even when we tried to trap it. Are there any work-arounds that allow you to raise a signal explicitly when the system won't do it for you? Yes. Look at the code that follows.

```
signal(SIGFPE, handler);
printf("Enter two numbers:  ");
gets(line);
sscanf(line, "%f %f", &i, &j);
if (j == 0.0) raise(SIGFPE);  /****  Explicitly raise
                                     SIGFPE!  ****/
else i /= j;
```

The `raise()` function generates the signal type given as its argument. Thus if `j` is `0.0` in the foregoing program, control will be transferred to `handler()`.

There are some signal types that are not part of "official" ANSI C but are handled by virtually every compiler on the market. The most important of these is `SIGALRM`. The `SIGALRM` signal is generally used to time a program out, as in the following example.

Example 10.4 Timing Programs Out with `SIGALRM`

```
#include <stdio.h>
#include <signal.h>
main()
{
```

```
    int num;
    void myalarm();

    signal(SIGALRM, myalarm);

    alarm(5);
    printf("You have 5 seconds to enter a number! ");
    scanf("%d",&num);
    alarm(0);
    printf("Good kid—you did it!\n");
}

void myalarm()
{
    printf("\nUser is timed out!\n");
    exit(1);
}
/**************  Sample Session Output Below  *************/

$ sigalrm
You have 5 seconds to enter a number!
User is timed out!
$ sigalrm
You have 5 seconds to enter a number! 6
Good kid—you did it!
```

Notice that the `alarm()` function takes an integer number-of-seconds argument. If that number of seconds expires before an `alarm(0)` (turn off alarm clock) call, the `SIGALRM` signal is raised.

As we noted before, on real-world hardware platforms, many more signals can be trapped than are specified in the ANSI C standard. It is not uncommon for a real-world program to have three, four, or more signal-handling functions. The problem is that there might be a lot of code redundancy in these handlers, because they might all have to perform the same cleanup work, such as completing file writes/closes, sending a message to some system program, and so on.

Rather than duplicating such functionality in four or five places, it is best to use the `atexit()` function from the `stdlib.h` library. `Atexit()` takes a function pointer argument. Whenever an `exit()` occurs anywhere in a program or `main()` completes, the function name given to `atexit()` will be called. Here's a "bare bones" illustration of `atexit()`.

Example 10.5 Demonstration of the `Atexit` Function

```
#include <stdio.h>
#include <signal.h>
```

```
#include <stdlib.h>
main()
{
    void handler(int signum), cleanup(void);
    int i;

    atexit(cleanup);
    signal(SIGINT,  handler);
    for (i = 0; i < 8; i++)
    {
        sleep(1);
        printf("Ouch!\n");
    }
}

void handler(int signum)
{
    printf("Aborting due to terminal interrupt!\n");
    exit(1);  /***  Should cause cleanup() to be called. ***/
}
void cleanup(void)
{
    printf("I'm in the exit handler!\n");
}
/*************  Sample Program Session Below ************/

Ouch!
Ouch!
Ouch!   /*** I hit CTRL-C here! ***/
Aborting due to terminal interrupt!
I'm in the exit handler!
```

Notice that the `cleanup()` function does not need an `exit()` call as its last statement. Through the `atexit()` call, the program knows that it is supposed to terminate when this function is called—it does not have to be told to do that explicitly.

You also need to be aware that the function given to `atexit()` *must* have a `void` return type and parameter list. Unfortunately, this means that any variables accessed in the exit-handling function must be declared either locally or globally. They cannot be passed in as parameters.

Finally, let's deal with error detection during program execution. During the debugging phase of program development, we might want the program to fail at runtime if certain variables have improper values or if a certain condition is not true. The `assert()` function in `assert.h` causes a program to abort with an error message if the value of the expression given as a parameter is zero. Here's how it works.

Example 10.6 Demonstration of the Assert Function

```
#include <assert.h>  /****  Contains assert() function. ****/
main()
{
    void handler(int signum);
    int i = 5;

    assert(i == 2);
}
```

In this example, because the assert condition is false, it has a value of zero. This causes the program to terminate with an error message. The error message always gives the assert condition that caused termination so you'll know exactly where the program failed. The message for Example 10.6 might be

```
Assert 'i == 2' failed.
Abort (core dumped)
```

Another function that is useful for error reporting is perror(). Here is a demonstration of it.

Example 10.7 Demonstration of the Perror Function

```
#include <stdio.h>      /**** Has perror(). ****/
#include <errno.h>      /**** Has errno variable. ****/
#include <stdlib.h>     /**** Has strtol(). ****/
main()
{
    char *string = "22222222222222222222222222222222222222";
    long num;

    errno = 0;  /**** Good habit to get into!  ****/
    num = strtol(string, NULL, 10);
    if (errno)
    {
        perror("Strtol failure!");
        exit(1);
    }
}
/*****************  Program Output Below  ****************/

Strtol failure!:  Result too large.
```

The perror() function dumps to the screen the string you give it plus any additional system information it obtains from looking at the type of error that occurred (which will be encoded in the value of errno).

Before we move to Section 10.3, I want to caution you that much of the material in Section 10.2 functions in a very individual way from platform to platform. Also, your platform may have slightly more reliable methods for handling signals and performing error detection. For example, the government POSIX standard specifies a new signal-handling function called `sigaction()` that eliminates all of the deficiencies and problems with `signal()`.

Whatever your destination platform, if you understand the material in this chapter and the preceding chapters in this book, you'll be able to move to systems programming on *any* platform with little difficulty. Our intention here is to introduce the basic ideas of signal, interrupt, and error detection and handling. Realize, though, that any programs you sell will contain much non-ANSI code when it comes to such detection and handling.

10.3 File-Related Functions

Some algorithms need disk files even though they need them only temporarily. For example, some *merge sorts* sort little pieces of a file into many files and then merge the sorted pieces back into the original file. Sometimes an application will not know immediately whether a new file needs to be saved. The application may wait for a yes/no response from a user to save a newly created file.

When applications create temporary files, they may wish to "clean up" by removing any files thus created. Though such occasions are rare, there may even be times when we wish to rename a file. We might want to take a temporary file (which might be in some directory other than ours) and make it "permanent" by renaming it so that it is part of our directory structure. Thus we need functions to do the following:

1. Create a file name that does not conflict with any other file name in the user's directory (function: `tmpnam()`).
2. Rename a file. The user might want to keep the file opened with a name given by the function performing task 1 above (function: `rename()`)!
3. Delete a file (function: `remove()`).
4. Create a file that exists only for the duration of the program and that is then automatically deleted (function: `tmpfile()`).

Finally, we may need to access the computer's operating system to call a command that either uses the file(s) created by the program or creates file(s) needed by the program. Operating system programs are accessed via the `system()` function. `System()` is in the `stdlib.h` header file, whereas the four functions listed above are all in `stdio.h`.

The following example illustrates all of the functions described in this section and also illustrates the great value of the underappreciated `sprintf()`

function. The output shows, for the first time in this entire book, a library function that *fails*. The rename() function returns an error value. We'll explain why after the example.

Example 10.8 Demonstration of File-Related Library Calls

```
#include <errno.h>
#include <stdio.h>
#include <stdlib.h>
#include <string.h>
main()
{
    char filename[L_tmpnam]; /* L_tmpnam defined in stdio.h.*/
    char *strs[] = {"Hello\n",
                    "Goodbye\n",
                    "Cat\n",
                    "Dog\n",
                    NULL };
    char **mover = strs;
    char line[80], command[80];
    FILE *fp;

    /****************  Open temporary file  *****************/
    fp = tmpfile();  /*** Opened in w+ mode. ***/
    for (; *mover != NULL; mover++) fputs(*mover, fp);
    rewind(fp);
    while (fgets(line, 80, fp)) printf("%s",line);
    fclose(fp);

    /**********  Get name for a file that will not   *********/
    /**********  conflict with existing names.       *********/
    if (tmpnam(filename) == NULL)
    {
        printf("Could not get non-conflicting filename.\n");
        exit(1);
    }
    printf("\nFilename obtained is: %s\n\n", filename);
    fp = fopen(filename, "w+");
    for (mover = strs; *mover != NULL; mover++)
    {
        fputs(*mover, fp);
    }
    rewind(fp);
    while (fgets(line, 80, fp)) printf("%s",line);
    putchar('\n');
    fclose(fp);
```

```
    /***************  Is "filename" there?  ****************/
    sprintf(command, "ls -l %s", filename);
    system(command);
    if (rename(filename, "/home/jwp2286/garbage.dat") != 0)
    {
        printf("Could not rename: %s\n", filename);
        remove(filename);
        system(command);  /**** File not found error!? ****/
        exit(2);
    }

    /*********  If we got here, rename succeeded.  **********/
    system("ls -l garbage.dat");
}
/****************  Program Output Below  ******************/

Hello   /***** Written on file opened with tmpfile(). *****/
Goodbye
Cat
Dog

Filename obtained is: /tmp/13676aaa

Hello  /*****  Written on /tmp/13676aaa.  *****/
Goodbye
Cat
Dog

-rw-r--r--   1 jwp2286  staff    22 Nov 28 23:34 /tmp/13676aaa
Could not rename: /tmp/13676aaa
ls: /tmp/13676aaa: No such file or directory
```

As you can see, the temporary file obtained with `tmpfile()` was properly opened. The proof is that when we did a `rewind()` and read what we wrote on that file, we read the correct file contents as shown in the output of the `printf()` in the first `while`.

`Tmpnam()` did, indeed, give us a nonconflicting name for a file. Notice, however, that this file was not placed in the *jwp2286* directory (my login directory on a Silicon Graphics computer). `Rename()` will usually work fine, but beware of trying to rename files that do not reside within your directory structure, such as files named by `tmpnam()`—the operating system may not like it!

`Remove()` did its job fine. That's why the last directory listing (the *ls -l* command on the Silicon Graphics computer) could not find the (`remove`'d) file named by `tmpnam()`. When using `remove()` and `rename()`, use full directory path specs whenever possible.

Facts About Functions

<stdlib.h> Functions

Function: `void qsort(void *start, size_t num_elements, size_t bytes_per_element,int (*compare) (void *element1, void *element2);`

Fact: 1) *You* must write the `compare()` function whose name you pass as the fourth and final parameter.

Fact: 2) `Qsort()` insists that the two parameters of `compare()` be of type `void *`. Therefore, if you wish to refer to some components of, say, `structs`, you should copy the parameters into local variables of the proper type. Then your `struct` component references won't cause compile time problems.

Fact: 3) Your `compare()` function should return `-1` if `element1` is "less than" `element2`, where your code defines *less than.* `Compare()` should return `0` if `element1` and `element2` are "equal" (again, you define *equal*). Finally, it should return `1` if `element1` is "greater than" `element2`.

Fact: 4) Be careful! You will note that `qsort()` has no error-return value. Your local compiler may change `errno` in some platform-specific way. The message here is to make sure you understand `qsort()` by testing it on a small example!

Fact: 5) Items are sorted in ascending order.

Fact: 6) Starts sort at the address given in `start`. Yes, this *does* allow you to sort subarrays.

Function: `void *bsearch(void *key, void *start, size_t num_elements,size_t bytes_per_element, int (*compare)(void *element1, void *element2));`

Fact: 1) `Bsearch()` is useless on unsorted arrays.

Fact: 2) The `compare()` function works the same way as it did in `qsort()`, except that the three return values may be negative, zero, and positive instead of `-1`, `0`, and `1`. See item 3 under `void qsort()`.

Fact: 3) `Bsearch()` returns a pointer to the array element with key value `key` if there is such an element. It returns `NULL` if no such element exists.

Fact: 4) Because `bsearch()` starts searching at address `start`, it is possible to do searches on sorted subarrays. For example, say you had an array of `int` like this:

```
13  7  23  9  3  6  9  14  23  34  45  22  19
```

You could do a `bsearch()` of seven elements starting at the 3, since the seven `int`s starting at the 3 are properly sorted.

Fact: 5) It is good to practice using `bsearch()` in a little "toy" program because it is difficult to tell whether a `NULL` return occurs because the element can't be found or because you have erred.

Function: `int atexit(void (*function_name)(void));`

Fact: 1) Registers the name of a function that should be called whenever `main()` ends or when the `exit()` function is called.

Fact: 2) ANSI C allows at least 32 function names to be so registered.

Fact: 3) Returns zero on success and non-zero on failure.

Fact: 4) The "exit handler" function registered is usually one that performs vital cleanup work such as closing files, writing out data structures to a file, and so on. Because this function cannot accept parameters, you may need to declare some variables (such as `FILE *` variables) *global* so that they can be accessed in the exit-handling function.

Function: `int system(char *command);`

Fact: 1) Usually returns a zero if it succeeds. Return value, however, is platform-specific.

Fact: 2) Executes `command` in the operating system environment of your computer. These commands (which perform things like file copying and deletion) differ from one hardware platform to another, so you may need `#ifdefs` to execute a specific command on a specific piece of hardware.

Fact: 3) `Command` is often constructed with the underappreciated `sprintf()` function. Think of this function when using `system()`!

<assert.h> Functions

Function: `void assert(boolean_expression);`

Fact: 1) Used most frequently for debugging purposes.

Fact: 2) Causes the program to terminate when the `boolean_expression` is false.

Fact: 3) The `boolean_expression` that caused the program to fail will be printed on the screen. Thus, if you have many `assert`s embedded in your program, you can tell which one caused the program to terminate.

Fact: 4) No return value! Once again, you might have to play with this function a little to make sure you understand it.

<stdio.h> Functions

Function: `void perror(char *error_message);`

Fact: 1) Used often after failure-prone functions (like `strtol()`) to dump `error_message` (which *you* specify) plus additional information from the operating system.

Fact: 2) Often used when `errno` is set by the aforementioned failure-prone calls.

Function: `int rename(char *old_filename, *new_filename);`

Fact: 1) Returns zero on success and non-zero on failure.

Fact: 2) Failure can be caused by

a) `old_filename` being nonexistent or inaccessible,

b) `new_filename` existing prior to `rename()`,

c) `new_filename` being on a directory that cannot be accessed, or

d) either file name containing file name characters that are not legal on the current operating system.

Fact: 3) Changes `old_filename` to `new_filename` on your disk directory.

Fact: 4) May *not* be useful for renaming files named via `tmpnam()`. In fact, this function is the most error-prone of the `stdio.h` functions reviewed in this section.

Fact: 5) Give complete directory path names of file parameters, if possible.

Function: `int remove(char *filename);`

Fact: 1) Deletes `filename` from your disk directory.

Fact: 2) Returns zero on success and non-zero on failure.

Fact: 3) Fails for reasons similar to those given in item 3 of `int rename()`.

Fact: 4) As for `int rename()`, give a complete directory path as part of the `filename` if this is possible.

Function: `FILE *tmpfile(void);`

Fact: 1) Creates a temporary file and opens it in `w+` mode.

Fact: 2) Deletes the file after it is closed either by `fclose()` or because the program ended.

Fact: 3) Useful when you do merge sorts or when you need file space to swap parts of memory out to disk. Such swapping is usually needed when your program burdens memory excessively.

Fact: 4) Returns `NULL` (like `fopen()`) if it cannot open a temporary file.

Fact: 5) There is no way to discover the name of the file it is opening!

Function: `char *tmpnam(char *filename);`

Fact: 1) Usually called as `tmpnam(filename)`—return value is same address as `filename` unless failure occurs. Returns `NULL` on failure.

Fact: 2) `Filename` should be dimensioned to `L_tmpnam` size. `L_tmpnam` is a built-in constant in `stdio.h`.

Fact: 3) If it succeeds, it guarantees that it will create a file name that will not conflict with any other file name on your computer. What this means is that you do not have to worry about accidentally wiping out an existing file if you use `fopen()` to open the file whose name is provided by `tmpnam()`.

Fact: 4) You are *not guaranteed* that the file name given you will be within your directory structure. Usually, the operating system will give you a file that can be created and read, but it might not give you one that can be `remove`'d or `rename`'d.

<signal.h> Functions

Function: `void (*signal(int signal_type, void (*signal_handler)(int signal_type))) (int);`

Fact: 1) Traps events or interrupts of type `signal_type`.

Fact: 2) Goes to `signal_handler()` when `signal_type` occurs.

Fact: 3) `Signal_handler()` will be one of three possible values:

- **a)** `SIG_IGN` if you want your program to ignore the `signal_type` when it occurs,
- **b)** `SIG_DFL` if you want the signal to be handled in the default manner, or
- **c)** the name of a signal-handling function you have written.

Fact: 4) If you write your own signal-handling function, the `signal_type` that invoked the handler function is passed as a parameter to this function.

Fact: 5) Excellent for preventing abnormal program terminations while a critical resource (such as a file) is being created or manipulated.

Fact: 6) The most important `signal_types` of the small group specified in ANSI C are `SIGINT` (usually a CTRL-C keyboard interrupt) and `SIGSEGV` (for trapping illegal memory accesses such as dereferencing a `NULL` pointer).

Fact: 7) `SIGALRM`, though not specified by ANSI C, is trappable on virtually all computers and is useful for timing out a program that is idle.

Fact: 8) If your computer supports the POSIX library standards, use `sigaction()` instead of `signal()`. It is far superior.

Fact: 9) The return value (which is rarely used) is a function pointer to the previous handler for `signal_type` before the current call to `signal()`. Remember that this can be any of the values mentioned in item 3.

Fact: 10) If you are not exiting the program from the `signal_handler()`, you should reinstall handling for the `signal_type` that got you into the `signal_handler()`. On some computers, the `signal_handler()` reverts to `SIG_DFL` unless you reinstall as just described.

Fact: 11) If you are not calling `exit()` from the `signal_handler()`, you should return from `signal_handler()` via a `longjmp()` to a `setjmp()` (see the following `setjmp.h` functions). Otherwise, you could return to the middle of a non-reentrant function, which may hang the program or cause a fatal error.

Function: `int raise(int signal_type);`

Fact: 1) Explicitly generates a signal of type `signal_type`. If you have installed a `signal()` call for handling that `signal_type`, your program will transfer control according to the `signal()` call's `signal_handler` value. See item 3 above. If you haven't installed a `signal()` call for that `signal_type`, the signal will be handled in the default manner.

Fact: 2) The significance of the return value is not specified in the ANSI standard. Because you know which signals you are trapping, an error return value for `raise()` is not really necessary.

Function: `unsigned int alarm(unsigned int seconds);`

Fact: 1) Causes a `SIGALRM` signal to be generated after `seconds` time elapses.

Fact: 2) Returns the number of seconds left from the previous call to `alarm()`. Seldom used.

Fact: 3) `Alarm(0)` turns off the alarm clock.

Fact: 4) Expired alarm clocks are the only way to generate `SIGALRM` aside from explicit calls to `raise()` or, on some systems, a function called `kill()`.

<setjmp.h> Functions

Function: `int setjmp(jmp_buf env);`

Fact: 1) Returns zero when executed directly and non-zero when executed via a transfer of control from a `longjmp()` call in a signal-handling function.

Fact: 2) Used for controlled re-entry from a signal-handling function to some predetermined point in the program. Remember that *uncontrolled* re-entries can result in the program hanging or fatally terminating.

Fact: 3) The `jmp_buf` variable always needs to be declared *globally* so that a `longjmp()` call in a signal-handling function can access its name. Remember that the only value passed into a signal-handling function is the `signal_type`.

Function: `void longjmp(jmp_buf env, int return_value_of_setjmp);`

Fact: 1) Returns program control to a `setjmp()` call that uses the same `jmp_buf` variable.

Fact: 2) The `return_value_of_setjmp` thrown back to the `setjmp()` call can be used in an `if`, `switch`, or other statement to determine what code to execute. `Longjmp()` cannot throw a `setjmp()` return value of zero back to a `setjmp()`. An attempt to do so will actually throw a 1.

Fact: 3) Values of variables are not altered from their most recent settings after a `longjmp()` is executed. Be sure to remember this vital fact!

The following function may be in either `stdlib.h` or `signal.h` or in both:

Function: `void sleep(unsigned int seconds);`

Fact: 1) Makes the program halt execution for `seconds` seconds of elapsed time.

Fact: 2) Very useful for test programs where you need to see whether alarm or other signal-related calls are working correctly.

Exercises

1. Write a program that does the following:

   a. Reads integer test scores from a text file called `scores.dat`. Test scores are separated by whitespace until `EOF`.

   b. Throws out any test score that is not a valid `int` between 0 and 100.

   c. Uses `malloc()` and `realloc()` to control space management so that no more than 100 `int`'s worth of space are wasted in the array of scores.

   d. Computes and displays the median test score. The median of a group of numbers is defined as the `(N/2) + 1` highest score if there are an odd number of scores and as the average of the `(N/2)` and `(N/2) + 1` highest scores if there are an even number of scores. `N` is the total number of scores.

   e. Pay attention to modularity. You ought to have a function to read the file from disk and one that computes the median. Report results in `main()`.

   f. You will not be given any hints about how to read the file or error-check its tokens. Good luck!

■ 2. Write statements that accomplish the following objectives.

   a. Explicitly generate the `SIGINT` signal if the variable `j` is zero.

   b. Transfer control to function `finish()` whenever `exit()` is called or the program's `main()` function terminates.

   c. Transfer control to function `time_out()` if any alarm clock expires.

   d. Suspend program execution for 20 seconds.

   e. Return control to a `setjmp()` call that uses the `jmp_buf` variable `eptr`. Make sure that when you return to this `setjmp()`, the `setjmp()` returns with a value of 5.

   f. Set the variable `j` to 5 if a `setjmp()` has been executed directly and to 10 if it has been executed via a control transfer from a `longjmp()`. Use the `jmp_buf` variable `env` in your answer.

   g. Change the name of file `oldfile.dat` to `newfile.dat`.

   h. Search for the value 25 in an array of 100 sorted `int`s called `array`. Assume that the searcher expects to call a function called `compare_int()`. Do not write the `compare_int()` function! Declare variables except for `array`.

i. Make your program terminate if a variable `j` is equal to zero. The Boolean test of `j` should be part of the termination message.

j. Make your program terminate with system information if a `malloc()` returns `NULL` on an attempt to allocate 10 `int`s and assign to the `int *` variable `ptr`. You may include your own error output as well.

k. Make your program transfer control to function `out_of_bounds()` whenever it tries to access a region of memory that is "illegal."

l. Turn off any ticking alarm clocks in your program.

m. Transfer control to function `handler()` if a binary search of `int` array `arr` fails to find the value 25. The array has 100 elements. Assume that 25 is in `key` and that the comparison function is `comp`. Do not explicitly call `handler()`!

n. Open a new binary file for reading and writing in such a way that there is no danger of clobbering an existing file. This file should continue to exist after the program terminates. Use the `FILE *` variable `fp` and the `char *` variable `fname`.

o. Same as part n, but the file should disappear when the program terminates.

■ 3. Write a function that accepts an array of file names as its only parameter and that returns an array containing a subset of those names representing files that could be successfully deleted. The input parameter has a `NULL` sentinel value in it. Your return array should also have a `NULL` sentinel in it and should waste absolutely no space.

4. Write a signal-handling function that

a. Asks users if they really wish to quit if they have just hit a CTRL-C. If they say "yes," your program should terminate. If they say "no," you should return to a `setjmp()` with the `jmp_buf` variable `env2`. If they say neither "yes" nor "no," reprompt them for a correct response.

b. Exits the program when a memory access error has occurred. Delivers a descriptive error message to the screen.

c. Tells the user that the program is going to terminate in 10 seconds because an alarm clock has expired. The program should unconditionally terminate in 10 seconds.

5. Write a function that accepts an array of file names (`NULL`-terminated) as its only argument. This function should try to rename all of the files by attaching `.new` to the ends of their current names. The return value should be a `NULL`-terminated array of names that cannot be changed. Your return array should waste no space.

■ **6.** Write a function that builds a command string and executes it, given a `NULL`-terminated array of strings with command tokens as the only function parameter. Assume that no command token has whitespace in it. Return void.

7. Write a signal-handling function that closes and deletes a file attached to the `FILE *` variable `fp` with a name kept in the `char *` variable `filename`.

8. A program needs to perform a merge sort and, therefore, needs to open ten temporary files that will disappear when the program terminates. Write a function that opens these ten files and returns the file pointers to the caller. Assume that the caller does not know how many file pointers are in the return value (that is, `NULL`-terminate the array of pointers).

Appendix

Answers to Selected Exercises

Chapter 2 Answers

1. a. 10 **b.** 1016
c. 2 **d.** 2
e. 1012 **f.** 24
g. 4 **h.** 4
i. 36 **j.** 20

4. a. The pointer `pi` has not been allocated any space.
b. The variable `i` cannot be dereferenced because it is not a pointer.
c. The variable `i` is not a `long int`. Therefore,the `%ld` format is inappropriate.
d. The variable c should be an `int` so that it is big enough to hold the value of `EOF`.
e. Nothing is wrong with this code.
f. The argument to `toupper()` should be `*p`, not `p`.
g. The argument to `printf()` should be `s`, not `*s`.
h. Nothing is wrong with this code.
i. The expression `i != 9`, not the `printf()`, should be the right-hand expression. Remember, the value of a comma-delimited expression is the value of the rightmost expression.

j. The character `p[3]` is after the `'\0'` character of `s`. Thus this is a memory access error.

5. a. –1 **b.** 1
c. 1003 **d.** 1001
e. 2 **f.** 1
g. 'B' or 66 **h.** 'l' or 108
i. 'e' or 101 **j.** 'c' or 99

6. a.
```
pc = pa;
pa = pb;
pb = pc;
```
d.
```
if  ((pc = (int *) malloc(10 * sizeof(int))) ==
     NULL)
{
     printf("Fatal malloc error!\n");
     exit(1);
}
pd = pc + 3;
```
e. `for (pc = pa; *pc != 6; pc++) printf("%d\n", *pc);`

g. `pc = pb + 2;`

7.
```
long count_elements(int *p)
{
     int *mover = p;

     while (*mover++ != -1); /*** Empty loop body! ***/
     return (long) (mover - p - 1); /*** Cast expression!***/
}
```

8.
```
int *greater_than_10(int *p, int num_elements)
{
     int *p_new_array, *mover, index = 0;

     p_new_array = (int *) malloc(num_elements *
                                  sizeof(int));
     mover = p_new_array;
     while (num_elements--) /*** Terse while header.***/
     {
          if (*p > 10) *p_new_array++ = index;
          index++;
          p++;
     }
     *p_new_array = -1;
     return mover;
}
```

Chapter 3 Answers

2.
```
NODE  *reverse_stack(NODE  *stack)
{
    NODE  *newstack = NULL,  *temp;

    while (stack)
    {
        temp = newstack;
        newstack = stack;
        stack = stack->next;
        newstack->next = temp;
    }
    return newstack;
}
```

4.
```
/******  Delete a node from ordered linked list.  ******/
int delete(NODE *list, char *string, NODE **freestack)
{
    NODE *current = list->next;
    NODE *previous = list;

    while(strcmp(string, current->string) != 0 &&
          current->string[0] != DUMMY_TRAILER)
    {
        previous = current;
        current  = current->next;
    }
    if  (current->string[0] == DUMMY_TRAILER)
    {
        return NOT_FOUND;
    }
    else
    {
        previous->next = current->next;
        current->next = *freestack;
        *freestack = current;
        return FOUND;
    }
 }
```

6.
```
/**************************************************/
/*                                                */
/*  This program reads a file (accounts) that    */
/*  contains records with two fields: a 4-digit  */
/*  account number and a current balance.  The   */
/*  program reads the account records into a     */
/*  linked list ordered by account number.       */
/*                                                */
```

```
/*  Then the user is prompted for records of      */
/*  recent transactions with positive amounts     */
/*  representing deposits and negative            */
/*  amounts representing withdrawals.  Net        */
/*  transaction amounts for each account are in   */
/*  a node of a transaction linked list.  Each    */
/*  account with at least one transaction will    */
/*  have ONE node in this list that is updated    */
/*  when further transactions take place.         */
/*                                                */
/*  After all user input, 3 files are created:    */
/*  a new balances file in account order, a       */
/*  file with the transaction list node contents,*/
/*  and a file with records of accounts with      */
/*  negative balances (after updating).           */
/************************************************/

#define BLOCK_SIZE 10
#define FILE_OPEN_ERROR 1
#define MALLOC_ERROR 2

#include <stdio.h>
#include <string.h>

typedef struct account ACCOUNT;

struct account
{
   int account_num;
   double amount;
   struct account *next;
};

main()
{
    ACCOUNT *balance_list, *transactions_list;
    ACCOUNT *init_list(void);
    void read_file_into_list(ACCOUNT *balance_list),
        get_transaction_records(ACCOUNT *transactions_list),
        adjust_balances(ACCOUNT *balance_list,
                        ACCOUNT *transactions_list),
        create_transactions_file(ACCOUNT
                                  *transactions_list),
        create_balance_files(ACCOUNT *balance_list);

   /************* Initialize the two lists. ***************/
   balance_list =      init_list();
   transactions_list = init_list();
```

```
    read_file_into_list(balance_list);
    get_transaction_records(transactions_list);
    adjust_balances(balance_list, transactions_list);
    create_transactions_file(transactions_list);
    create_balance_files(balance_list);
}


/*************** Get a pointer to a new *****************/
/*************** account node.          *****************/
ACCOUNT *get_free_node(int account_num, float amount)
{
    ACCOUNT *new;
    static ACCOUNT *freerecs = NULL, *rear;

    if (freerecs == NULL)
    {
        if ((freerecs = (ACCOUNT *)
            calloc(BLOCK_SIZE, sizeof(ACCOUNT))) == NULL)
        {
             printf("Fatal malloc error!\n");
             exit(MALLOC_ERROR);
        }
        rear = freerecs + BLOCK_SIZE - 1;
    }
    new = freerecs;
    if (freerecs == rear) freerecs = NULL;
    else freerecs++;
    new->account_num = account_num;
    new->amount = amount;
    return new;
}


/**** Create dummy header/trailer for an account list. ****/
ACCOUNT *init_list(void)
{
     ACCOUNT *list;

     list = get_free_node(-1, 0.00);
     list->next = get_free_node(10000, 0.00);
     return list;
}


/*************** Inserts node into list or **************/
/*************** updates record if the node **************/
/*************** exists.                    **************/
```

```
void insert_node(int account_num, float amount, ACCOUNT
                 *list)
{
    ACCOUNT *current = list->next, *previous = list, *new;

    while ( account_num > current->account_num)
    {
         previous = current;
         current  = current->next;
    }
    if (account_num == current->account_num) /* Old node! */
    {
         current->amount = current->amount + amount;
    }
    else  /* New node!! */
    {
         new = get_free_node(account_num, amount);
         new->next  = current;
         previous->next = new;
    }
}


/************ This function reads the current ************/
/************ balances file (accounts) into a ************/
/************ linked list ordered by 4-digit  ************/
/************ account number.                ************/
void read_file_into_list(ACCOUNT *balance_list)
{
    FILE *curbal;
    char line[80];
    int account_num;
    float amount;
    void insert_node(int account_num, float amount,
                     ACCOUNT *balance_list);

    if ((curbal = fopen("accounts", "r")) == NULL)
    {
         printf("Could not open balances file!\n");
         exit(FILE_OPEN_ERROR);
    }
    while (fgets(line, 80, curbal))
    {
         sscanf(line, "%d %f", &account_num, &amount);
         insert_node(account_num, amount, balance_list);
    }
    fclose(curbal);
}
```

```
/************** Get input records from the     ************/
/************** user.  Records are account     ************/
/************** number and transaction         ************/
/************** amount (positive for           ************/
/************** deposits and negative for      ************/
/************** withdrawals).                  ************/
/**************                                ************/
/************** If it is the first trans-      ************/
/************** action for an account, make    ************/
/************** a new list node in the trans-  ************/
/**************  action list. Update node if   ************/
/**************  account is already repre-     ************/
/**************  sented in the list.           ************/
void get_transaction_records(ACCOUNT *transactions_list)
{
    char line[80];
    int account_num;
    float amount;
    ACCOUNT *new;
    void insert_node(int account_num, float amount,
                     ACCOUNT *transactions_list);

    while (printf("Enter transaction record:"),
          strcmp(gets(line), "quit"))
    {
        sscanf(line, "%d %f", &account_num, &amount);
        insert_node(account_num, amount,
                    transactions_list);
    }
}


/** Adjust account balances by net transaction amounts. **/
void adjust_balances(ACCOUNT *balance_list,
                     ACCOUNT *transactions_list)
{
    transactions_list = transactions_list->next;

    while (transactions_list->account_num != 10000)
    {
        balance_list = balance_list->next;


        while (transactions_list->account_num !=
               balance_list->account_num)
        {
               balance_list = balance_list->next;
        }
```

```
            balance_list->amount += transactions_list->amount;
            transactions_list = transactions_list->next;
        }
    }


    /******* Output transaction list records to file. *******/
    void create_transactions_file(ACCOUNT *transactions_list)
    {
        FILE *transactions;

        if ((transactions = fopen("transactions", "w")) ==
             NULL)
        {
             printf("Could not make transactions file!\n");
             exit(FILE_OPEN_ERROR);
        }

        transactions_list = transactions_list->next;
        while (transactions_list->account_num != 10000)
        {
             fprintf(transactions, "%04d %.2f\n",
                     transactions_list->account_num,
                     transactions_list->amount);
             transactions_list = transactions_list->next;
        }
        fclose(transactions);
    }


    /*********** Create new files for updated      ************/
    /*********** balances and overdrawn accounts. ************/
    void create_balance_files(ACCOUNT *balance_list)
    {
        FILE *balances, *overdrawn;

        if ((balances = fopen("balances","w")) == NULL)
        {
             printf("Couldn't make new balances file!\n");
             exit(FILE_OPEN_ERROR);
        }
        if ((overdrawn = fopen("overdrawn","w")) == NULL)
        {
             printf("Couldn't make overdrawn file!\n");
             exit(FILE_OPEN_ERROR);
        }

        balance_list = balance_list->next;
```

```
    while (balance_list->account_num != 10000)
    {
         fprintf(balances, "%04d %.2f\n",
                 balance_list->account_num,
                 balance_list->amount);
         if (balance_list->amount < 0.0)
         {
             fprintf(overdrawn, "%04d %.2f\n",
                     balance_list->account_num,
                     balance_list->amount);
         }
         balance_list = balance_list->next;
    }
    fclose(balances);
    fclose(overdrawn);
}
/**********  CONTENTS OF ORIGINAL ACCOUNTS FILE  *********/
4444 6000.00
2222 2400.55
6767 100000.34
5555 100.56
7878 4567.67
3431 1000.00
6898 23.23
8906 40000.00
0043 7600.34
0154 87000000.00
4356 567.43
5656 0.98
4698 3456.21
7744 9807.99
4378 909.67
3333 20087.87
7777 9876.56
9999 4209.89
1111 342.78
/**************  INTERACTIVE SESSION  ************/

Enter transaction record:1111 150.22
Enter transaction record:2222 -2000.00
Enter transaction record:3431 233.77
Enter transaction record:1111 -1000.00
Enter transaction record:5656 -20.00
Enter transaction record:5656 400.00
Enter transaction record:7744 -10000.00
Enter transaction record:3431 100.00
Enter transaction record:quit
$ /* Operating system prompt. */
```

```
/**********  BALANCES FILE CREATED BY PROGRAM  ***********/

0043 7600.34
0154 87000000.00
1111 -507.00
2222 400.55
3333 20087.87
3431 1333.77
4356 567.43
4378 909.67
4444 6000.00
4698 3456.21
5555 100.56
5656 380.98
6767 100000.34
6898 23.23
7744 -192.01
7777 9876.56
7878 4567.67
8906 40000.00
9999 4209.89

/*********  TRANSACTIONS FILE CREATED BY PROGRAM  *********/

1111 -849.78
2222 -2000.00
3431 333.77
5656 380.00
7744 -10000.00

/********** OVERDRAWN FILE CREATED BY PROGRAM ************/

1111 -507.00
7744 -192.01
```

8.
```
void transpose_pairs(NODE *list)
{
    NODE *current   = list->forward->forward;
    NODE *previous  = list->forward;

    while (strcmp(previous->key, "ZZZZ") != 0 &&
           strcmp(previous->forward->key, "ZZZZ") !=0)
    {
           previous->backward->forward = current;
           previous->forward = current->forward;
           current->forward->backward = previous;
           current->backward  = previous->backward;
           current->forward   = previous;
           previous->backward = current;
```

```
            previous = previous->forward;
            current  = previous->forward;
        }
    }
```

10.
```
void process_user(SERVICE *list, char *qname)
{
    NODE *temp;

    list = list->next;
    while(strcmp(qname,list->qname) > 0)list = list->next;
    if (strcmp(qname, list->qname) != 0)
    {
        printf("Queue: %s : not found.\n", qname);
        return;
    }
     if (list->front == NULL)
    {
        printf("No user in queue: %s.\n", qname);
        return;
    }
    temp = list->front;
    if (list->front == list->rear) list->rear = NULL;
    list->front = list->front->next;
    free(temp);
}
```

13.
```
void transpose_pairs(NODE *list)
{
    NODE *hold = list, *prev, *cur, *after;

    while (hold->next->next != NULL)
    {
        prev  = hold->next;
        cur   = prev->next;
        after = cur->next;
        cur->next    = prev;
        prev->next   = after;
        hold->next   = cur;
        hold  = prev;
    }
}   /***  End of transpose_pairs here! ***/
```

Chapter 4 Answers

1.
```
char **substr_addresses(char *string, char *substr)
{
    static char *substrs[100];
    char *ptr, **mover = substrs;
```

```
    for (ptr = string; ptr = strstr(ptr, substr); mover++)
    {
        *mover = ptr;
        ptr += strlen(substr);
    }
    *mover = NULL;
    return substrs;
}
```

2. a. `pp`
   b. `c`
   c. `A bat is an animal.`
   d. `Bullwinkle is a caboose.`
   e. `What's up?`
   f. `foobar`
   g. `foobar`
   h. `3`
   i. `here here here!`
   j. `cdefg`

3. a.
```
char *p1, *p2;
p1 = strrchr(s, '.');
if (p1) *p1 = '\0';
p2 = strrchr(s, '.');
if (!p1 || !p2) printf("Not enough periods.\n");
else if (p2) printf("%s\n", p2 + 1);
```
   b.
```
char *ptr, *token;
for (ptr = s; token = strtok(ptr, "0123456789");
     ptr = NULL)
{
     printf("%s\n", token);
}
```
   c.
```
int i,j;
for (ptr = s; (i=strcspn(ptr, "0123456789")) <
strlen(ptr); ptr += i + j)
{
    j = strspn(ptr + i, "0123456789");
    printf("%.*s\n", j, ptr + i);
}
```

OR

```
int i,j;
for (ptr = s; ptr = strpbrk(ptr,"0123456789"); ptr += i )
{
    i = strspn(ptr, "0123456789");
```

```
        printf("%.*s\n", i, ptr);
    }
```

d.
```
    long num;
    char *endp;
    num = strtol(s, &endp, 2);
    if (*endp != '\0' || errno == ERANGE)
    {
        printf("Bad number or out of range!\n");
    }
    else
    {
        printf("Number is: %ld\n", num);
    }
```

e.
```
    char *ptr;
    for (ptr = s; ptr = strchr(ptr, '#'); ptr++)
    {
        *ptr = '.';
    }
```

6.
```
long *no_digits(char *filename)
{
    FILE *fp;
    char line[1024];
    long count = 0, linenum = 0, *linenums;

    if ((linenums = (long *)malloc(5 * sizeof(long)))
        == NULL)
    {
        printf("Fatal malloc error!\n");
        return NULL;
    }
    if ((fp = fopen(filename, "r")) == NULL)
    {
        printf("Could not open %s\n", filename);
        return NULL;
    }
    while (fgets(line, 1024, fp))
    {
        linenum++;
        if (strpbrk(line, "0123456789") == NULL)
        {
            linenums[count++] = linenum;
        }
        if (linenum % 5 == 0)
        {
            if ((linenums = (long *) realloc(linenums,
            (linenum + 5) * sizeof(long))) == NULL)
            {
```

```
                    printf("Fatal realloc error!\n");
                    return NULL;
                }
            }
        }
        linenums[count] = 0;
        return linenums;
    }
```

7. **a.** 5002 **b.** 3
c. 'm' **d.** 'c'
e. 3 **f.** 'e'
g. 'o' **h.** 1012
i. NULL **j.** 1012

8.
```
#include <stdio.h>
#include <string.h>
#include <stdlib.h>
main(int argc, char *argv[])
{
    FILE *fp, *fpout;
    char line[257], *punc;

    fp = fopen(argv[1], "r");
    fpout = fopen(argv[2], "w");

    if (fp == NULL)
    {
        printf("Input file could not be opened!\
        Aborting!\n");
        exit(1);
    }
    if (fpout == NULL)
    {
        printf("Output file could not be opened!
                Aborting!\n");
        exit(2);
    }

    while (fgets(line, 256, fp) != NULL)
    {
        punc = line;
        while ((punc = strpbrk(punc, ".!?;:,()")) != NULL)
        {
            *punc = '\040';  /** ASCII space character. **/
             punc++;  /*** Move past punctuation. ***/
        }
        fputs(line, fpout);
    }
```

```
    fclose(fp);    fclose(fpout);
}   /**** End of program. ****/
```

9.
```
#include <stdio.h>
#include <string.h>
#include <stdlib.h>
main(int argc, char *argv[])
{
    FILE *fp;
    char line[257], *digit, *endp;
    int sum = 0, number;

    fp = fopen(argv[1], "r");

    if (fp == NULL)
    {
        printf("Input file could not be opened!
                Aborting!\n");
        exit(1);
    }

    while (fgets(line, 256, fp) != NULL)
    {
        endp = line;
        while ((digit = strpbrk(endp,"0123456789")) != NULL)
        {
            number = (int) strtol(digit, &endp, 10);
               sum += number;
        }
    }
    printf("The total is = %d\n", sum);
    fclose(fp);
}   /********  End of program. *******/
```

Chapter 5 Answers

1. a.
```
fp = fopen("foobar.dat", "r+");
```

b.
```
long pos;
fseek(fp, 0, SEEK_END);
pos = ftell(fp)/sizeof(struct foo);
printf("There are %ld struct foo in the file.\n", pos);
```

c.
```
struct foo temp;  middle = pos/2 - 1;
fseek(fp, middle * sizeof(struct foo), SEEK_SET);
fread(&temp, sizeof(struct foo), 1, fp);
```

d.
```
struct foo temp, *all_records;
long records, i;

fseek(fp, 0L, SEEK_END);
```

```
records = ftell(fp)/sizeof(struct foo);
all_records = (struct foo) malloc(records *
                    sizeof(struct foo));
rewind(fp);
fread(all_records, sizeof(struct foo), records, fp);
for (i = 0; i < records; i += 2)
{
    temp = all_records[i];
    all_records[i] = all_records[i + 1];
    all_records[i + 1] = temp;
}
rewind(fp);
fwrite(all_records, sizeof(struct foo), records, fp);
```

e. Same as part d through the `fread()`. Then...

```
for (i = 0, j = records - 1; i <= records/2; i++, j--)
{
    temp = all_records[i];
    all_records[i] = all_records[j];
    all_records[j] = temp;
}
rewind(fp);
fwrite(all_records, sizeof(struct foo), records, fp);
```

2.

```
struct foo *read_whole_file(char *filename)
{
    struct foo *all_records;
    FILE *fp;
    long records;

    fp = fopen(filename, "r+b");
    fseek(fp, 0, SEEK_END);
    records = ftell(fp)/sizeof(struct foo);
    rewind(fp);
    all_records = (struct foo *)malloc((records + 1) *
                                sizeof(struct foo));
    fread(all_records, sizeof(struct foo), records, fp);
    fclose(fp);
    memset(&all_records[records], 0, sizeof(struct foo));
    return all_records;
}
```

5 a. `00100`

b. `40`

c. `23.12`

d. `abcd`

e. `abcdefghij`

f. `This`

g. `This is a sentence.`

h. `What's up, Elmer Fudd?`

i. `AFGH`

j. `Doc?`

7.
```
#include <stdio.h>
#include <stdlib.h>
main(int argc, char *argv[])
{
    char line[256];
    FILE *fout;

    if ((fout = fopen(argv[1], "wb")) == NULL)
    {
        printf("Can't open %s! Goodbye!\n", argv[1]);
        exit(1);
    }

    while(fgets(line, 256, stdin), strncmp(line, "quit", 4))
    {
        fwrite(line, strlen(line), 1, fout);
    }
}
```

8.
```
#include <stdio.h>
#include <stdlib.h>
main(int argc, char *argv[])
{
    FILE *fp;
    long offset, middle;
    char startchar, endchar;

    if ((fp = fopen(argv[1], "r+b")) == NULL)
    {
        printf("Can't open %s!  Goodbye!\n", argv[1]);
        exit(1);
    }
    fseek(fp, 0L, SEEK_END);
    middle = ftell(fp) / 2;
    rewind(fp);
    offset = 0L;
    while (offset != middle)
    {
        fseek(fp, offset, SEEK_SET);
        startchar = fgetc(fp);
        fseek(fp, -(offset + 1L) , SEEK_END);
        endchar   = fgetc(fp);
        fseek(fp, -1L, SEEK_CUR);
        fputc(startchar, fp);
        fseek(fp, offset, SEEK_SET);
```

```
        fputc(endchar, fp);
        offset++;
    }
fclose(fp);
}   /****  End of Program. ****/
```

Chapter 6 Answers

1. **a.** 0 **b.** 0
   c. 8 **d.** 7
   e. 1 **f.** 10
   g. 14 **h.** 0
   i. 63 **j.** 0

5.
```
int find_pattern(char *pattern, unsigned short u)
{
    char *endp, bit[2],
        cu[8 * sizeof(unsigned short) + 1] = "", *match;
    int i;

    if (strlen(pattern) > 8 * sizeof(unsigned short))
    {
        return -1;
    }
    strtol(pattern, &endp, 2);
    if (*endp != '\0') return -2;
    for (i = 0; i < 8 * sizeof(unsigned short); i++)
    {
        sprintf(bit, "%1d", (u >> i) & 1);
        strcat(cu, bit);
    }
    if (match = strstr(cu, pattern))
    {
        return  match - cu;
    }
    else
    {
        return -3;
    }
}
```

10.
```
unsigned short toggle_bits(unsigned short word, int
                           numbits,int startbit)

{
    word ^= ~((unsigned short) ~0 << numbits) << startbit;
    return word;
}
```

11.
```
char *bit_pattern(unsigned short word, int startbit,
                  int endbit)
{
    int bits = sizeof(unsigned short) * 8, i;
    /*** Next declaration must be static or else the    ***/
    /*** memory is deallocated when the function        ***/
    /*** terminates!                                    ***/
    static char string[sizeof(unsigned short) * 8 + 1];

    memset(string, 0, bits + 1); /***  Zero out string. ***/
    if (startbit >= bits || startbit < 0 ||
        endbit >= bits || endbit < 0 || endbit < startbit)
    {
        return NULL;
    }
    for (i = endbit; i >= startbit; i--)
    {
        if ((word >> i) & 1) strcat(string, "1");
        else strcat(string, "0");
    }
    return string;
}
```

Chapter 7 Answers

1.
```
void print_backwards(void)
{
    char c;
    if ((c = getchar()) == '\n') return;
    print_backwards();
    putchar(c);
}
```

2.
```
int count_tree_nodes(NODE *root)
{
    static int count = 0; /*** Init. happens once only!!***/

    if (!root) return count;
    printtree(root->left);
    count++;
    printtree(root->right);
}
```

5.
```
/****  No change at all because asterisk is in key!!  ****/
NODE *find(char *word, NODE *tree)
{
    int  compare;
    NODE *mover;
```

```
        for (mover = tree; mover != NULL; )
        {
            compare = strcmp(word,mover->word);
            if (compare < 0)            mover = mover->left;
            else if (compare > 0)       mover = mover->right;
            else return mover;          /**** Found it!! ****/
        }
        return NULL;    /****  Got to the end of the tree   ****/
                        /****  without finding the node!!   ****/
    }

    void printtree(NODE *tree)
    {
        if (!tree) return;
        printtree(tree->left);
        if (strchr(tree->word, '*') == NULL)
        {
             printf("%s\n",tree->word);
        }
        printtree(tree->right);
    }
```

7.
```
    void printtree(char *word, NODE *root)
    {
        if (!root) return;
        printtree(word, root->left);
        if (strcmp(root->word, word) >= 0)
        {
            printf("%s\n",root->word);
        }
        printtree(word, root->right);
    }
```

10.
```
    #include <stdio.h>
    #include <string.h>
    #include <errno.h>
    #include <stdlib.h>
    main(int argc, char *argv[])
    {
        FILE *fp;
        void write_file(FILE *fp);
        int i;

        /******  Open file for write and read so we can  ******/
        /******  verify correctness of file write.       ******/
        if ((fp = fopen(argv[1], "w+b")) == NULL)
        {
            printf("Can't open %s.  Goodbye!\n", argv[1]);
            exit(1);
```

```
    }

    write_file(fp);

    rewind(fp);  /***  Obviates need for fflush() call. ***/
    while (fread(&i, sizeof(int), 1, fp) != 0)
    {
        printf("%d\n", i);
    }
    fclose(fp);
}



void write_file(FILE *fp)
{
    char line[512], *token, *endp;
    int errflag;
    long number;

    do  /****  Repeat prompt on empty response. ****/
        /****  Repeat prompt on error.          ****/
    {
        errflag = 0;
        errno   = 0;
        printf("Enter an integer:  ");
        gets(line);
        token = strtok(line, "\040\t");
        if (!token) continue;
        if (strcmp(token, "quit") == 0) return;
        number = strtol(token, &endp, 10);
        if (errno == ERANGE) /* Errno declared in errno.h */
        {
            errflag = 1;
            printf("Number cannot fit on your machine!\n");
            printf("Try again!\n");
            continue;
        }
        if (*endp != '\0')
        {
            errflag = 1;
            printf("Improper integer. Try again!\n");
            continue;
        }
    }
    while (token == NULL || errflag);
    write_file(fp);
    fwrite(&number, sizeof(int), 1, fp);
}
```

Chapter 8 Answers

1. `int matrix[4][4] = {{1}, {0, 1}, {0, 0, 1}, {0, 0, 0, 1}};`

2.

a. error	**b.** 4
c. 4 (3 + 1)	**d.** 4
e. 1	**f.** 4
g. 48	**h.** 6
i. 0	**j.** 4
k. 1020	**l.** 1
m. 5	**n.** 4
o. 2	**p.** 6
q. error	**r.** error
s. 1004	**t.** 1028

4.
```
int zero_elements(int **array)
{
    int **mover = array, count = 0;

    for ( ; *mover != NULL; mover++) count++;
    return count;
}
```

5. `*(&a[0][0][0][0] + (4*3*2*q) + (3*2*r) + (2*s) + t)`

8.
```
int sum_ragged(int **p)
{
    int **mover = p, *rowmover, sum = 0;

    for ( ; *mover != NULL; mover++)
        for (rowmover = *mover; *rowmover != -1; rowmover++)
        {
            sum += *rowmover;
        }
    return sum;
}
```

10.
```
/****** Just remember that memset is byte oriented! ******/
memset(array, 255, N * sizeof(unsigned long));
```

11. and **12.** plus `main()` driver.
```
#include <stdio.h>
#include <string.h>
#include <stdlib.h>
main()
{
    int sizes[] = {4, 2, 3, 4, 3}, **ragged;
```

```
    int **create_ragged(int *sizes);
    void print_ragged(int *sizes, int **ragged);

    ragged = create_ragged(sizes);

    /******  Populate ragged array with values.  ******/
    /******  Row 0.  ******/
    ragged[0][0] = 3;   ragged[0][1] = 6;
    /******  Row 1.  ******/
    ragged[1][0] = 4;  ragged[1][1] = 7;  ragged[1][2] = 10;
    /******  Row 2.  ******/
    ragged[2][0] = 1;   ragged[2][1] = 5;
    ragged[2][2] = 11;  ragged[2][3] = 13;
    /******  Row 3.  ******/
    ragged[3][0] = 17;  ragged[3][1] = 14;
    ragged[3][2] = 11;
    print_ragged(sizes, ragged);
}
/*********  Create space for the ragged array.  **********/
int **create_ragged(int *sizes)
{
    int rows, **ragged, **mover;

    rows = *sizes++;  /*** Move sizes to row lengths. ***/
    /******  Allocate room for row pointers.  ******/
    if ((ragged = (int **) malloc(rows * sizeof(int *)))
          == NULL)
    {
          return (int **) NULL;
    }
    mover = ragged;
    while (rows--)
    {
        if ((*mover++ = (int *) malloc(*sizes *
            sizeof(int))) == NULL)
            {
                return (int **) NULL;
            }
            sizes++;
    }
    return ragged;
}

/***********  Print contents of ragged array.  **********/
void print_ragged(int *sizes, int **ragged)
{
    int rows = 0, numrows = *sizes, i,
        **mover = ragged, *rowptr;

    while (rows < numrows)
    {
```

```
            printf("Values in row %d:\n", rows);
            sizes++;
            for (rowptr = *mover, i = 0; i < *sizes;
                 i++, rowptr++)
            {
                printf("%d\n", *rowptr);
            }
            printf("\n");
            mover++;
            rows++;
        }
    }
```

Chapter 9 Answers

2.
```
time_t timeval;
struct tm *timeptr;
char buf[80];

time(&timeval);
timeptr = localtime(&timeval);
strftime(buf, 80, "%A, %b. %d, %I:%M %p", timeptr);
printf("%s", buf);
```

3.
```
int hours_from_greenwich(void)
{
        int diff;
        time_t timeval;
        struct tm *local, *greenwich;

        time(&timeval);
        local = localtime(&timeval);
        greenwich = gmtime(&timeval);
        diff = greenwich->tm_hour - local->tm_hour;
        diff = (diff < 0) ? diff + 24: diff;
        if (local->tm_isdst) diff -= 1;
        return diff;
}
```

5. **a.** `char *(*X)[20];`
   b. `char *X[20];`
   c. `char X[20][10];`
   d. `int *X[20];`
   e. `int (*X)[20];`
   f. `int X[20][10];`
   g. `int (*X)(int i, double (*func)(int i));`

h. `void (*X (int signum)) (void *);`

i. `char *(*X[5])(int);`

j. `int (*X)[20][10];`

6.
```
#include <stdio.h>  /***** Demo of 5a Ideas.  *****/
main()
{
    char *(*x)[3];
    char *p[3][3]= {{"Hi", "Bye", "What"},
                    {"There", "Over", "Who"},
                    {"John", "Guy", "Man"}};

    x = p;
    printf("%s\n", **x);
    x++;    /******  Skips over THREE strings.      ******/
    printf("%s\n", **x);  /****  Should print "There". ****/
    x++;
    printf("%s\n", **x);  /****  Should print "John".  ****/
}
/***************** Program Output Below ***************/

Hi   /**** Data type of **x is char *. ****/
There
John
/**************  Demo of 5j Ideas Below  ***************/
#include <stdio.h>
main()
{
    int a[3][20][10], (*x)[20][10];

    x = a;
    a[0][0][0] = 2; a[1][0][0] = 5;  a[2][0][0] = 9;
    printf("%d\n", ***x);
    x++; /**** Skips 200 ints (20*10) ****/
    printf("%d\n", ***x);   /*** Should print 5. ***/
    x++;
    printf("%d\n", ***x);   /*** Should print 9. ***/
}

/**************  Program Output Below  ***************/
2
5
9
```

7.
```
void login_times(void)
{
    FILE *rawlogin, *textlogin;
    struct login temp;
```

```
    struct tm *timeptr;
    time_t now, secs_logged_in;

    if ((rawlogin = fopen("users.dat", "rb")) == NULL)
    {
        printf("Cannot open users.dat. Aborting!\n\n");
        return;
    }
    if ((textlogin = fopen("login.dat", "w")) == NULL)
    {
        printf("Cannot open login.dat. Aborting!\n\n");
        return;
    }
    time(&now);
    while (fread(&temp, sizeof(struct login), 1, rawlogin))
    {
        secs_logged_in = now - temp.login_time;
        timeptr = gmtime(&secs_logged_in);
        fprintf(textlogin, "%s %d %d %d %d\n",
                temp.username,
                timeptr->tm_yday, timeptr->tm_hour,
                timeptr->tm_min, timeptr->tm_sec);
    }
    fclose(rawlogin);   fclose(textlogin);
}
```

10.

```
int run_funcs(int dummy, ...)
{
    va_list argp;
    int (*f)(int), i;
    struct execute *execptr;

    va_start(argp,dummy);
    while (execptr = va_arg(argp, struct execute *))
    {
        i = execptr->function(execptr->i);
        printf("f(i) = %d\n", i);
    }
    va_end(argp);
    return 0;
}
```

Chapter 10 Answers

2 **a.** `if (j == 0) raise(SIGINT);`

b. `atexit(finish);`

c. `signal(SIGALRM, time_out);`

d. `sleep(20);`

e. `longjmp(eptr, 5);`

f.
```
if (setjmp(env) == 0)
{
    j = 5;
}
else
{
    j = 10;
}
```

g. `rename("oldfile.dat", "newfile.dat");`

h.
```
int *ptr;
int key = 25;
ptr = bsearch(&key, array, 100, sizeof(int),
      compare_int);
```

i. `assert(j == 0);`

j.
```
if ((ptr = (int *)malloc(10 * sizeof(int))) == NULL)
{
    perror("Fatal malloc error!");
    exit(1);
}
```

k. `signal(SIGSEGV, out_of_bounds);`
or, on some computers . . .
`signal(SIGBUS, out_of_bounds);`

l. `alarm(0);`

m.
```
int key = 25;
signal(SIGINT, handler);
if (bsearch(&key, arr, 100, sizeof(int), comp) == NULL
{
    raise(SIGINT);
}
```

n.
```
tmpnam(fname);
fp = fopen(fname, "w+b");
```

o. `fp = tmpfile();`

3.
```
char **delete_file(char **files)
{
    char **success, **mover, count = 0;

    if ((success = (char **)malloc(5 * sizeof(char *)))
        == NULL)
    {
        printf("Fatal malloc error!\n");
        return NULL;
```

```
    }
    mover = files;

    while (*mover)  /* fgets keeps \n in line */
    {
    /**** Zero success return is unofficial but ****/
    /**** widespread. ****/
        if (remove(*mover) == 0)
        {
            if ((success[count] =
                (char *)malloc(strlen(*mover)+1))== NULL)
            {
                printf("Malloc failed!\n");
                return NULL;
            }
            strcpy(success[count], *mover);
            count++;
        }

        if (count % 5 == 0)  /*** Need more pointers!! ***/
        {
            if ((success = (char **) realloc(success,
                (count + 5) * sizeof(char *))) == NULL)
            {
                printf("Fatal realloc error!\n");
                return NULL;
            }
        }
        mover++;
    }
    success[count] = NULL;
    return success;
}
```

6.
```
void execute(char **command)
{
    char run_this[512] = "";  /**** Nice, safe size.  ****/

    while (*command)
    {
        strcat(run_this, *command);
        strcat(run_this, "\040");
        command++;
    }
    run_this[strlen(run_this) - 1] = '\0';
    system(run_this);
}
```

Index